NON SANZ DROICT.

Twelfe Night, Or what you will.

Decorative headband from the earliest printed edition, 1623

William Shakespeare

Twelfth Night, or, What You Will

With New and Updated Critical Essays and a Revised Bibliography

Edited by Herschel Baker

THE SIGNET CLASSIC SHAKESPEARE
General Editor: Sylvan Barnet

A SIGNET CLASSIC

SIGNET CLASSIC
Published by New American Library, a division of
Penguin Group (USA) Inc., 375 Hudson Street,
New York, New York 10014, U.S.A.
Penguin Books Ltd, 80 Strand,
London WC2R 0RL, England
Penguin Books Australia Ltd, 250 Camberwell Road,
Camberwell, Victoria 3124, Australia
Penguin Books Canada Ltd, 10 Alcorn Avenue,
Toronto, Ontario, Canada M4V 3B2
Penguin Books (N.Z.) Ltd, Cnr Rosedale and Airborne Roads,
Albany, Auckland 1310, New Zealand

Penguin Books Ltd, Registered Offices:
80 Strand, London WC2R 0RL, England

Published by Signet Classic, an imprint of New American Library, a division of Penguin Group (USA) Inc. The Signet Classic edition of *Twelfth Night* was first published in 1965, and an updated edition was published in 1986.

First Signet Classic Printing (Second Revised Edition), April 1998
25 24 23 22 21 20 19

Orsino, Duke of Illyria
Sebastian, brother of Viola
Antonio, a sea captain, friend to Sebastian
A Sea Captain, friend to Viola
Valentine
Curio   } gentlemen attending on the Duke
Sir Toby Belch, uncle to Olivia
Sir Andrew Aguecheek
Malvolio, steward to Olivia
Fabian
Feste, a clown } servants to Olivia
Olivia, a countess
Viola, sister to Sebastian
Maria, Olivia's woman
Lords, a Priest, Sailors, Officers, Musicians, and
   Attendants

Scene: Illyria]

Shakespeare: An Overview

Biographical Sketch

Between the record of his baptism in Stratford on 26 April 1564 and the record of his burial in Stratford on 25 April 1616, some forty official documents name Shakespeare, and many others name his parents, his children, and his grandchildren. Further, there are at least fifty literary references to him in the works of his contemporaries. More facts are known about William Shakespeare than about any other playwright of the period except Ben Jonson. The facts should, however, be distinguished from the legends. The latter, inevitably more engaging and better known, tell us that the Stratford boy killed a calf in high style, poached deer and rabbits, and was forced to flee to London, where he held horses outside a playhouse. These traditions are only traditions; they may be true, but no evidence supports them, and it is well to stick to the facts.

Mary Arden, the dramatist's mother, was the daughter of a substantial landowner; about 1557 she married John Shakespeare, a tanner, glove-maker, and trader in wool, grain, and other farm commodities. In 1557 John Shakespeare was a member of the council (the governing body of Stratford), in 1558 a constable of the borough, in 1561 one of the two town chamberlains, in 1565 an alderman (entitling him to the appellation of "Mr."), in 1568 high bailiff—the town's highest political office, equivalent to mayor. After 1577, for an unknown reason he drops out of local politics. What *is* known is that he had to mortgage his wife's property, and that he was involved in serious litigation.

The birthday of William Shakespeare, the third child and the eldest son of this locally prominent man, is unrecorded, but the Stratford parish register records that the infant was baptized on 26 April 1564. (It is quite possible that he was born on 23 April, but this date has probably been assigned by tradition because it is the date on which, fifty-two years later, he died, and perhaps because it is the feast day of St. George, patron saint of England.) The attendance records of the Stratford grammar school of the period are not extant, but it is reasonable to assume that the son of a prominent local official attended the free school—it had been established for the purpose of educating males precisely of his class—and received substantial training in Latin. The masters of the school from Shakespeare's seventh to fifteenth years held Oxford degrees; the Elizabethan curriculum excluded mathematics and the natural sciences but taught a good deal of Latin rhetoric, logic, and literature, including plays by Plautus, Terence, and Seneca.

On 27 November 1582 a marriage license was issued for the marriage of Shakespeare and Anne Hathaway, eight years his senior. The couple had a daughter, Susanna, in May 1583. Perhaps the marriage was necessary, but perhaps the couple had earlier engaged, in the presence of witnesses, in a formal "troth plight" which would render their children legitimate even if no further ceremony were performed. In February 1585, Anne Hathaway bore Shakespeare twins, Hamnet and Judith.

That Shakespeare was born is excellent; that he married and had children is pleasant; but that we know nothing about his departure from Stratford to London or about the beginning of his theatrical career is lamentable and must be admitted. We would gladly sacrifice details about his children's baptism for details about his earliest days in the theater. Perhaps the poaching episode is true (but it is first reported almost a century after Shakespeare's death), or perhaps he left Stratford to be a schoolmaster, as another tradition holds; perhaps he was moved (like Petruchio in *The Taming of the Shrew*) by

> Such wind as scatters young men through the world,
> To seek their fortunes farther than at home
> Where small experience grows.   (1.2.49–51)

In 1592, thanks to the cantankerousness of Robert Greene, we have our first reference, a snarling one, to Shakespeare as an actor and playwright. Greene, a graduate of St. John's College, Cambridge, had become a playwright and a pamphleteer in London, and in one of his pamphlets he warns three university-educated playwrights against an actor who has presumed to turn playwright:

> There is an upstart crow, beautified with our feathers, that with his *tiger's heart wrapped in a player's hide* supposes he is as well able to bombast out a blank verse as the best of you, and being an absolute Johannes-factotum [i.e., jack-of-all-trades] is in his own conceit the only Shake-scene in a country.

The reference to the player, as well as the allusion to Aesop's crow (who strutted in borrowed plumage, as an actor struts in fine words not his own), makes it clear that by this date Shakespeare had both acted and written. That Shakespeare is meant is indicated not only by *Shake-scene* but also by the parody of a line from one of Shakespeare's plays, *3 Henry VI*: "O, tiger's heart wrapped in a woman's hide" (1.4.137). If in 1592 Shakespeare was prominent enough to be attacked by an envious dramatist, he probably had served an apprenticeship in the theater for at least a few years.

In any case, although there are no extant references to Shakespeare between the record of the baptism of his twins in 1585 and Greene's hostile comment about "Shake-scene" in 1592, it is evident that during some of these "dark years" or "lost years" Shakespeare had acted and written. There are a number of subsequent references to him as an actor. Documents indicate that in 1598 he is a "principal comedian," in 1603 a "principal tragedian," in 1608 he is one of the "men players." (We do not have, however, any solid information about which roles he may have played; later traditions say he played Adam in *As You Like It* and the ghost in *Hamlet*, but nothing supports the assertions. Probably his role as dramatist came to supersede his role as actor.) The profession of actor was not for a gentleman, and it occasionally drew the scorn of university men like Greene who resented writing speeches for persons less educated than themselves, but it was respectable enough; players, if prosperous, were in effect members of the bourgeoisie, and there is nothing to suggest that Stratford considered William Shakespeare less than a solid citizen. When, in 1596, the Shakespeares were granted a coat of arms—i.e., the right to be considered gentlemen—the grant was made to Shakespeare's father, but probably William Shakespeare had arranged the matter on his own behalf. In subsequent transactions he is occasionally styled a gentleman.

Although in 1593 and 1594 Shakespeare published two narrative poems dedicated to the Earl of Southampton, *Venus and Adonis* and *The Rape of Lucrece*, and may well have written most or all of his sonnets in the middle nineties, Shakespeare's literary activity seems to have been almost entirely devoted to the theater. (It may be significant that the two narrative poems were written in years when the plague closed the theaters for several months.) In 1594 he was a charter member of a theatrical company called the Chamberlain's Men, which in 1603 became the royal company, the King's Men, making Shakespeare the king's playwright. Until he retired to Stratford (about 1611, apparently), he was with this remarkably stable company. From 1599 the company acted primarily at the Globe theater, in which Shakespeare held a one-tenth interest. Other Elizabethan dramatists are known to have acted, but no other is known also to have been entitled to a share of the profits.

Shakespeare's first eight published plays did not have his name on them, but this is not remarkable; the most popular play of the period, Thomas Kyd's *The Spanish Tragedy*, went through many editions without naming Kyd, and Kyd's authorship is known only because a book on the profession of acting happens to quote (and attribute to Kyd) some lines on the interest of Roman emperors in the drama. What is remarkable is that after 1598 Shakespeare's name commonly appears on printed plays—some of which are not his. Presumably his name was a drawing card, and publishers used it to attract potential buyers. Another indication of his popularity comes from Francis Meres, author of *Palladis Tamia: Wit's Treasury* (1598). In this anthology of snippets accompanied by an essay on literature, many playwrights are mentioned, but Shakespeare's name occurs

more often than any other, and Shakespeare is the only playwright whose plays are listed.

From his acting, his play writing, and his share in a
playhouse, Shakespeare seems to have made considerable
money. He put it to work, making substantial investments in
Stratford real estate. As early as 1597 he bought New Place,
the second-largest house in Stratford. His family moved in
soon afterward, and the house remained in the family until a
granddaughter died in 1670. When Shakespeare made his
will in 1616, less than a month before he died, he sought
to leave his property intact to his descendants. Of small
bequests to relatives and to friends (including three actors,
Richard Burbage, John Heminges, and Henry Condell), that
to his wife of the second-best bed has provoked the most
comment. It has sometimes been taken as a sign of an
unhappy marriage (other supposed signs are the apparently hasty marriage, his wife's seniority of eight years, and
his residence in London without his family). Perhaps the
second-best bed was the bed the couple had slept in, the best
bed being reserved for visitors. In any case, had Shakespeare
not excepted it, the bed would have gone (with the rest of his
household possessions) to his daughter and her husband.

On 25 April 1616 Shakespeare was buried within the
chancel of the church at Stratford. An unattractive monument to his memory, placed on a wall near the grave, says
that he died on 23 April. Over the grave itself are the lines,
perhaps by Shakespeare, that (more than his literary fame)
have kept his bones undisturbed in the crowded burial
ground where old bones were often dislodged to make way
for new:

> Good friend, for Jesus' sake forbear
> To dig the dust enclosed here.
> Blessed be the man that spares these stones
> And cursed be he that moves my bones.

A Note on the Anti-Stratfordians, Especially Baconians and Oxfordians

Not until 1769—more than a hundred and fifty years
after Shakespeare's death—is there any record of anyone

expressing doubt about Shakespeare's authorship of the plays and poems. In 1769, however, Herbert Lawrence nominated Francis Bacon (1561–1626) in *The Life and Adventures of Common Sense*. Since then, at least two dozen other nominees have been offered, including Christopher Marlowe, Sir Walter Raleigh, Queen Elizabeth I, and Edward de Vere, 17th earl of Oxford. The impulse behind all anti-Stratfordian movements is the scarcely concealed snobbish opinion that "the man from Stratford" simply could not have written the plays because he was a country fellow without a university education and without access to high society. Anyone, the argument goes, who used so many legal terms, medical terms, nautical terms, and so forth, and who showed some familiarity with classical writing, must have attended a university, and anyone who knew so much about courtly elegance and courtly deceit must himself have moved among courtiers. The plays do indeed reveal an author whose interests were exceptionally broad, but specialists in any given field—law, medicine, arms and armor, and so on—soon find that the plays do not reveal deep knowledge in specialized matters; indeed, the playwright often gets technical details wrong.

The claim on behalf of Bacon, forgotten almost as soon as it was put forth in 1769, was independently reasserted by Joseph C. Hart in 1848. In 1856 it was reaffirmed by W. H. Smith in a book, and also by Delia Bacon in an article; in 1857 Delia Bacon published a book, arguing that Francis Bacon had directed a group of intellectuals who wrote the plays.

Francis Bacon's claim has largely faded, perhaps because it was advanced with such evident craziness by Ignatius Donnelly, who in *The Great Cryptogram* (1888) claimed to break a code in the plays that proved Bacon had written not only the plays attributed to Shakespeare but also other Renaissance works, for instance the plays of Christopher Marlowe and the essays of Montaigne.

Consider the last two lines of the Epilogue in *The Tempest*:

As you from crimes would pardoned be,
Let your indulgence set me free.

What was Shakespeare—sorry, Francis Bacon, Baron Verulam—*really* saying in these two lines? According to Baconians, the lines are an anagram reading, "Tempest of Francis Bacon, Lord Verulam; do ye ne'er divulge me, ye words." Ingenious, and it is a pity that in the quotation the letter *a* appears only twice in the cryptogram, whereas in the deciphered message it appears three times. Oh, no problem; just alter "Verulam" to "Verul'm" and it works out very nicely.

Most people understand that with sufficient ingenuity one can torture any text and find in it what one wishes. For instance: Did Shakespeare have a hand in the King James Version of the Bible? It was nearing completion in 1610, when Shakespeare was forty-six years old. If you look at the 46th Psalm and count forward for forty-six words, you will find the word *shake*. Now if you go to the end of the psalm and count backward forty-six words, you will find the word *spear*. Clear evidence, according to some, that Shakespeare slyly left his mark in the book.

Bacon's candidacy has largely been replaced in the twentieth century by the candidacy of Edward de Vere (1550–1604), 17th earl of Oxford. The basic ideas behind the Oxford theory, advanced at greatest length by Dorothy and Charlton Ogburn in *This Star of England* (1952, rev. 1955), a book of 1297 pages, and by Charlton Ogburn in *The Mysterious William Shakespeare* (1984), a book of 892 pages, are these: (1) The man from Stratford could not possibly have had the mental equipment and the experience to have written the plays—only a courtier could have written them; (2) Oxford had the requisite background (social position, education, years at Queen Elizabeth's court); (3) Oxford did not wish his authorship to be known for two basic reasons: writing for the public theater was a vulgar pursuit, and the plays show so much courtly and royal disreputable behavior that they would have compromised Oxford's position at court. Oxfordians offer countless details to support the claim. For example, Hamlet's phrase "that ever I was born to set it right" (1.5.89) barely conceals "E. Ver, I was born to set it right," an unambiguous announcement of de Vere's authorship, according to *This Star of England* (p. 654). A second example: Consider Ben

Jonson's poem entitled "To the Memory of My Beloved Master William Shakespeare," prefixed to the first collected edition of Shakespeare's plays in 1623. According to Oxfordians, when Jonson in this poem speaks of the author of the plays as the "swan of Avon," he is alluding not to William Shakespeare, who was born and died in Stratford-on-Avon and who throughout his adult life owned property there; rather, he is alluding to Oxford, who, the Ogburns say, used "William Shakespeare" as his pen name, and whose manor at Bilton was on the Avon River. Oxfordians do not offer any evidence that Oxford took a pen name, and they do not mention that Oxford had sold the manor in 1581, forty-two years before Jonson wrote his poem. Surely a reference to the Shakespeare who was born in Stratford, who had returned to Stratford, and who had died there only seven years before Jonson wrote the poem is more plausible. And exactly why Jonson, who elsewhere also spoke of Shakespeare as a playwright, and why Heminges and Condell, who had acted with Shakespeare for about twenty years, should speak of Shakespeare as the author in their dedication in the 1623 volume of collected plays is never adequately explained by Oxfordians. Either Jonson, Heminges and Condell, and numerous others were in on the conspiracy, or they were all duped—equally unlikely alternatives. Another difficulty in the Oxford theory is that Oxford died in 1604, and some of the plays are clearly indebted to works and events later than 1604. Among the Oxfordian responses are: At his death Oxford left some plays, and in later years these were touched up by hacks, who added the material that points to later dates. *The Tempest*, almost universally regarded as one of Shakespeare's greatest plays and pretty clearly dated to 1611, does indeed date from a period after the death of Oxford, but it is a crude piece of work that should not be included in the canon of works by Oxford.

The anti-Stratfordians, in addition to assuming that the author must have been a man of rank and a university man, usually assume two conspiracies: (1) a conspiracy in Elizabethan and Jacobean times, in which a surprisingly large number of persons connected with the theater knew that the actor Shakespeare did not write the plays attributed to him but for some reason or other pretended that he did; (2) a conspiracy of today's Stratfordians, the professors who teach Shakespeare in the colleges and universities, who are said to have a vested interest in preserving Shakespeare as the author of the plays they teach. In fact, (1) it is inconceivable that the secret of Shakespeare's non-authorship could have been preserved by all of the people who supposedly were in on the conspiracy, and (2) academic fame awaits any scholar today who can disprove Shakespeare's authorship.

The Stratfordian case is convincing not only because hundreds or even thousands of anti-Stratford arguments—of the sort that say "ever I was born" has the secret double meaning "E. Ver, I was born"—add up to nothing at all but also because irrefutable evidence connects the man from Stratford with the London theater and with the authorship of particular plays. The anti-Stratfordians do not seem to understand that it is not enough to dismiss the Stratford case by saying that a fellow from the provinces simply couldn't have written the plays. Nor do they understand that it is not enough to dismiss all of the evidence connecting Shakespeare with the plays by asserting that it is perjured.

The Shakespeare Canon

We return to William Shakespeare. Thirty-seven plays as well as some nondramatic poems are generally held to constitute the Shakespeare canon, the body of authentic works. The exact dates of composition of most of the works are highly uncertain, but evidence of a starting point and/or of a final limiting point often provides a framework for informed guessing. For example, *Richard II* cannot be earlier than 1595, the publication date of some material to which it is indebted; *The Merchant of Venice* cannot be later than 1598, the year Francis Meres mentioned it. Sometimes arguments for a date hang on an alleged topical allusion, such as the lines about the unseasonable weather in *A Midsummer Night's Dream*, 2.1.81–117, but such an allusion, if indeed it is an allusion to an event in the real world, can be variously interpreted, and in any case there is always the possibility that a topical allusion was inserted years later, to bring the play up to date. (The issue of alterations in a text between the time that Shakespeare drafted it and the time that it was printed—alterations due to censorship or playhouse practice or Shakespeare's own second thoughts—will be discussed in "The Play Text as a Collaboration" later in this overview.) Dates are often attributed on the basis of style, and although conjectures about style usually rest on other conjectures (such as Shakespeare's development as a playwright, or the appropriateness of lines to character), sooner or later one must rely on one's literary sense. There is no documentary proof, for example, that *Othello* is not as early as *Romeo and Juliet*, but one feels that *Othello* is a later, more mature work, and because the first record of its performance is 1604, one is glad enough to set its composition at that date and not push it back into Shakespeare's early years. (*Romeo and Juliet* was first published in 1597, but evidence suggests that it was written a little earlier.) The following chronology, then, is indebted not only to facts but also to informed guesswork and sensitivity. The dates, necessarily imprecise for some works, indicate something like a scholarly consensus concerning the time of original composition. Some plays show evidence of later revision.

Plays. The first collected edition of Shakespeare, published in 1623, included thirty-six plays. These are all accepted as Shakespeare's, though for one of them, *Henry VIII*, he is thought to have had a collaborator. A thirty-seventh play, *Pericles*, published in 1609 and attributed to Shakespeare on the title page, is also widely accepted as being partly by Shakespeare even though it is not included in the 1623 volume. Still another play not in the 1623 volume, *The Two Noble Kinsmen*, was first published in 1634, with a title page attributing it to John Fletcher and Shakespeare. Probably most students of the subject now believe that Shakespeare did indeed have a hand in it. Of the remaining plays attributed at one time or another to Shakespeare, only one, *Edward III*, anonymously published in 1596, is now regarded by some scholars as a serious candidate. The prevailing opinion, however, is that this rather simple-minded play is not Shakespeare's; at most he may have revised some passages, chiefly scenes with the Countess of

Salisbury. We include *The Two Noble Kinsmen* but do not include *Edward III* in the following list.

1588–94	*The Comedy of Errors*
1588–94	*Love's Labor's Lost*
1589–91	*2 Henry VI*
1590–91	*3 Henry VI*
1589–92	*1 Henry VI*
1592–93	*Richard III*
1589–94	*Titus Andronicus*
1593–94	*The Taming of the Shrew*
1592–94	*The Two Gentlemen of Verona*
1594–96	*Romeo and Juliet*
1595	*Richard II*
1595–96	*A Midsummer Night's Dream*
1596–97	*King John*
1594–96	*The Merchant of Venice*
1596–97	*1 Henry IV*
1597	*The Merry Wives of Windsor*
1597–98	*2 Henry IV*
1598–99	*Much Ado About Nothing*
1598–99	*Henry V*
1599	*Julius Caesar*
1599–1600	*As You Like It*
1599–1600	*Twelfth Night*
1600–1601	*Hamlet*
1601–1602	*Troilus and Cressida*
1602–1604	*All's Well That Ends Well*
1603–1604	*Othello*
1604	*Measure for Measure*
1605–1606	*King Lear*
1605–1606	*Macbeth*
1606–1607	*Antony and Cleopatra*
1605–1608	*Timon of Athens*
1607–1608	*Coriolanus*
1607–1608	*Pericles*
1609–10	*Cymbeline*
1610–11	*The Winter's Tale*
1611	*The Tempest*

| 1612–13 | *Henry VIII* |
| 1613 | *The Two Noble Kinsmen* |

Poems. In 1989 Donald W. Foster published a book in which he argued that "A Funeral Elegy for Master William Peter," published in 1612, ascribed only to the initials W.S., *may* be by Shakespeare. Foster later published an article in a scholarly journal, *PMLA* 111 (1996), in which he asserted the claim more positively. The evidence begins with the initials, and includes the fact that the publisher and the printer of the elegy had published Shakespeare's *Sonnets* in 1609. But such facts add up to rather little, especially because no one has found any connection between Shakespeare and William Peter (an Oxford graduate about whom little is known, who was murdered at the age of twenty-nine). The argument is based chiefly on statistical examinations of word patterns, which are said to correlate with Shakespeare's known work. Despite such correlations, however, many readers feel that the poem does not sound like Shakespeare. True, Shakespeare has a great range of styles, but his work is consistently imaginative and interesting. Many readers find neither of these qualities in "A Funeral Elegy."

1592–93	*Venus and Adonis*
1593–94	*The Rape of Lucrece*
1593–1600	*Sonnets*
1600–1601	*The Phoenix and the Turtle*

Shakespeare's English

1. Spelling and Pronunciation. From the philologist's point of view, Shakespeare's English is modern English. It requires footnotes, but the inexperienced reader can comprehend substantial passages with very little help, whereas for the same reader Chaucer's Middle English is a foreign language. By the beginning of the fifteenth century the chief grammatical changes in English had taken place, and the final unaccented -*e* of Middle English had been lost (though it survives even today in spelling, as in *name*); during the fifteenth century the dialect of London, the commercial and political center, gradually displaced the provincial dialects, at least in writing; by the end of the century, printing had helped to regularize and stabilize the language, especially spelling. Elizabethan spelling may seem erratic to us (there were dozens of spellings of *Shakespeare*, and a simple word like *been* was also spelled *beene* and *bin*), but it had much in common with our spelling. Elizabethan spelling was conservative in that for the most part it reflected an older pronunciation (Middle English) rather than the sound of the language as it was then spoken, just as our spelling continues to reflect medieval pronunciation—most obviously in the now silent but formerly pronounced letters in a word such as *knight*. Elizabethan pronunciation, though not identical with ours, was much closer to ours than to that of the Middle Ages. Incidentally, though no one can be certain about what Elizabethan English sounded like, specialists tend to believe it was rather like the speech of a modern stage Irishman (*time* apparently was pronounced *toime*, *old* pronounced *awld*, *day* pronounced *die*, and *join* pronounced *jine*) and not at all like the Oxford speech that most of us think it was.

An awareness of the difference between our pronunciation and Shakespeare's is crucial in three areas—in accent, or number of syllables (many metrically regular lines may look irregular to us); in rhymes (which may not look like rhymes); and in puns (which may not look like puns). Examples will be useful. Some words that were at least on occasion stressed differently from today are *aspèct*, *còmplete*, *fòrlorn*, *revènue*, and *sepùlcher*. Words that sometimes had an additional syllable are *emp[e]ress*, *Hen[e]ry*, *mon[e]th*, and *villain* (three syllables, *vil-lay-in*). An additional syllable is often found in possessives, like *moon*'s (pronounced *moones*) and in words ending in *-tion* or *-sion*. Words that had one less syllable than they now have are *needle* (pronounced *neel*) and *violet* (pronounced *vilet*). Among rhymes now lost are *one* with *loan*, *love* with *prove*, *beast* with *jest*, *eat* with *great*. (In reading, trust your sense of metrics and your ear, more than your eye.) An example of a pun that has become obliterated by a change in pronunciation is Falstaff's reply to Prince Hal's "Come, tell us your reason" in *1 Henry IV*: "Give you a reason on compulsion? If reasons were as plentiful as blackberries, I would give no man a reason upon compulsion, I" (2.4.237–40). The *ea* in *reason* was pronounced rather like a long *a*, like the *ai* in *raisin*, hence the comparison with blackberries.

Puns are not merely attempts to be funny; like metaphors they often involve bringing into a meaningful relationship areas of experience normally seen as remote. In *2 Henry IV*, when Feeble is conscripted, he stoically says, "I care not. A man can die but once. We owe God a death" (3.2.242–43), punning on *debt*, which was the way *death* was pronounced. Here an enormously significant fact of life is put into simple commercial imagery, suggesting its commonplace quality. Shakespeare used the same pun earlier in *1 Henry IV*, when Prince Hal says to Falstaff, "Why, thou owest God a death," and Falstaff replies, " 'Tis not due yet: I would be loath to pay him before his day. What need I be so forward with him that calls not on me?" (5.1.126–29).

Sometimes the puns reveal a delightful playfulness; sometimes they reveal aggressiveness, as when, replying to Claudius's "But now, my cousin Hamlet, and my son," Hamlet says, "A little more than kin, and less than kind!" (1.2.64–65). These are Hamlet's first words in the play, and we already hear him warring verbally against Claudius. Hamlet's "less than kind" probably means (1) Hamlet is not of Claudius's family or nature, *kind* having the sense it still has in our word *mankind*; (2) Hamlet is not kindly (affectionately) disposed toward Claudius; (3) Claudius is not naturally (but rather unnaturally, in a legal sense incestuously) Hamlet's father. The puns evidently were not put in as sops to the groundlings; they are an important way of communicating a complex meaning.

2. *Vocabulary.* A conspicuous difficulty in reading Shakespeare is rooted in the fact that some of his words are no longer in common use—for example, words concerned with armor, astrology, clothing, coinage, hawking, horsemanship, law, medicine, sailing, and war. Shakespeare had a large vocabulary—something near thirty thousand words— but it was not so much a vocabulary of big words as a vocabulary drawn from a wide range of life, and it is partly

his ability to call upon a great body of concrete language that gives his plays the sense of being in close contact with life. When the right word did not already exist, he made it up. Among words thought to be his coinages are *accommodation, all-knowing, amazement, bare-faced, countless, dexterously, dislocate, dwindle, fancy-free, frugal, indistinguishable, lackluster, laughable, overawe, premeditated, sea change, star-crossed*. Among those that have not survived are the verb *convive*, meaning to feast together, and *smilet*, a little smile.

Less overtly troublesome than the technical words but more treacherous are the words that seem readily intelligible to us but whose Elizabethan meanings differ from their modern ones. When Horatio describes the Ghost as an "erring spirit," he is saying not that the ghost has sinned or made an error but that it is wandering. Here is a short list of some of the most common words in Shakespeare's plays that often (but not always) have a meaning other than their most usual modern meaning:

'a	he
abuse	deceive
accident	occurrence
advertise	inform
an, and	if
annoy	harm
appeal	accuse
artificial	skillful
brave	fine, splendid
censure	opinion
cheer	(1) face (2) frame of mind
chorus	a single person who comments on the events
closet	small private room
competitor	partner
conceit	idea, imagination
cousin	kinsman
cunning	skillful
disaster	evil astrological influence
doom	judgment
entertain	receive into service

envy	malice
event	outcome
excrement	outgrowth (of hair)
fact	evil deed
fancy	(1) love (2) imagination
fell	cruel
fellow	(1) companion (2) low person (often an insulting term if addressed to someone of approximately equal rank)
fond	foolish
free	(1) innocent (2) generous
glass	mirror
hap, haply	chance, by chance
head	army
humor	(1) mood (2) bodily fluid thought to control one's psychology
imp	child
intelligence	news
kind	natural, acting according to nature
let	hinder
lewd	base
mere(ly)	utter(ly)
modern	commonplace
natural	a fool, an idiot
naughty	(1) wicked (2) worthless
next	nearest
nice	(1) trivial (2) fussy
noise	music
policy	(1) prudence (2) stratagem
presently	immediately
prevent	anticipate
proper	handsome
prove	test
quick	alive
sad	serious
saw	proverb
secure	without care, incautious
silly	innocent

sensible	capable of being perceived by the senses
shrewd	sharp
so	provided that
starve	die
still	always
success	that which follows
tall	brave
tell	count
tonight	last night
wanton	playful, careless
watch	keep awake
will	lust
wink	close both eyes
wit	mind, intelligence

All glosses, of course, are mere approximations; sometimes one of Shakespeare's words may hover between an older meaning and a modern one, and as we have seen, his words often have multiple meanings.

3. Grammar. A few matters of grammar may be surveyed, though it should be noted at the outset that Shakespeare sometimes made up his own grammar. As E.A. Abbott says in *A Shakespearian Grammar,* "Almost any part of speech can be used as any other part of speech": a noun as a verb ("he childed as I fathered"); a verb as a noun ("She hath made compare"); or an adverb as an adjective ("a seldom pleasure"). There are hundreds, perhaps thousands, of such instances in the plays, many of which at first glance would not seem at all irregular and would trouble only a pedant. Here are a few broad matters.

Nouns: The Elizabethans thought the *-s* genitive ending for nouns (as in *man's*) derived from *his*; thus the line " 'gainst the count his galleys I did some service," for "the count's galleys."

Adjectives: By Shakespeare's time adjectives had lost the endings that once indicated gender, number, and case. About the only difference between Shakespeare's adjectives and ours is the use of the now redundant *more* or *most* with the comparative ("some more fitter place") or superlative

("This was the most unkindest cut of all"). Like double comparatives and double superlatives, double negatives were acceptable; Mercutio "will not budge for no man's pleasure."

Pronouns: The greatest change was in pronouns. In Middle English *thou, thy,* and *thee* were used among familiars and in speaking to children and inferiors; *ye, your,* and *you* were used in speaking to superiors (servants to masters, nobles to the king) or to equals with whom the speaker was not familiar. Increasingly the "polite" forms were used in all direct address, regardless of rank, and the accusative *you* displaced the nominative *ye.* Shakespeare sometimes uses *ye* instead of *you,* but even in Shakespeare's day *ye* was archaic, and it occurs mostly in rhetorical appeals.

Thou, thy, and *thee* were not completely displaced, however, and Shakespeare occasionally makes significant use of them, sometimes to connote familiarity or intimacy and sometimes to connote contempt. In *Twelfth Night* Sir Toby advises Sir Andrew to insult Cesario by addressing him as *thou:* "If thou thou'st him some thrice, it shall not be amiss" (3.2.46–47). In *Othello* when Brabantio is addressing an unidentified voice in the dark he says, "What are you?" (1.1.91), but when the voice identifies itself as the foolish suitor Roderigo, Brabantio uses the contemptuous form, saying, "I have charged thee not to haunt about my doors" (93). He uses this form for a while, but later in the scene, when he comes to regard Roderigo as an ally, he shifts back to the polite *you,* beginning in line 163, "What said she to you?" and on to the end of the scene. For reasons not yet satisfactorily explained, Elizabethans used *thou* in addresses to God—"O God, thy arm was here," the king says in *Henry V* (4.8.108)—and to supernatural characters such as ghosts and witches. A subtle variation occurs in *Hamlet.* When Hamlet first talks with the Ghost in 1.5, he uses *thou,* but when he sees the Ghost in his mother's room, in 3.4, he uses *you,* presumably because he is now convinced that the Ghost is not a counterfeit but is his father.

Perhaps the most unusual use of pronouns, from our point of view, is the neuter singular. In place of our *its, his* was often used, as in "How far that little candle throws *his* beams." But the use of a masculine pronoun for a neuter noun came to seem unnatural, and so *it* was used for the possessive as well as the nominative: "The hedge-sparrow fed the cuckoo so long / That it had it head bit off by it young." In the late sixteenth century the possessive form *its* developed, apparently by analogy with the *-s* ending used to indicate a genitive noun, as in *book*'s, but *its* was not yet common usage in Shakespeare's day. He seems to have used *its* only ten times, mostly in his later plays. Other usages, such as "you have seen Cassio and she together" or the substitution of *who* for *whom,* cause little problem even when noticed.

Verbs, Adverbs, and Prepositions: Verbs cause almost no difficulty: The third person singular present form commonly ends in *-s,* as in modern English (e.g., "He blesses"), but sometimes in *eth* (Portia explains to Shylock that mercy "blesseth him that gives and him that takes"). Broadly speaking, the *-eth* ending was old-fashioned or dignified or "literary" rather than colloquial, except for the words *doth, hath,* and *saith.* The *-eth* ending (regularly used in the King James Bible, 1611) is very rare in Shakespeare's dramatic prose, though not surprisingly it occurs twice in the rather formal prose summary of the narrative poem *Lucrece.* Sometimes a plural subject, especially if it has collective force, takes a verb ending in *-s,* as in "My old bones aches." Some of our strong or irregular preterites (such as *broke*) have a different form in Shakespeare (*brake*); some verbs that now have a weak or regular preterite (such as *helped*) in Shakespeare have a strong or irregular preterite (*holp*). Some adverbs that today end in *-ly* were not inflected: "grievous sick," "wondrous strange." Finally, prepositions often are not the ones we expect: "We are such stuff as dreams are made on," "I have a king here to my flatterer."

Again, none of the differences (except meanings that have substantially changed or been lost) will cause much difficulty. But it must be confessed that for some elliptical passages there is no widespread agreement on meaning. Wise editors resist saying more than they know, and when they are uncertain they add a question mark to their gloss.

Shakespeare's Theater

In Shakespeare's infancy, Elizabethan actors performed wherever they could—in great halls, at court, in the courtyards of inns. These venues implied not only different audiences but also different playing conditions. The innyards must have made rather unsatisfactory theaters: on some days they were unavailable because carters bringing goods to London used them as depots; when available, they had to be rented from the innkeeper. In 1567, presumably to avoid such difficulties, and also to avoid regulation by the Common Council of London, which was not well disposed toward theatricals, one John Brayne, brother-in-law of the carpenter turned actor James Burbage, built the Red Lion in an eastern suburb of London. We know nothing about its shape or its capacity; we can say only that it may have been the first building in Europe constructed for the purpose of giving plays since the end of antiquity, a thousand years earlier. Even after the building of the Red Lion theatrical activity continued in London in makeshift circumstances, in marketplaces and inns, and always uneasily. In 1574 the Common Council required that plays and playing places in London be licensed because

> sundry great disorders and inconveniences have been found to ensue to this city by the inordinate haunting of great multitudes of people, specially youth, to plays, interludes, and shows, namely occasion of frays and quarrels, evil practices of incontinency in great inns having chambers and secret places adjoining to their open stages and galleries.

The Common Council ordered that innkeepers who wished licenses to hold performance put up a bond and make contributions to the poor.

The requirement that plays and innyard theaters be licensed, along with the other drawbacks of playing at inns and presumably along with the success of the Red Lion, led James Burbage to rent a plot of land northeast of the city walls, on property outside the jurisdiction of the city. Here he built England's second playhouse, called simply the Theatre. About all that is known of its construction is that it was wood. It soon had imitators, the most famous being the Globe (1599), essentially an amphitheater built across the Thames (again outside the city's jurisdiction), constructed with timbers of the Theatre, which had been dismantled when Burbage's lease ran out.

Admission to the theater was one penny, which allowed spectators to stand at the sides and front of the stage that jutted into the yard. An additional penny bought a seat in a covered part of the theater, and a third penny bought a more comfortable seat and a better location. It is notoriously difficult to translate prices into today's money, since some things that are inexpensive today would have been expensive in the past and vice versa—a pipeful of tobacco (imported, of course) cost a lot of money, about three pennies, and an orange (also imported) cost two or three times what a chicken cost—but perhaps we can get some idea of the low cost of the penny admission when we realize that a penny could also buy a pot of ale. An unskilled laborer made about five or sixpence a day, an artisan about twelve pence a day, and the hired actors (as opposed to the sharers in the company, such as Shakespeare) made about ten pence a performance. A printed play cost five or sixpence. Of course a visit to the theater (like a visit to a baseball game today) usually cost more than the admission since the spectator probably would also buy food and drink. Still, the low entrance fee meant that the theater was available to all except the very poorest people, rather as movies and most athletic events are today. Evidence indicates that the audience ranged from apprentices who somehow managed to scrape together the minimum entrance fee and to escape from their masters for a few hours, to prosperous members of the middle class and aristocrats who paid the additional fee for admission to the galleries. The exact proportion of men to women cannot be determined, but women of all classes certainly were present. Theaters were open every afternoon but Sundays for much of the year, except in times of plague, when they were closed because of fear of infection. By the way, no evidence suggests the presence of toilet facilities. Presumably the patrons relieved themselves by making a quick trip to the fields surrounding the playhouses.

There are four important sources of information about the

structure of Elizabethan public playhouses—drawings, a contract, recent excavations, and stage directions in the plays. Of drawings, only the so-called de Witt drawing (c. 1596) of the Swan—really his friend Aernout van Buchell's copy of Johannes de Witt's drawing—is of much significance. The drawing, the only extant representation of the interior of an Elizabethan theater, shows an amphitheater of three tiers, with a stage jutting from a wall into the yard or

Johannes de Witt, a Continental visitor to London, made a drawing of the Swan theater in about the year 1596. The original drawing is lost; this is Aernout van Buchell's copy of it.

center of the building. The tiers are roofed, and part of the stage is covered by a roof that projects from the rear and is supported at its front on two posts, but the groundlings, who paid a penny to stand in front of the stage or at its sides, were exposed to the sky. (Performances in such a playhouse were held only in the daytime; artificial illumination was not used.) At the rear of the stage are two massive doors; above the stage is a gallery.

The second major source of information, the contract for the Fortune (built in 1600), specifies that although the Globe (built in 1599) is to be the model, the Fortune is to be square, eighty feet outside and fifty-five inside. The stage is to be forty-three feet broad, and is to extend into the middle of the yard, i.e., it is twenty-seven and a half feet deep.

The third source of information, the 1989 excavations of the Rose (built in 1587), indicate that the Rose was fourteen-sided, about seventy-two feet in diameter with an inner yard almost fifty feet in diameter. The stage at the Rose was about sixteen feet deep, thirty-seven feet wide at the rear, and twenty-seven feet wide downstage. The relatively small dimensions and the tapering stage, in contrast to the rectangular stage in the Swan drawing, surprised theater historians and have made them more cautious in generalizing about the Elizabethan theater. Excavations at the Globe have not yielded much information, though some historians believe that the fragmentary evidence suggests a larger theater, perhaps one hundred feet in diameter.

From the fourth chief source, stage directions in the plays, one learns that entrance to the stage was by the doors at the rear (*"Enter one citizen at one door, and another at the other"*). A curtain hanging across the doorway—or a curtain hanging between the two doorways—could provide a place where a character could conceal himself, as Polonius does, when he wishes to overhear the conversation between Hamlet and Gertrude. Similarly, withdrawing a curtain from the doorway could "discover" (reveal) a character or two. Such discovery scenes are very rare in Elizabethan drama, but a good example occurs in *The Tempest* (5.1.171), where a stage direction tells us, *"Here Prospero discovers Ferdinand and Miranda playing at chess."* There was also some sort of playing space "aloft" or "above" to represent, for instance, the top of a city's walls or a room above the street. Doubtless each theater had its own peculiarities, but perhaps we can talk about a "typical" Elizabethan theater if we realize that no theater need exactly fit the description, just as no mother is the average mother with 2.7 children.

This hypothetical theater is wooden, round, or polygonal (in *Henry V* Shakespeare calls it a "wooden *O*") capable of holding some eight hundred spectators who stood in the yard around the projecting elevated stage—these spectators were the "groundlings"—and some fifteen hundred additional spectators who sat in the three roofed galleries. The stage, protected by a "shadow" or "heavens" or roof, is entered from two doors; behind the doors is the "tiring house" (attiring house, i.e., dressing room), and above the stage is some sort of gallery that may sometimes hold spectators but can be used (for example) as the bedroom from which Romeo—according to a stage direction in one text—"goeth down." Some evidence suggests that a throne can be lowered onto the platform stage, perhaps from the "shadow"; certainly characters can descend from the stage through a trap or traps into the cellar or "hell." Sometimes this space beneath the stage accommodates a sound-effects man or musician (in *Antony and Cleopatra* "*music of the hautboys* [oboes] *is under the stage*") or an actor (in *Hamlet* the "*Ghost cries under the stage*"). Most characters simply walk on and off through the doors, but because there is no curtain in front of the platform, corpses will have to be carried off (Hamlet obligingly clears the stage of Polonius's corpse, when he says, "I'll lug the guts into the neighbor room"). Other characters may have fallen at the rear, where a curtain on a doorway could be drawn to conceal them.

Such may have been the "public theater," so called because its inexpensive admission made it available to a wide range of the populace. Another kind of theater has been called the "private theater" because its much greater admission charge (sixpence versus the penny for general admission at the public theater) limited its audience to the wealthy or the prodigal. The private theater was basically a large room, entirely roofed and therefore artificially illuminated, with a stage at one end. The theaters thus were distinct in two ways: One was essentially an amphitheater that

catered to the general public; the other was a hall that catered
to the wealthy. In 1576 a hall theater was established in
Blackfriars, a Dominican priory in London that had been
suppressed in 1538 and confiscated by the Crown and thus
was not under the city's jurisdiction. All the actors in this
Blackfriars theater were boys about eight to thirteen years
old (in the public theaters similar boys played female parts;
a boy Lady Macbeth played to a man Macbeth). Near the
end of this section on Shakespeare's theater we will talk at
some length about possible implications in this convention
of using boys to play female roles, but for the moment we
should say that it doubtless accounts for the relative lack of
female roles in Elizabethan drama. Thus, in *A Midsummer
Night's Dream*, out of twenty-one named roles, only four are
female; in *Hamlet*, out of twenty-four, only two (Gertrude
and Ophelia) are female. Many of Shakespeare's characters
have fathers but no mothers—for instance, King Lear's
daughters. We need not bring in Freud to explain the dis-
parity; a dramatic company had only a few boys in it.

To return to the private theaters, in some of which all of
the performers were children—the "eyrie of . . . little cyases"
(nest of unfledged hawks—2.2.347–48) which Rosencrantz
mentions when he and Guildenstern talk with Hamlet. The
theater in Blackfriars had a precarious existence, and ceased
operations in 1584. In 1596 James Burbage, who had already
made theatrical history by building the Theatre, began to
construct a second Blackfriars theater. He died in 1597, and
for several years this second Blackfriars theater was used by
a troupe of boys, but in 1608 two of Burbage's sons and five
other actors (including Shakespeare) became joint operators
of the theater, using it in the winter when the open-air Globe
was unsuitable. Perhaps such a smaller theater, roofed, artificially illuminated, and with a tradition of a wealthy audience, exerted an influence in Shakespeare's late plays.

Performances in the private theaters may well have had
intermissions during which music was played, but in the
public theaters the action was probably uninterrupted,
flowing from scene to scene almost without a break. Actors
would enter, speak, exit, and others would immediately
enter and establish (if necessary) the new locale by a few
properties and by words and gestures. To indicate that the

scene took place at night, a player or two would carry a torch. Here are some samples of Shakespeare establishing the scene:

This is Illyria, lady.   (*Twelfth Night*, 1.2.2)

Well, this is the Forest of Arden.   (*As You Like It*, 2.4.14)

This castle has a pleasant seat; the air
Nimbly and sweetly recommends itself
Unto our gentle senses.   (*Macbeth*, 1.6.1–3)

The west yet glimmers with some streaks of day.
                                          (*Macbeth*, 3.3.5)

Sometimes a speech will go far beyond evoking the minimal setting of place and time, and will, so to speak, evoke the social world in which the characters move. For instance, early in the first scene of *The Merchant of Venice* Salerio suggests an explanation for Antonio's melancholy. (In the following passage, *pageants* are decorated wagons, floats, and *cursy* is the verb "to curtsy," or "to bow.")

Your mind is tossing on the ocean,
There where your argosies with portly sail—
Like signiors and rich burghers on the flood,
Or as it were the pageants of the sea—
Do overpeer the petty traffickers
That cursy to them, do them reverence,
As they fly by them with their woven wings.   (1.1.8–14)

Late in the nineteenth century, when Henry Irving produced the play with elaborate illusionistic sets, the first scene showed a ship moored in the harbor, with fruit vendors and dock laborers, in an effort to evoke the bustling and exotic life of Venice. But Shakespeare's words give us this exotic, rich world of commerce in his highly descriptive language when Salerio speaks of "argosies with portly sail" that fly with "woven wings"; equally important, through Salerio Shakespeare conveys a sense of the orderly, hierarchical society in which the lesser ships, "the petty traffickers," curtsy and thereby "do . . . reverence" to their superiors, the merchant prince's ships, which are "Like signiors and rich burghers."

On the other hand, it is a mistake to think that except for verbal pictures the Elizabethan stage was bare. Although Shakespeare's Chorus in *Henry V* calls the stage an "unworthy scaffold" (Prologue 1.10) and urges the spectators to "eke out our performance with your mind" (Prologue 3.35), there was considerable spectacle. The last act of *Macbeth*, for instance, has five stage directions calling for *"drum and colors,"* and another sort of appeal to the eye is indicated by the stage direction *"Enter Macduff, with Macbeth's head."* Some scenery and properties may have been substantial; doubtless a throne was used, but the pillars supporting the roof would have served for the trees on which Orlando pins his poems in *As You Like It*.

Having talked about the public theater—"this wooden *O*"—at some length, we should mention again that Shakespeare's plays were performed also in other locales. Alvin Kernan, in *Shakespeare, the King's Playwright: Theater in the Stuart Court 1603–1613* (1995) points out that "several of [Shakespeare's] plays contain brief theatrical performances, set always in a court or some noble house. When Shakespeare portrayed a theater, he did not, except for the choruses in *Henry V*, imagine a public theater" (p. 195). (Examples include episodes in *The Taming of the Shrew*, *A Midsummer Night's Dream*, *Hamlet*, and *The Tempest*.)

A Note on the Use of Boy Actors in Female Roles

Until fairly recently, scholars were content to mention that the convention existed; they sometimes also mentioned that it continued the medieval practice of using males in female roles, and that other theaters, notably in ancient Greece and in China and Japan, also used males in female roles. (In classical Noh drama in Japan, males still play the female roles.) Prudery may have been at the root of the academic failure to talk much about the use of boy actors, or maybe there really is not much more to say than that it was a convention of a male-centered culture (Stephen Greenblatt's view, in *Shakespearean Negotiations* [1988]). Further, the very nature of a convention is that it is not thought about: Hamlet is a Dane and Julius Caesar is a Roman, but in Shakespeare's plays they speak English, and we in the audience never give this odd fact a thought. Similarly, a character may speak in the presence of others and we understand, again without thinking about it, that he or she is not heard by the figures on the stage (the aside); a character alone on the stage may speak (the soliloquy), and we do not take the character to be unhinged; in a realistic (box) set, the fourth wall, which allows us to see what is going on, is miraculously missing. The no-nonsense view, then, is that the boy actor was an accepted convention, accepted unthinkingly—just as today we know that Kenneth Branagh is not Hamlet, Al Pacino is not Richard III, and Denzel Washington is not the Prince of Aragon. In this view, the audience takes the performer for the role, and that is that; such is the argument we now make for race-free casting, in which African-Americans and Asians can play roles of persons who lived in medieval Denmark and ancient Rome. But gender perhaps is different, at least today. It is a matter of abundant academic study: The Elizabethan theater is now sometimes called a transvestite theater, and we hear much about cross-dressing.

Shakespeare himself in a very few passages calls attention to the use of boys in female roles. At the end of *As You Like It* the boy who played Rosalind addresses the audience, and says, "O men, . . . if I were a woman, I would kiss as many of you as had beards that pleased me." But this is in the Epilogue; the plot is over, and the actor is stepping out of the play and into the audience's everyday world. A second reference to the practice of boys playing female roles occurs in *Antony and Cleopatra*, when Cleopatra imagines that she and Antony will be the subject of crude plays, her role being performed by a boy:

> The quick comedians
> Extemporally will stage us, and present
> Our Alexandrian revels: Antony
> Shall be brought drunken forth, and I shall see
> Some squeaking Cleopatra boy my greatness.   (5.2.216–20)

In a few other passages, Shakespeare is more indirect. For instance, in *Twelfth Night* Viola, played of course by a boy, disguises herself as a young man and seeks service in the house of a lord. She enlists the help of a Captain, and (by way of explaining away her voice and her beardlessness) says,

> I'll serve this duke
> Thou shalt present me as an eunuch to him.   (1.2.55–56)

In *Hamlet*, when the players arrive in 2.2, Hamlet jokes with the boy who plays a female role. The boy has grown since Hamlet last saw him: "By'r Lady, your ladyship is nearer to heaven than when I saw you last by the altitude of a chopine" (a lady's thick-soled shoe). He goes on: "Pray God your voice . . . be not cracked" (434–38).

Exactly how sexual, how erotic, this material was and is, is now much disputed. Again, the use of boys may have been unnoticed, or rather not thought about—an unexamined convention—by most or all spectators most of the time, perhaps *all* of the time, except when Shakespeare calls the convention to the attention of the audience, as in the passages just quoted. Still, an occasional bit seems to invite erotic thoughts. The clearest example is the name that Rosalind takes in *As You Like It*, Ganymede—the beautiful youth whom Zeus abducted. Did boys dressed to play female roles carry homoerotic appeal for straight men (Lisa Jardine's view, in *Still Harping on Daughters* [1983]), or for gay men, or for some or all women in the audience? Further, when the boy actor played a woman who (for the purposes of the plot) disguised herself as a male, as Rosalind, Viola, and Portia do—so we get a boy playing a woman playing a man—what sort of appeal was generated, and for what sort of spectator?

Some scholars have argued that the convention empowered women by letting female characters display a freedom unavailable in Renaissance patriarchal society; the convention, it is said, undermined rigid gender distinctions. In this view, the convention (along with plots in which female characters for a while disguised themselves as young men) allowed Shakespeare to say what some modern gender

critics say: Gender is a constructed role rather than a biological given, something we make, rather than a fixed binary
opposition of male and female (see Juliet Dusinberre, in
Shakespeare and the Nature of Women [1975]). On the other
hand, some scholars have maintained that the male disguise
assumed by some female characters serves only to reaffirm
traditional social distinctions since female characters who
don male garb (notably Portia in *The Merchant of Venice*
and Rosalind in *As You Like It*) return to their female garb
and at least implicitly (these critics say) reaffirm the status
quo. (For this last view, see Clara Claiborne Park, in an
essay in *The Woman's Part*, ed. Carolyn Ruth Swift Lenz et
al. [1980].) Perhaps no one answer is right for all plays; in
As You Like It cross-dressing empowers Rosalind, but in
Twelfth Night cross-dressing comically traps Viola.

Shakespeare's Dramatic Language: Costumes, Gestures and Silences; Prose and Poetry

Because Shakespeare was a dramatist, not merely a poet,
he worked not only with language but also with costume,
sound effects, gestures, and even silences. We have already
discussed some kinds of spectacle in the preceding section,
and now we will begin with other aspects of visual language;
a theater, after all, is literally a "place for seeing." Consider
the opening stage direction in *The Tempest*, the first play in
the first published collection of Shakespeare's plays: *"A
tempestuous noise of thunder and Lightning heard: Enter a
Ship-master, and a Boteswain."*

Costumes: What did that shipmaster and that boatswain
wear? Doubtless they wore something that identified them
as men of the sea. Not much is known about the costumes
that Elizabethan actors wore, but at least three points are
clear: (1) many of the costumes were splendid versions of
contemporary Elizabethan dress; (2) some attempts were
made to approximate the dress of certain occupations and of
antique or exotic characters such as Romans, Turks, and
Jews; (3) some costumes indicated that the wearer was

supernatural. Evidence for elaborate Elizabethan clothing can be found in the plays themselves and in contemporary comments about the "sumptuous" players who wore the discarded clothing of noblemen, as well as in account books that itemize such things as "a scarlet cloak with two broad gold laces, with gold buttons down the sides."

The attempts at approximation of the dress of certain occupations and nationalities also can be documented from the plays themselves, and it derives additional confirmation from a drawing of the first scene of Shakespeare's *Titus Andronicus*—the only extant Elizabethan picture of an identifiable episode in a play. (See pp. xxxviii–xxxix.) The drawing, probably done in 1594 or 1595, shows Queen Tamora pleading for mercy. She wears a somewhat medieval-looking robe and a crown; Titus wears a toga and a wreath, but two soldiers behind him wear costumes fairly close to Elizabethan dress. We do not know, however, if the drawing represents an actual stage production in the public theater, or perhaps a private production, or maybe only a reader's visualization of an episode. Further, there is some conflicting evidence: In *Julius Caesar* a reference is made to Caesar's doublet (a close-fitting jacket), which, if taken literally, suggests that even the protagonist did not wear Roman clothing; and certainly the lesser characters, who are said to wear hats, did not wear Roman garb.

It should be mentioned, too, that even ordinary clothing can be symbolic: Hamlet's "inky cloak," for example, sets him apart from the brightly dressed members of Claudius's court and symbolizes his mourning; the fresh clothes that are put on King Lear partly symbolize his return to sanity. Consider, too, the removal of disguises near the end of some plays. For instance, Rosalind in *As You Like It* and Portia and Nerissa in *The Merchant of Venice* remove their male attire, thus again becoming fully themselves.

Gestures and Silences: Gestures are an important part of a dramatist's language. King Lear kneels before his daughter Cordelia for a benediction (4.7.57–59), an act of humility that contrasts with his earlier speeches banishing her and that contrasts also with a comparable gesture, his ironic

kneeling before Regan (2.4.153–55). Northumberland's failure to kneel before King Richard II (3.3.71–72) speaks volumes. As for silences, consider a moment in *Coriolanus*: Before the protagonist yields to his mother's entreaties (5.3.182), there is this stage direction: *"Holds her by the hand, silent."* Another example of "speech in dumbness" occurs in *Macbeth*, when Macduff learns that his wife and children have been murdered. He is silent at first, as Malcolm's speech indicates: "What, man! Ne'er pull your hat upon your brows. Give sorrow words" (4.3.208–09). (For a discussion of such moments, see Philip C. McGuire's *Speechless Dialect: Shakespeare's Open Silences* [1985].)

Of course when we think of Shakespeare's work, we think primarily of his language, both the poetry and the prose.

Prose: Although two of his plays (*Richard II* and *King John*) have no prose at all, about half the others have at least one quarter of the dialogue in prose, and some have notably more: *1 Henry IV* and *2 Henry IV*, about half; *As You Like It*

and *Twelfth Night*, a little more than half; *Much Ado About Nothing*, more than three quarters; and *The Merry Wives of Windsor*, a little more than five sixths. We should remember that despite Molière's joke about M. Jourdain, who was amazed to learn that he spoke prose, most of us do not speak prose. Rather, we normally utter repetitive, shapeless, and often ungrammatical torrents; prose is something very different—a sort of literary imitation of speech at its most coherent.

Today we may think of prose as "natural" for drama; or even if we think that poetry is appropriate for high tragedy we may still think that prose is the right medium for comedy. Greek, Roman, and early English comedies, however, were written in verse. In fact, prose was not generally considered a literary medium in England until the late fifteenth century; Chaucer tells even his bawdy stories in verse. By the end of the 1580s, however, prose had established itself on the English comic stage. In tragedy, Marlowe made some use of prose, not simply in the speeches of clownish servants but even in the speech of a tragic hero, Doctor Faustus. Still, before Shakespeare, prose normally was used in the theater only for special circumstances: (1) letters and proclamations, to set them off from the poetic dialogue; (2) mad characters, to indicate that normal thinking has become disordered; and (3) low comedy, or speeches uttered by clowns even when they are not being comic. Shakespeare made use of these conventions, but he also went far beyond them. Sometimes he begins a scene in prose and then shifts into verse as the emotion is heightened; or conversely, he may shift from verse to prose when a speaker is lowering the emotional level, as when Brutus speaks in the Forum.

Shakespeare's prose usually is not prosaic. Hamlet's prose includes not only small talk with Rosencrantz and Guildenstern but also princely reflections on "What a piece of work is a man" (2.2.312). In conversation with Ophelia, he shifts from light talk in verse to a passionate prose denunciation of women (3.1.103), though the shift to prose here is perhaps also intended to suggest the possibility of madness. (Consult Brian Vickers, *The Artistry of Shakespeare's Prose* [1968].)

Poetry: Drama in rhyme in England goes back to the Middle Ages, but by Shakespeare's day rhyme no longer dominated poetic drama; a finer medium, blank verse (strictly speaking, unrhymed lines of ten syllables, with the stress on every second syllable) had been adopted. But before looking at unrhymed poetry, a few things should be said about the chief uses of rhyme in Shakespeare's plays. (1) A couplet (a pair of rhyming lines) is sometimes used to convey emotional heightening at the end of a blank verse speech; (2) characters sometimes speak a couplet as they leave the stage, suggesting closure; (3) except in the latest plays, scenes fairly often conclude with a couplet, and sometimes, as in *Richard II*, 2.1.145–46, the entrance of a new character within a scene is preceded by a couplet, which wraps up the earlier portion of that scene; (4) speeches of two characters occasionally are linked by rhyme, most notably in *Romeo and Juliet*, 1.5.95–108, where the lovers speak a sonnet between them; elsewhere a taunting reply occasionally rhymes with the previous speaker's last line; (5) speeches with sententious or gnomic remarks are sometimes in rhyme, as in the duke's speech in *Othello* (1.3.199–206); (6) speeches of sardonic mockery are sometimes in rhyme—for example, Iago's speech on women in *Othello* (2.1.146–58)—and they sometimes conclude with an emphatic couplet, as in Bolingbroke's speech on comforting words in *Richard II* (1.3.301–2); (7) some characters are associated with rhyme, such as the fairies in *A Midsummer Night's Dream*; (8) in the early plays, especially *The Comedy of Errors* and *The Taming of the Shrew*, comic scenes that in later plays would be in prose are in jingling rhymes; (9) prologues, choruses, plays-within-the-play, inscriptions, vows, epilogues, and so on are often in rhyme, and the songs in the plays are rhymed.

Neither prose nor rhyme immediately comes to mind when we first think of Shakespeare's medium: It is blank verse, unrhymed iambic pentameter. (In a mechanically exact line there are five iambic feet. An iambic foot consists of two syllables, the second accented, as in *away*; five feet make a pentameter line. Thus, a strict line of iambic pentameter contains ten syllables, the even syllables being stressed more heavily than the odd syllables. Fortunately, Shakespeare usually varies the line somewhat.) The first speech in *A Midsummer Night's Dream*, spoken by Duke Theseus to his betrothed, is an example of blank verse:

> Now, fair Hippolyta, our nuptial hour
> Draws on apace. Four happy days bring in
> Another moon; but, O, methinks, how slow
> This old moon wanes! She lingers my desires,
> Like to a stepdame, or a dowager,
> Long withering out a young man's revenue.   (1.1.1–6)

As this passage shows, Shakespeare's blank verse is not mechanically unvarying. Though the predominant foot is the iamb (as in *apace* or *desires*), there are numerous variations. In the first line the stress can be placed on "fair," as the regular metrical pattern suggests, but it is likely that "Now" gets almost as much emphasis; probably in the second line "Draws" is more heavily emphasized than "on," giving us a

trochee (a stressed syllable followed by an unstressed one);
and in the fourth line each word in the phrase "This old
moon wanes" is probably stressed fairly heavily, conveying
by two spondees (two feet, each of two stresses) the oppressive tedium that Theseus feels.

In Shakespeare's early plays much of the blank verse is
end-stopped (that is, it has a heavy pause at the end of each
line), but he later developed the ability to write iambic pentameter verse paragraphs (rather than lines) that give the
illusion of speech. His chief techniques are (1) enjambing,
i.e., running the thought beyond the single line, as in the first
three lines of the speech just quoted; (2) occasionally
replacing an iamb with another foot; (3) varying the position
of the chief pause (the caesura) within a line; (4) adding an
occasional unstressed syllable at the end of a line, traditionally called a feminine ending; (5) and beginning or ending a
speech with a half line.

Shakespeare's mature blank verse has much of the
rhythmic flexibility of his prose; both the language, though
richly figurative and sometimes dense, and the syntax seem
natural. It is also often highly appropriate to a particular
character. Consider, for instance, this speech from *Hamlet*,
in which Claudius, King of Denmark ("the Dane"), speaks
to Laertes:

> And now, Laertes, what's the news with you?
> You told us of some suit. What is't, Laertes?
> You cannot speak of reason to the Dane
> And lose your voice. What wouldst thou beg, Laertes,
> That shall not be my offer, not thy asking?   (1.2.42–46)

Notice the short sentences and the repetition of the name
"Laertes," to whom the speech is addressed. Notice, too, the
shift from the royal "us" in the second line to the more intimate "my" in the last line, and from "you" in the first three
lines to the more intimate "thou" and "thy" in the last two
lines. Claudius knows how to ingratiate himself with
Laertes.

For a second example of the flexibility of Shakespeare's
blank verse, consider a passage from *Macbeth*. Distressed

by the doctor's inability to cure Lady Macbeth and by the imminent battle, Macbeth addresses some of his remarks to the doctor and others to the servant who is arming him. The entire speech, with its pauses, interruptions, and irresolution (in "Pull't off, I say," Macbeth orders the servant to remove the armor that the servant has been putting on him), catches Macbeth's disintegration. (In the first line, *physic* means "medicine," and in the fourth and fifth lines, *cast the water* means "analyze the urine.")

> Throw physic to the dogs, I'll none of it.
> Come, put mine armor on. Give me my staff.
> Seyton, send out.—Doctor, the thanes fly from me.—
> Come, sir, dispatch. If thou couldst, doctor, cast
> The water of my land, find her disease
> And purge it to a sound and pristine health,
> I would applaud thee to the very echo,
> That should applaud again.—Pull't off, I say.—
> What rhubarb, senna, or what purgative drug,
> Would scour these English hence? Hear'st thou of them?
>
> (5.3.47–56)

Blank verse, then, can be much more than unrhymed iambic pentameter, and even within a single play Shakespeare's blank verse often consists of several styles, depending on the speaker and on the speaker's emotion at the moment.

The Play Text as a Collaboration

Shakespeare's fellow dramatist Ben Jonson reported that the actors said of Shakespeare, "In his writing, whatsoever he penned, he never blotted out line," i.e., never crossed out material and revised his work while composing. None of Shakespeare's plays survives in manuscript (with the possible exception of a scene in *Sir Thomas More*), so we cannot fully evaluate the comment, but in a few instances the published work clearly shows that he revised his manuscript. Consider the following passage (shown here in facsimile) from the best early text of *Romeo and Juliet*, the Second Quarto (1599):

> *Ro.* Would I were sleepe and peace so sweet to rest
> The grey eyde morne smiles on the frowning night,
> Checkring the Easterne Clouds with streaks of light,
> And darknesse fleckted like a drunkard reeles,
> From forth daies pathway, made by *Tytans* wheeles.
> Hence will I to my ghostly Friers close cell,
> His helpe to craue, and my deare hap to tell.
>
> > *Exit.*
>
> *Enter Frier alone with a basket.*   (night,
> *Fri.* The grey-eyed morne smiles on the frowning
> Checking the Easterne clowdes with streaks of light:
> And fleckeld darknesse like a drunkard reeles,
> From forth daies path, and *Titans* burning wheeles:
> Now ere the sun aduance his burning eie,

Romeo rather elaborately tells us that the sun at dawn is
dispelling the night (morning is smiling, the eastern clouds
are checked with light, and the sun's chariot—Titan's
wheels—advances), and he will seek out his spiritual father,
the Friar. He exits and, oddly, the Friar enters and says pretty
much the same thing about the sun. Both speakers say that
"the gray-eyed morn smiles on the frowning night," but there
are small differences, perhaps having more to do with the
business of printing the book than with the author's
composition: For Romeo's "checkring," "fleckted," and
"pathway," we get the Friar's "checking," "fleckeld," and
"path." (Notice, by the way, the inconsistency in Elizabethan
spelling: Romeo's "clouds" become the Friar's "clowdes.")
     Both versions must have been in the printer's copy, and it
seems safe to assume that both were in Shakespeare's manuscript. He must have written one version—let's say he first
wrote Romeo's closing lines for this scene—and then he
decided, no, it's better to give this lyrical passage to the
Friar, as the opening of a new scene, but he neglected to
delete the first version. Editors must make a choice, and they
may feel that the reasonable thing to do is to print the text as
Shakespeare intended it. But how can we know what he
intended? Almost all modern editors delete the lines from

Romeo's speech, and retain the Friar's lines. They don't do this because they know Shakespeare's intention, however. They give the lines to the Friar because the first published version (1597) of *Romeo and Juliet* gives only the Friar's version, and this text (though in many ways inferior to the 1599 text) is thought to derive from the memory of some actors, that is, it is thought to represent a performance, not just a script. Maybe during the course of rehearsals Shakespeare—an actor as well as an author—unilaterally decided that the Friar should speak the lines; if so (remember that we don't know this to be a fact) his final intention was to give the speech to the Friar. Maybe, however, the actors talked it over and settled on the Friar, with or without Shakespeare's approval. On the other hand, despite the 1597 version, one might argue (if only weakly) on behalf of giving the lines to Romeo rather than to the Friar, thus: (1) Romeo's comment on the coming of the daylight emphasizes his separation from Juliet, and (2) the figurative language seems more appropriate to Romeo than to the Friar. Having said this, in the Signet edition we have decided in this instance to draw on the evidence provided by earlier text and to give the lines to the Friar, on the grounds that since Q1 reflects a production, in the theater (at least on one occasion) the lines were spoken by the Friar.

A playwright sold a script to a theatrical company. The script thus belonged to the company, not the author, and author and company alike must have regarded this script not as a literary work but as the basis for a play that the actors would create on the stage. We speak of Shakespeare as the author of the plays, but readers should bear in mind that the texts they read, even when derived from a single text, such as the First Folio (1623), are inevitably the collaborative work not simply of Shakespeare with his company—doubtless during rehearsals the actors would suggest alterations—but also with other forces of the age. One force was governmental censorship. In 1606 parliament passed "an Act to restrain abuses of players," prohibiting the utterance of oaths and the name of God. So where the earliest text of *Othello* gives us "By heaven" (3.3.106), the first Folio gives "Alas," presumably reflecting the compliance of stage practice with the law. Similarly, the 1623 version of *King Lear* omits the oath "Fut" (probably from "By God's foot") at 1.2.142, again presumably reflecting the line as it was spoken on the stage. Editors who seek to give the reader the play that Shakespeare initially conceived—the "authentic" play conceived by the solitary Shakespeare—probably will restore the missing oaths and references to God. Other editors, who see the play as a collaborative work, a construction made not only by Shakespeare but also by actors and compositors and even government censors, may claim that what counts is the play as it was actually performed. Such editors regard the censored text as legitimate, since it is the play that was (presumably) finally put on. A performed text, they argue, has more historical reality than a text produced by an editor who has sought to get at what Shakespeare initially wrote. In this view, the text of a play is rather like the script of a film; the script is not the film, and the play text is not the performed play. Even if we want to talk about the play that Shakespeare "intended," we will find ourselves talking about a script that he handed over to a company with the intention that it be implemented by actors. The "intended" play is the one that the actors—we might almost say "society"—would help to construct.

Further, it is now widely held that a play is also the work of readers and spectators, who do not simply receive meaning, but who create it when they respond to the play. This idea is fully in accord with contemporary post-structuralist critical thinking, notably Roland Barthes's "The Death of the Author," in *Image-Music-Text* (1977) and Michel Foucault's "What Is an Author?," in *The Foucault Reader* (1984). The gist of the idea is that an author is not an isolated genius; rather, authors are subject to the politics and other social structures of their age. A dramatist especially is a worker in a collaborative project, working most obviously with actors—parts may be written for particular actors—but working also with the audience. Consider the words of Samuel Johnson, written to be spoken by the actor David Garrick at the opening of a theater in 1747:

> The stage but echoes back the public voice;
> The drama's laws, the drama's patrons give,
> For we that live to please, must please to live.

The audience—the public taste as understood by the playwright—helps to determine what the play is. Moreover, even members of the public who are not part of the playwright's immediate audience may exert an influence through censorship. We have already glanced at governmental censorship, but there are also other kinds. Take one of Shakespeare's most beloved characters, Falstaff, who appears in three of Shakespeare's plays, the two parts of *Henry IV* and *The Merry Wives of Windsor*. He appears with this name in the earliest printed version of the first of these plays, *1 Henry IV*, but we know that Shakespeare originally called him (after an historical figure) Sir John Oldcastle. Oldcastle appears in Shakespeare's source (partly reprinted in the Signet edition of *1 Henry IV*), and a trace of the name survives in Shakespeare's play, 1.2.43–44, where Prince Hal punningly addresses Falstaff as "my old lad of the castle." But for some reason—perhaps because the family of the historical Oldcastle complained—Shakespeare had to change the name. In short, the play as we have it was (at least in this detail) subject to some sort of censorship. If we think that a text should present what we take to be the author's intention, we probably will want to replace *Falstaff* with *Oldcastle*. But if we recognize that a play is a collaboration, we may welcome the change, even if it was forced on Shakespeare. Somehow *Falstaff*, with its hint of *false-staff*, i.e., inadequate prop, seems just right for this fat knight who, to our delight, entertains the young prince with untruths. We can go as far as saying that, at least so far as a play is concerned, an insistence on the author's original intention (even if we could know it) can sometimes impoverish the text.

The tiny example of Falstaff's name illustrates the point that the text we read is inevitably only a version—something in effect produced by the collaboration of the playwright with his actors, audiences, compositors, and editors—of a fluid text that Shakespeare once wrote, just as the *Hamlet* that we see on the screen starring Kenneth Branagh is not the *Hamlet* that Shakespeare saw in an open-air playhouse starring Richard Burbage. *Hamlet* itself, as we shall note in a moment, also exists in several versions. It is not surprising that there is now much talk about the *instability* of Shakespeare's texts.

Because he was not only a playwright but was also an actor and a shareholder in a theatrical company, Shakespeare probably was much involved with the translation of the play from a manuscript to a stage production. He may or may not have done some rewriting during rehearsals, and he may or may not have been happy with cuts that were made. Some plays, notably *Hamlet* and *King Lear*, are so long that it is most unlikely that the texts we read were acted in their entirety. Further, for both of these plays we have more than one early text that demands consideration. In *Hamlet*, the Second Quarto (1604) includes some two hundred lines not found in the Folio (1623). Among the passages missing from the Folio are two of Hamlet's reflective speeches, the "dram of evil" speech (1.4.13–38) and "How all occasions do inform against me" (4.4.32–66). Since the Folio has more numerous and often fuller stage directions, it certainly looks as though in the Folio we get a theatrical version of the play, a text whose cuts were probably made—this is only a hunch, of course—not because Shakespeare was changing his conception of Hamlet but because the playhouse demanded a modified play. (The problem is complicated, since the Folio not only cuts some of the Quarto but adds some material. Various explanations have been offered.)

Or take an example from *King Lear*. In the First and Second Quarto (1608, 1619), the final speech of the play is given to Albany, Lear's surviving son-in-law, but in the First Folio version (1623), the speech is given to Edgar. The Quarto version is in accord with tradition—usually the highest-ranking character in a tragedy speaks the final words. Why does the Folio give the speech to Edgar? One possible answer is this: The Folio version omits some of Albany's speeches in earlier scenes, so perhaps it was decided (by Shakespeare? by the players?) not to give the final lines to so pale a character. In fact, the discrepancies are so many between the two texts, that some scholars argue we do not simply have texts showing different theatrical productions. Rather, these scholars say, Shakespeare substantially revised the play, and we really have two versions of *King Lear* (and of *Othello* also, say some)—two different plays—not simply two texts, each of which is in some ways imperfect.

In this view, the 1608 version of *Lear* may derive from Shakespeare's manuscript, and the 1623 version may derive from his later revision. The Quartos have almost three hundred lines not in the Folio, and the Folio has about a hundred lines not in the Quartos. It used to be held that all the texts were imperfect in various ways and from various causes—some passages in the Quartos were thought to have been set from a manuscript that was not entirely legible, other passages were thought to have been set by a compositor who was new to setting plays, and still other passages were thought to have been provided by an actor who misremembered some of the lines. This traditional view held that an editor must draw on the Quartos and the Folio in order to get Shakespeare's "real" play. The new argument holds (although not without considerable strain) that we have two authentic plays, Shakespeare's early version (in the Quarto) and Shakespeare's—or his theatrical company's—revised version (in the Folio). Not only theatrical demands but also Shakespeare's own artistic sense, it is argued, called for extensive revisions. Even the titles vary: Q1 is called *True Chronicle Historie of the life and death of King Lear and his three Daughters*, whereas the Folio text is called *The Tragedie of King Lear*. To combine the two texts in order to produce what the editor thinks is the play that Shakespeare intended to write is, according to this view, to produce a text that is false to the history of the play. If the new view is correct, and we do have texts of two distinct versions of *Lear* rather than two imperfect versions of one play, it supports in a textual way the poststructuralist view that we cannot possibly have an unmediated vision of (in this case) a play by Shakespeare; we can only recognize a plurality of visions.

Editing Texts

Though eighteen of his plays were published during his lifetime, Shakespeare seems never to have supervised their publication. There is nothing unusual here; when a playwright sold a play to a theatrical company he surrendered his ownership to it. Normally a company would not publish the play, because to publish it meant to allow competitors to acquire the piece. Some plays did get published: Apparently hard-up actors sometimes pieced together a play for a publisher; sometimes a company in need of money sold a play; and sometimes a company allowed publication of a play that no longer drew audiences. That Shakespeare did not concern himself with publication is not remarkable; of his contemporaries, only Ben Jonson carefully supervised the publication of his own plays.

In 1623, seven years after Shakespeare's death, John Heminges and Henry Condell (two senior members of Shakespeare's company, who had worked with him for about twenty years) collected his plays—published and unpublished—into a large volume, of a kind called a folio. (A folio is a volume consisting of large sheets that have been folded once, each sheet thus making two leaves, or four pages. The size of the page of course depends on the size of the sheet—a folio can range in height from twelve to sixteen inches, and in width from eight to eleven; the pages in the 1623 edition of Shakespeare, commonly called the First Folio, are approximately thirteen inches tall and eight inches wide.) The eighteen plays published during Shakespeare's lifetime had been issued one play per volume in small formats called quartos. (Each sheet in a quarto has been folded twice, making four leaves, or eight pages, each page being about nine inches tall and seven inches wide, roughly the size of a large paperback.)

Heminges and Condell suggest in an address "To the great variety of readers" that the republished plays are presented in better form than in the quartos:

> Before you were abused with diverse stolen and surreptitious copies, maimed and deformed by the frauds and stealths of injurious impostors that exposed them; even those, are now offered to your view cured and perfect of their limbs, and all the rest absolute in their numbers, as he [i.e., Shakespeare] conceived them.

There is a good deal of truth to this statement, but some of the quarto versions are better than others; some are in fact preferable to the Folio text.

Whoever was assigned to prepare the texts for publication

in the first Folio seems to have taken the job seriously and yet not to have performed it with uniform care. The sources of the texts seem to have been, in general, good unpublished copies or the best published copies. The first play in the collection, *The Tempest*, is divided into acts and scenes, has unusually full stage directions and descriptions of spectacle, and concludes with a list of the characters, but the editor was not able (or willing) to present all of the succeeding texts so fully dressed. Later texts occasionally show signs of carelessness: in one scene of *Much Ado About Nothing* the names of actors, instead of characters, appear as speech prefixes, as they had in the Quarto, which the Folio reprints; proofreading throughout the Folio is spotty and apparently was done without reference to the printer's copy; the pagination of *Hamlet* jumps from 156 to 257. Further, the proofreading was done while the presses continued to print, so that each play in each volume contains a mix of corrected and uncorrected pages.

Modern editors of Shakespeare must first select their copy; no problem if the play exists only in the Folio, but a considerable problem if the relationship between a Quarto and the Folio—or an early Quarto and a later one—is unclear. In the case of *Romeo and Juliet*, the First Quarto (Q1), published in 1597, is vastly inferior to the Second (Q2), published in 1599. The basis of Q1 apparently is a version put together from memory by some actors. Not surprisingly, it garbles many passages and is much shorter than Q2. On the other hand, occasionally Q1 makes better sense than Q2. For instance, near the end of the play, when the parents have assembled and learned of the deaths of Romeo and Juliet, in Q2 the Prince says (5.3.208–9),

Come, *Montague;* for thou art early vp
To see thy sonne and heire, now earling downe.

The last three words of this speech surely do not make sense, and many editors turn to Q1, which instead of "now earling downe" has "more early downe." Some modern editors take only "early" from Q1, and print "now early down"; others take "more early," and print "more early down." Further, Q1 (though, again, quite clearly a garbled and abbreviated text) includes some stage directions that are not found in Q2, and today many editors who base their text on Q2 are glad to add these stage directions, because the directions help to give us a sense of what the play looked like on Shakespeare's stage. Thus, in 4.3.58, after Juliet drinks the potion, Q1 gives us this stage direction, not in Q2: *"She falls upon her bed within the curtains."*

In short, an editor's decisions do not end with the choice of a single copy text. First of all, editors must reckon with Elizabethan spelling. If they are not producing a facsimile, they probably modernize the spelling, but ought they to preserve the old forms of words that apparently were pronounced quite unlike their modern forms—*lanthorn, alablaster*? If they preserve these forms are they really preserving Shakespeare's forms or perhaps those of a compositor in the printing house? What is one to do when one finds *lanthorn* and *lantern* in adjacent lines? (The editors of this series in general, but not invariably, assume that words should be spelled in their modern form, unless, for instance, a rhyme is involved.) Elizabethan punctuation, too, presents problems. For example, in the First Folio, the only text for the play, Macbeth rejects his wife's idea that he can wash the blood from his hand (2.2.60–62):

> No: this my Hand will rather
> The multitudinous Seas incarnardine,
> Making the Greene one, Red.

Obviously an editor will remove the superfluous capitals, and will probably alter the spelling to "incarnadine," but what about the comma before "Red"? If we retain the comma, Macbeth is calling the sea "the green one." If we drop the comma, Macbeth is saying that his bloody hand will make the sea ("the Green") *uniformly* red.

An editor will sometimes have to change more than spelling and punctuation. Macbeth says to his wife (1.7.46–47):

> I dare do all that may become a man,
> Who dares no more, is none.

For two centuries editors have agreed that the second line is unsatisfactory, and have emended "no" to "do": "Who dares do more is none." But when in the same play (4.2.21–22) Ross says that fearful persons

> Floate vpon a wilde and violent Sea
> Each way, and moue,

need we emend the passage? On the assumption that the compositor misread the manuscript, some editors emend "each way, and move" to "and move each way"; others emend "move" to "none" (i.e., "Each way and none"). Other editors, however, let the passage stand as in the original. The editors of the Signet Classic Shakespeare have restrained themselves from making abundant emendations. In their minds they hear Samuel Johnson on the dangers of emendation: "I have adopted the Roman sentiment, that it is more honorable to save a citizen than to kill an enemy." Some departures (in addition to spelling, punctuation, and lineation) from the copy text have of course been made, but the original readings are listed in a note following the play, so that readers can evaluate the changes for themselves.

Following tradition, the editors of the Signet Classic Shakespeare have prefaced each play with a list of characters, and throughout the play have regularized the names of the speakers. Thus, in our text of *Romeo and Juliet*, all speeches by Juliet's mother are prefixed "Lady Capulet," although the 1599 Quarto of the play, which provides our copy text, uses at various points seven speech tags for this one character: *Capu. Wi.* (i.e., Capulet's wife), *Ca. Wi., Wi., Wife, Old La.* (i.e., Old Lady), *La.,* and *Mo.* (i.e., Mother). Similarly, in *All's Well That Ends Well*, the character whom we regularly call "Countess" is in the Folio (the copy text) variously identified as *Mother, Countess, Old Countess, Lady,* and *Old Lady.* Admittedly there is some loss in regularizing, since the various prefixes may give us a hint of the way Shakespeare (or a scribe who copied Shakespeare's manuscript) was thinking of the character in a particular scene—for instance, as a mother, or as an old lady. But too much can be made of these differing prefixes, since the social relationships implied are *not* always relevant to the given scene.

We have also added line numbers and in many cases act and scene divisions as well as indications of locale at the beginning of scenes. The Folio divided most of the plays into acts and some into scenes. Early eighteenth-century editors increased the divisions. These divisions, which provide a convenient way of referring to passages in the plays, have been retained, but when not in the text chosen as the basis for the Signet Classic text they are enclosed within square brackets, [ ], to indicate that they are editorial additions. Similarly, though no play of Shakespeare's was equipped with indications of the locale at the heads of scene divisions, locales have here been added in square brackets for the convenience of readers, who lack the information that costumes, properties, gestures, and scenery afford to spectators. Spectators can tell at a glance they are in the throne room, but without an editorial indication the reader may be puzzled for a while. It should be mentioned, incidentally, that there are a few authentic stage directions—perhaps Shakespeare's, perhaps a prompter's—that suggest locales, such as *"Enter Brutus in his orchard,"* and *"They go up into the Senate house."* It is hoped that the bracketed additions in the Signet text will provide readers with the sort of help provided by these two authentic directions, but it is equally hoped that the reader will remember that the stage was not loaded with scenery.

Shakespeare on the Stage

Each volume in the Signet Classic Shakespeare includes a brief stage (and sometimes film) history of the play. When we read about earlier productions, we are likely to find them eccentric, obviously wrongheaded—for instance, Nahum Tate's version of *King Lear*, with a happy ending, which held the stage for about a century and a half, from the late seventeenth century until the end of the first quarter of the nineteenth. We see engravings of David Garrick, the greatest actor of the eighteenth century, in eighteenth-century garb

as King Lear, and we smile, thinking how absurd the production must have been. If we are more thoughtful, we say,
with the English novelist L. P. Hartley, "The past is a foreign
country: they do things differently there." But if the eighteenth-century staging is a foreign country, what of the plays
of the late sixteenth and seventeenth centuries? A foreign
language, a foreign theater, a foreign audience.

Probably all viewers of Shakespeare's plays, beginning
with Shakespeare himself, at times have been unhappy with
the plays on the stage. Consider three comments about production that we find in the plays themselves, which suggest
Shakespeare's concerns. The Chorus in *Henry V* complains
that the heroic story cannot possibly be adequately staged:

> But pardon, gentles all,
> The flat unraisèd spirits that hath dared
> On this unworthy scaffold to bring forth
> So great an object. Can this cockpit hold
> The vasty fields of France? Or may we cram
> Within this wooden *O* the very casques
> That did affright the air at Agincourt?
>
> . . . .
>
> Piece out our imperfections with your thoughts.
>
> (Prologue 1.8–14,23)

Second, here are a few sentences (which may or may not
represent Shakespeare's own views) from Hamlet's longish
lecture to the players:

> Speak the speech, I pray you, as I pronounced it to you, trippingly
> on the tongue. But if you mouth it, as many of our players do, I had
> as lief the town crier spoke my lines. . . . O, it offends me to the
> soul to hear a robustious periwig-pated fellow tear a passion to tat-
> ters, to very rags, to split the ears of the groundlings. . . . And let
> those that play your clowns speak no more than is set down for
> them, for there be of them that will themselves laugh, to set on
> some quantity of barren spectators to laugh too, though in the
> meantime some necessary question of the play be then to be con-
> sidered. That's villainous and shows a most pitiful ambition in the
> fool that uses it. (3.2.1–47)

Finally, we can quote again from the passage cited earlier in this introduction, concerning the boy actors who played the female roles. Cleopatra imagines with horror a theatrical version of her activities with Antony:

> The quick comedians
> Extemporally will stage us, and present
> Our Alexandrian revels: Antony
> Shall be brought drunken forth, and I shall see
> Some squeaking Cleopatra boy my greatness
> I' th' posture of a whore.   (5.2.216–21)

It is impossible to know how much weight to put on such passages—perhaps Shakespeare was just being modest about his theater's abilities—but it is easy enough to think that he was unhappy with some aspects of Elizabethan production. Probably no production can fully satisfy a playwright, and for that matter, few productions can fully satisfy *us;* we regret this or that cut, this or that way of costuming the play, this or that bit of business.

One's first thought may be this: Why don't they just do "authentic" Shakespeare, "straight" Shakespeare, the play as Shakespeare wrote it? But as we read the plays—words written to be performed—it sometimes becomes clear that we do not know *how* to perform them. For instance, in *Antony and Cleopatra* Antony, the Roman general who has succumbed to Cleopatra and to Egyptian ways, says, "The nobleness of life / Is to do thus" (1.1.36–37). But what is "thus"? Does Antony at this point embrace Cleopatra? Does he embrace and kiss her? (There are, by the way, very few scenes of kissing on Shakespeare's stage, possibly because boys played the female roles.) Or does he make a sweeping gesture, indicating the Egyptian way of life?

This is not an isolated example; the plays are filled with lines that call for gestures, but we are not sure what the gestures should be. *Interpretation* is inevitable. Consider a passage in *Hamlet*. In 3.1, Polonius persuades his daughter, Ophelia, to talk to Hamlet while Polonius and Claudius eavesdrop. The two men conceal themselves, and Hamlet encounters Ophelia. At 3.1.131 Hamlet suddenly says to her, "Where's your father?" Why does Hamlet, apparently out of nowhere—they have not been talking about Polonius—ask this question? Is this an example of the "antic disposition" (fantastic behavior) that Hamlet earlier (1.5.172) had told Horatio and others—including us—he would display? That is, is the question about the whereabouts of her father a seemingly irrational one, like his earlier question (3.1.103) to Ophelia, "Ha, ha! Are you honest?" Or, on the other hand, has Hamlet (as in many productions) suddenly glimpsed Polonius's foot protruding from beneath a drapery at the rear? That is, does Hamlet ask the question because he has suddenly seen something suspicious and now is testing Ophelia? (By the way, in productions that do give Hamlet a physical cue, it is almost always Polonius rather than Claudius who provides the clue. This itself is an act of interpretation on the part of the director.) Or (a third possibility) does Hamlet get a clue from Ophelia, who inadvertently betrays the spies by nervously glancing at their place of hiding? This is the interpretation used in the BBC television version, where Ophelia glances in fear toward the hiding place just after Hamlet says "Why wouldst thou be a breeder of sinners?" (121–22). Hamlet, realizing that he is being observed, glances here and there *before* he asks "Where's your father?" The question thus is a climax to what he has been doing while speaking the preceding lines. Or (a fourth interpretation) does Hamlet suddenly, without the aid of any clue whatsoever, intuitively (insightfully, mysteriously, wonderfully) sense that someone is spying? Directors must decide, of course—and so must readers.

Recall, too, the preceding discussion of the texts of the plays, which argued that the texts—though they seem to be before us in permanent black on white—are unstable. The Signet text of *Hamlet*, which draws on the Second Quarto (1604) and the First Folio (1623) is considerably longer than any version staged in Shakespeare's time. Our version, even if spoken very briskly and played without any intermission, would take close to four hours, far beyond "the two hours' traffic of our stage" mentioned in the Prologue to *Romeo and Juliet*. (There are a few contemporary references to the duration of a play, but none mentions more than three hours.) Of Shakespeare's plays, only *The Comedy of Errors*, *Macbeth*, and *The Tempest* can be done in less than three hours without cutting. And even if we take a play that exists only in a short text, *Macbeth*, we cannot claim that we are experiencing the very play that Shakespeare conceived, partly because some of the Witches' songs almost surely are non-Shakespearean additions, and partly because we are not willing to watch the play performed without an intermission and with boys in the female roles.

Further, as the earlier discussion of costumes mentioned, the plays apparently were given chiefly in contemporary, that is, in Elizabethan dress. If today we give them in the costumes that Shakespeare probably saw, the plays seem not contemporary but curiously dated. Yet if we use our own dress, we find lines of dialogue that are at odds with what we see; we may feel that the language, so clearly not our own, is inappropriate coming out of people in today's dress. A common solution, incidentally, has been to set the plays in the nineteenth century, on the grounds that this attractively distances the plays (gives them a degree of foreignness, allowing for interesting costumes) and yet doesn't put them into a museum world of Elizabethan England.

Inevitably our productions are adaptations, *our* adaptations, and inevitably they will look dated, not in a century but in twenty years, or perhaps even in a decade. Still, we cannot escape from our own conceptions. As the director Peter Brook has said, in *The Empty Space* (1968):

> It is not only the hair-styles, costumes and make-ups that look dated. All the different elements of staging—the shorthands of behavior that stand for emotions; gestures, gesticulations and tones of voice—are all fluctuating on an invisible stock exchange all the time. . . . A living theatre that thinks it can stand aloof from anything as trivial as fashion will wilt. (p. 16)

As Brook indicates, it is through today's hairstyles, costumes, makeup, gestures, gesticulations, tones of voice—this includes our *conception* of earlier hairstyles, costumes, and so forth if we stage the play in a period other than our own—that we inevitably stage the plays.

It is a truism that every age invents its own Shakespeare, just as, for instance, every age has invented its own classical world. Our view of ancient Greece, a slave-holding society in which even free Athenian women were severely circumscribed, does not much resemble the Victorians' view of ancient Greece as a glorious democracy, just as, perhaps, our view of Victorianism itself does not much resemble theirs. We cannot claim that the Shakespeare on our stage is the true Shakespeare, but in our stage productions we find a Shakespeare that speaks to us, a Shakespeare that our ancestors doubtless did not know but one that seems to us to be the true Shakespeare—at least for a while.

Our age is remarkable for the wide variety of kinds of staging that it uses for Shakespeare, but one development deserves special mention. This is the now common practice of race-blind or color-blind or nontraditional casting, which allows persons who are not white to play in Shakespeare. Previously blacks performing in Shakespeare were limited to a mere three roles, Othello, Aaron (in *Titus Andronicus*), and the Prince of Morocco (in *The Merchant of Venice*), and there were no roles at all for Asians. Indeed, African-Americans rarely could play even one of these three roles, since they were not welcome in white companies. Ira Aldridge (c.1806–1867), a black actor of undoubted talent, was forced to make his living by performing Shakespeare in England and in Europe, where he could play not only Othello but also—in whiteface—other tragic roles such as King Lear. Paul Robeson (1898–1976) made theatrical history when he played Othello in London in 1930, and there was some talk about bringing the production to the United States, but there was more talk about whether American audiences would tolerate the sight of a black man—a real black man, not a white man in blackface—kissing and then killing a white woman. The idea was tried out in summer stock in 1942, the reviews were enthusiastic, and in the following year Robeson opened on Broadway in a production that ran an astounding 296 performances. An occasional all-black company sometimes performed Shakespeare's plays, but otherwise blacks (and other minority members) were in effect shut out from performing Shakespeare. Only since about 1970 has it been common for nonwhites to play major roles along with whites. Thus, in a 1996–97 production of *Antony and Cleopatra*, a white Cleopatra, Vanessa Redgrave, played opposite a black Antony, David Harewood.

Multiracial casting is now especially common at the New York Shakespeare Festival, founded in 1954 by Joseph Papp, and in England, where even siblings such as Claudio and Isabella in *Measure for Measure* or Lear's three daughters may be of different races. Probably most viewers today soon stop worrying about the lack of realism, and move beyond the color of the performers' skin to the quality of the performance.

Nontraditional casting is not only a matter of color or race; it includes sex. In the past, occasionally a distinguished woman of the theater has taken on a male role—Sarah Bernhardt (1844–1923) as Hamlet is perhaps the most famous example—but such performances were widely regarded as eccentric. Although today there have been some performances involving cross-dressing (a drag *As You Like It* staged by the National Theatre in England in 1966 and in the United States in 1974 has achieved considerable fame in the annals of stage history), what is more interesting is the casting of women in roles that traditionally are male but that need not be. Thus, a 1993–94 English production of *Henry V* used a woman—*not* cross-dressed—in the role of the governor of Harfleur. According to Peter Holland, who reviewed the production in *Shakespeare Survey* 48 (1995), "having a female Governor of Harfleur feminized the city and provided a direct response to the horrendous threat of rape and murder that Henry had offered, his language and her body in direct connection and opposition" (p. 210). Ten years from now the device may not play so effectively, but today it speaks to us. Shakespeare, born in the Elizabethan Age, has been dead nearly four hundred years, yet he is, as Ben Jonson said, "not of an age but for all time." We must understand, however, that he is "for all time" precisely because each age finds in his abundance something for itself and something of itself.

And here we come back to two issues discussed earlier in this introduction—the instability of the text and, curiously, the Bacon/Oxford heresy concerning the authorship of the plays. *Of course* Shakespeare wrote the plays, and we should daily fall on our knees to thank him for them—and yet there is something to the idea that he is not their only author. Every editor, every director and actor, and every reader to some degree shapes them, too, for when we edit, direct, act, or read, we inevitably become Shakespeare's collaborator and re-create the plays. The plays, one might say, are so cunningly contrived that they guide our responses, tell us how we ought to feel, and make a mark on us, but (for better or for worse) we also make a mark on them.

—SYLVAN BARNET
Tufts University

Introduction

Although some readers and some directors have found considerable darkness in *Twelfth Night*—see Charles Lamb's essay on pages 136–38, and our brief account of the stage history of the play, pages 164–74—for most readers and viewers, *Twelfth Night* is a genial, charming play. Its charm, however, may be self-defeating. In the eighteenth century, for instance, Samuel Johnson admired its elegance and ease and its exquisite humor, and he conceded that it might be diverting on the stage; but because the principal action "wants credibility" and "exhibits no just picture of life," he remarked with disapproval, it cannot be instructive or tell us anything important. In short, it fails the test of relevance.

This great critic's cold opinion of the most profound of Shakespeare's so-called "golden comedies" presents us with a hard decision: either to dismiss *Twelfth Night* as false and fatuous or to accept it as a version of romance—deft and entertaining, to be sure, but remote from our concerns and exempt from any common-sense appraisal. As usual, Johnson, a man not given to unconsidered judgments, seems to argue from the facts. For one thing, what we know or may infer about the circumstances of its first production would indicate that *Twelfth Night* was conceived and written as a kind of bagatelle. If, as many scholars think, it was commissioned for performance by the fledgling lawyers of the Middle Temple at the romp that crowned their Christmas celebration, the play was tailored to an annual frolic when duty and convention were ignored, and when, in a saturnalian Feast of Misrule, mirth became the order of the day. Even the subtitle—*What You Will*—repudiates, or so it seems, the drab and probable for the promise of the

unexpected.[1] Life, as most of us come to know it, is a frayed
and tattered thing of unexpressed desires and disappointed
hopes, and its tumults rarely find repose. In the world de-
picted by *Twelfth Night*, however, it would seem that per-
turbation leads to calm and all suspensions are resolved, so
that by happy if implausible coincidence afflicted virtue is
rewarded, folly is exposed, and error yields to knowledge.

The ingredients of this consoling fiction are the staple
items of romance: shipwreck, alienation, and wandering in a
remote realm where a pair of high-born lovers melodiously
indulge a set of attitudes untested by experience, where a
maiden in distress by luck and pluck gets everything she
wants, and where the pretensions of an "affectioned ass"
(2.3.147) are demolished by a pack of high-spirited tormen-
tors. The main plot, articulated by the ancient devices of disguise and mistaken identity, presents a love story (or a brace
of interlocking love stories) that leads through skillful convolutions to a final recognition scene; and the subplot—a
kind of anti-masque—involves the "lighter people" (5.1.341)
in a complicated jest. Finally, all these knotted strands of
action are conducted in a language so precise that form and
function seem to coincide, with Orsino's artful "fancy"
(1.1.14) and Viola's deep but muted love as charmingly
conveyed as Sir Toby's burly humor and the wit and music
of the Clown.

Indeed, this play, which starts and ends with music, and
which is studded with so many lovely songs, might be said
to approach the condition of that art where form and style are

[1]Despite Leslie Hotson's interesting attempt in *The First Night of Twelfth
Night* (1954) to show that the play was commissioned for performance before
the Queen and court at Whitehall on Twelfth Night (6 January) in 1601 to
celebrate the splendid visit of Virginio Orsini, Duke of Bracchiano, most
scholars still accept an entry of 2 February, 1602, in the diary of John Manningham, a barrister of the Middle Temple, as pointing to its first production
in the Middle Temple hall on Twelfth Night of that year: "At our feast we had
a play called *Twelve Night, or What You Will*, much like the *Comedy of Errors*
or *Menechmi* in Plautus, but most like and near to that in Italian called
Inganni. A good practice in it to make the steward believe his Lady widow
was in love with him, by counterfeiting a letter as from his Lady in general
terms, telling him what she liked best in him, and prescribing his gesture in
smiling, his apparel, etc., and then when he came to practice making him
believe they took him to be mad." On Manningham's clever guess about
Nicolò Secchi's *Inganni*, see "The Source of *Twelfth Night*," p. 108.

everything, and where there is, or should be, no appeal to values and criteria not inherent in the work itself. In more severely imitative kinds of art, such as portrait painting and the novel, the reverse, of course, is true. Because Holbein's portrait of Sir Thomas More or Richardson's *Clarissa*— which, incidentally, was one of Johnson's favorite books— seek in different, complicated ways to represent contemporary experience with fidelity, at least a part of our response to them is based on what we know of life, and therefore we require that they express some aspect of the truth about the things they represent. On the other hand, a Mozart serenade stands for nothing but itself; it has a logic of its own, and it creates an independent frame of reference that baffles any moral or utilitarian test. *Twelfth Night* is not this kind of work, of course, but it is such a triumph of artifice and style, and shows such mastery of convention, that some readers might regard it as a self-subsistent artifact, or, at any rate, as a work invulnerable to the expectations and probabilities derived from everyday experience. Beguiled by its mazy plot and music, they would not even dare to ask if it is "true." For them, therefore, Johnson's test of relevance would appear to be irrelevant, and his common-sense, adverse opinion merely an impertinence.

To regard *Twelfth Night* either as escapist folderol or adroit but meaningless romance is, however, to forget its function as a play. But since it is a play, and since a play, as Aristotle said, is the imitation of an action, it must meet the test of relevance. This test can never be evaded in a literary production, because no true work of literature ignores what Johnson means by "life," and no honest writer, however much concerned with form and style, neglects his or her only proper subject, which is the human situation. It is not that we require an easy calculus of triumph for the good and disaster for the bad, but that a play reveal—or permit us to infer—a necessary connection between what happens to a person and the kind of person he or she is. When this requirement is evaded, as it seems to be evaded, for example, in the last act of *Measure for Measure*, we are baffled and uneasy because we feel a lack of moral sequence. Conversely, when the conduct of the action, however painful, satisfies our moral expectations we are forced to yield assent. Thus, although the conclusion of *King Lear* is as harrowing as anything in drama, we accept it, in our anguish, because we recognize its dreadful logic.

We do not look for dreadful logic in *Twelfth Night*, of course, but we do expect to find a real connection between its artful, entertaining fiction and those aspects of experience that it seeks to represent. We expect to find some reference, even if oblique and stylized, to the world which each of us inhabits—a refinement of our own perceptions, an enlargement of our knowledge or compassion, a demonstration of how men and women act, and why. Otherwise art deteriorates to mere technique, and literature becomes gesticulation.

What, then, is there in *Twelfth Night* to save it from this danger? For one thing, there is a shaping theme that enables us to view the conventions of romance as a paradigm of our own behavior; for another, there is, in the subplot, such skillful use of sharp and even topical detail in depicting various kinds of folly that the effect is almost photographic. These two features of the work remove it from the realm of pure romance and attach it to our own experience. They remind us that despite its old-fashioned apparatus, its lyric grace, and what Johnson called its lack of "credibility," *Twelfth Night* should not be thought of as a piece of music or as an empty virtuoso exercise in style, but as a play that we may verify by what we know of life.

Twelfth Night meets this test with ease, for it concerns a basic human problem; or, if that sounds too severe for such a gay and sprightly work of art, it records and comments on a mode of human action that all of us everywhere exhibit. This might be defined as our native bent for self-deception, or, conversely, as our difficulty in achieving self-awareness. (Pushed far, this interpretation leads to the "autumnal" or "Chekhovian" productions discussed in our account of the stage history of the play, pages 152–53.) Here the theme is given comic statement and presented as romance, but it has a universal application. Is it possible, *Twelfth Night* makes us wonder, for us to know the truth about ourselves? And even if we gain such knowledge, Shakespeare asks in other, darker plays, can such knowledge be endured? We see these questions posed when Richard II, stripped of crown and power and even of his misconceptions, sits in Pomfret Castle and explores his final, humbling recognition of himself; when Harry V, on the eve of Agincourt, expounds the wide distinction between the common notion of a king and the kingly burden that he bears; when Othello is compelled to face the horror of the deed he did "in honor"; when Lear tears off his clothing to reveal the "unaccommodated man." Such analogues in plays so different from *Twelfth Night* suggest how often, and in what varied contexts, Shakespeare used the theme. For him—as for Sophocles and Pirandello— to show one's growth toward self-awareness is almost coextensive with the art of drama.

This theme, so massive and protean, receives consummate comic statement in *Twelfth Night*. Here Shakespeare has to trim it not merely to the comic form (which requires a complex plot directed toward a happy ending) but also, presumably, to the interests of a special clientele—the debonair young lawyers at their revels in the Middle Temple. Almost inevitably, therefore, he writes a play of love: not love as the annihilating passion shared by Romeo and Juliet or the febrile lust of Troilus, but as a mode of social intercourse that works its way through opposition to eventual satisfaction. He had done this sort of thing before, of course, in such plays as *The Two Gentlemen of Verona* and *As You Like It*; but in *Twelfth Night* he makes a signal innovation, for here the lovers' triumph is delayed not by the customary impediments of parental disapproval or insolvency or politics, but by their own deceits and self-deceptions. To secure this innovation he manipulates the old conventions of romance—notably the stock devices of disguise and mistaken identity—not merely that they might complicate the action and so provide diversion but that they might serve almost as metaphors or emblems for mental obfuscation. The perplexity of the plot—where, among many other sources of confusion, a girl disguised as a boy loves a man who commissions her to woo a lady whose advances she must check—represents in concrete terms the intellectual and emotional bewilderment that almost every character in the play exhibits. As a consequence, the machinery of romance acquires the novel function of articulating theme. To be sure, the convolutions of the plot provide diversion of a sort, but they also bind the characters in a web of inter-woven error, and thus they underscore the meaning of the play: that most of us never know, and maybe never have a chance to know, the truth about ourselves.

But if, as the knotty and perplexing plot suggests, we are forced by circumstances into compounded misconceptions, we are also trapped by our illusions. Between the errors thrust upon us and those we generate ourselves, we are caught as in a vise—victims not merely of deceit but also of our own folly. Orsino, for example, though

> Of great estate, of fresh and stainless youth;
> In voices well divulged, free, learned, and valiant,
> And in dimension and the shape of nature
> A gracious person,   (1.5.260–4)

is in fact so blinded by his image of himself as an ardent but despairing lover that he is maimed by his obsession. We see him first as he indulges this obsession with his famous speech on music as the food of love, and this speech, how-ever lovely to the ear, reveals the speaker as a narcissistic fool. Much given to discussions about his complicated states of mind, he, like most self-centered persons, is really very simple. Whereas he tells Viola that

> such as I am all true lovers are,
> Unstaid and skittish in all motions else
> Save in the constant image of the creature
> That is beloved,   (2.4.17–20)

the only thing he loves is his romantic notion of the lover that he himself exemplifies, and he finds it so appealing that he never even asks if it is true. He leaves the play as he had entered it, with highfalutin talk about his "fancy" (1.1.14) but this "fancy" is no more to be confused with love than his lyric self-descriptions are to be confused with fact. His plea-sure in caressing his emotions, his delight in "old and antic" songs as a solace for his "passion" (2.4.3–4) even his petu-lant threat of violence against Olivia and "Cesario" for their presumed unfaithfulness reveal the sentimentalist who prefers the comfort of his own illusions to the dangers of candid self-appraisal.

In varying degrees, almost all the other characters in the play are shackled by their inability or refusal to comprehend their own emotions, or even to discern their blunders. Olivia's preoccupation with "a brother's dead love" (1.1.32) is so unreal that a single visit from "Cesario" is enough to shatter it—and to provide her with a new obsession that is even more absurd, because it rests upon a yet more rudimentary error. Malvolio, "sick of self-love" (1.5.90), is so easily led to self-exposure and humiliation that even as we laugh we pity him: "Alas, poor fool, how have they baffled thee!" (5.1.371) Sir Andrew's imposing list of follies, both natural and acquired, makes him everybody's fool; and although Sir Toby has a searching eye for other people's foibles, he is usually much too drunk to recognize his own. Even Viola, who at least is in possession of the facts that save her from Olivia's type of blunder, thinks she must embark upon a program of deceit in order to survive. "Conceal me what I am," she tells the captain,

> and be my aid
> For such disguise as haply shall become
> The form of my intent. (1.3.53–5)

Her finest moment in the play—the speech about the lovelorn girl who never told her love—is charming and pathetic, but it shows a certain pleasure in equivocation. Indeed, her skill and relish for the kind of organized deceit on which the action hangs are appropriate for the heroine of a play in which dissimulation and deception are routine. Only the Clown, it seems, is clear-eyed and wise enough to stand somewhat above the antics of the others and to comment on their follies. Knowing that foolery "does walk about the orb like the sun" (3.1.39), he is as quick to puncture Orsino's egomania as to expose Olivia's silly posture of bereavement; and it is he, in the amusing but disturbing interview with the "lunatic" Malvolio, who makes us trace the narrow line between the madman and the sage. The Clown alone is immune to the pandemic error in Illyria—but he must wear a mask against contagion and infection, and he must hide his wisdom as the babble of a licensed fool. In a world where everyone is slightly mad, his motley is a badge of knowledge.

Finally, the plotting, which Johnson found offensive, is also made to demonstrate the fact that most of us live by error and illusion. The three main lines of action—Orsino's languid courtship of Olivia, Olivia's imbroglio with Viola and Sebastian, and Malvolio's disgrace—do not appear as isolated plots that run their parallel and independent courses; they come to us instead as reciprocal and reverberating statements of a single situation, which is the gulling of a fool. Writers from Aristophanes to Shaw have used this situation, in one form or another, to pedagogic purpose, for they have brought the gull through ridicule to exposure and correction. It is significant that although Orsino, Olivia, and Malvolio are all the victims of deception fostered either by themselves or others, they learn nothing from experience. Two of them are unmolested in their folly, and the third, though harshly treated, clings to his absurd illusions. Malvolio's credulity—which is no sillier than that which goes unpunished in his betters—is chastised so severely that he becomes, as Lamb observed (see page 138), an almost tragic figure; but Orsino and Olivia are never even chided. None of them is changed, however, and none surrenders his obsession. The denouement affords a kind of liberation, to be sure, for the proper pairing off of lovers signifies release from labyrinthine misconception. But the ease with which Orsino shifts his "fancy" from Olivia to Viola matches that with which, earlier, Olivia turns from anchorite to ardent lover and then substitutes Sebastian for "Cesario." Neither of these self-indulgent egotists has been compelled to shake off his illusion, and in a sense, therefore, neither earns the triumph he enjoys. Perhaps, as Johnson thought, Sir Andrew's "natural fatuity" renders him ineligible for comic therapy, but at any rate he stays, as he will always stay, a fool. Sir Toby, too, remains what he had been before—a sot and parasite—and in addition he acquires Maria. As for Malvolio, he not only profits nothing from his hard instruction, but as he takes his angry leave we see his self-love stiffened by his sense of injured merit. "I'll be revenged on the whole pack of you" (5.1.380), he snarls as he departs.

Hazlitt thought that Shakespeare was "too good-natured and magnanimous" to treat his comic knaves and fools as they deserve. Perhaps for this reason or perhaps because he makes us recognize ourselves in them, we are glad for these deluded people in Illyria, for they teach us what, alas, we need to know: that since we rarely win our way to truth, we must settle for illusion.

—HERSCHEL BAKER
Harvard University

Twelfth Night,
or, What You Will

Orsino, Duke of Illyria
Sebastian, brother of Viola
Antonio, a sea captain, friend to Viola
A Sea Captain, friend to Viola
Valentine ⎱
Curio ⎰ gentlemen attending on the Duke
Sir Toby Belch, uncle to Olivia
Sir Andrew Aguecheek
Malvolio, steward to Olivia
Fabian ⎱
Feste, a clown ⎰ servants to Olivia
Olivia, a countess
Viola, sister to Sebastian
Maria, Olivia's woman
Lords, a Priest, Sailors, Officers, Musicians, and
   Attendants

Scene: Illyria]

Twelfth Night,
or, What You Will

ACT 1

Scene 1. [*The Duke's palace.*]

Enter Orsino, Duke of Illyria, Curio, and other Lords,
[with Musicians].

Duke. If music be the food of love, play on,
Give me excess of it, that, surfeiting,
The appetite°¹ may sicken, and so die.
That strain again! It had a dying fall;°
O, it came o'er my ear like the sweet sound   5
That breathes upon a bank of violets,
Stealing and giving odor. Enough, no more!
'Tis not so sweet now as it was before.
O spirit of love, how quick and fresh° art thou,
That,° notwithstanding thy capacity,   10
Receiveth as the sea. Nought enters there,°
Of what validity and pitch° soe'er,
But falls into abatement and low price°

---

¹The degree sign (°) indicates a footnote, which is keyed to the text by
line number. Text references are printed in **boldface** type; the annota-
tion follows in roman type.
1.1.3 **appetite** i.e., the lover's appetite for music   4 **fall** cadence
9 **quick and fresh** lively and eager   10 **That** in that   11 **there** i.e.,
in the lover's "capacity"   12 **validity and pitch** value and superiority
(in falconry, pitch is the highest point of a bird's flight)   13 **price**
esteem

3

Even in a minute. So full of shapes° is fancy°
15 That it alone is high fantastical.°

Curio. Will you go hunt, my lord?

Duke. What, Curio?

Curio. The hart.

Duke. Why, so I do, the noblest that I have.
20 O, when mine eyes did see Olivia first,
Methought she purged the air of pestilence.
That instant was I turned into a hart,
And my desires, like fell° and cruel hounds,
E'er since pursue me.°

Enter Valentine.

How now? What news from her?

25 *Valentine.* So please my lord, I might not be admitted;
But from her handmaid do return this answer:
The element° itself, till seven years' heat,°
Shall not behold her face at ample view;
But like a cloistress she will veilèd walk,
30 And water once a day her chamber round
With eye-offending brine: all this to season°
A brother's dead love, which she would keep fresh
And lasting in her sad remembrance.°

Duke. O, she that hath a heart of that fine frame
35 To pay this debt of love but to a brother,
How will she love when the rich golden shaft°
Hath killed the flock of all affections else°

14 **shapes** fantasies   14 **fancy** love   15 **high fantastical** preeminently
imaginative   23 **fell** fierce   22–24 **That instant … pursue me** (Orsino's mannered play on "hart-heart"—which exemplifies the lover's
"high fantastical" wit—derives from the story of Actaeon, a famous
hunter who, having seen Diana bathing, was transformed into a stag
and torn to pieces by his hounds)   27 **element** sky   27 **heat** course
31 **season** preserve (by the salt in her tears)   33 **remembrance** (pronounced with four syllables, "re-mem-ber-ance")   36 **golden shaft**
(the shaft, borne by Cupid, that causes love, as distinguished from the
leaden shaft, which causes aversion and disdain)   37 **all affections
else** i.e., all other emotions but love

That live in her; when liver, brain, and heart,°
These sovereign thrones, are all supplied and filled,
Her sweet perfections,° with one self° king.   40
Away before me to sweet beds of flow'rs;
Love-thoughts lie rich when canopied with bow'rs.

Exeunt.

Scene 2. [*The seacoast.*]

Enter Viola, a Captain, and Sailors.

Viola. What country, friends, is this?

Captain. This is Illyria,° lady.

Viola. And what should I do in Illyria?
My brother he is in Elysium.°
Perchance he is not drowned. What think you, sailors?   5

Captain. It is perchance that you yourself were saved.

Viola. O my poor brother, and so perchance may he be.

Captain. True, madam; and, to comfort you with
      chance,°
Assure yourself, after our ship did split,
When you, and those poor number saved with you,   10
Hung on our driving° boat, I saw your brother,
Most provident in peril, bind himself
(Courage and hope both teaching him the practice)°
To a strong mast that lived° upon the sea;
Where, like Arion° on the dolphin's back,   15

38 **liver, brain, and heart** (the seats respectively of sexual desire,
thought, and feeling) 40 **perfections** (pronounced with four syllables) 40 **self** sole 1.2.2 **Illyria** region bordering the east coast of
the Adriatic 4 **Elysium** heaven (in classical mythology, the abode
of the happy dead) 8 **chance** possibility 11 **driving** drifting 13
practice procedure 14 **lived** i.e., floated 15 **Arion** (in classical
mythology, a bard who, having leapt into the sea to escape from
murderous sailors, was borne to shore by a dolphin that he charmed
by his songs)

I saw him hold acquaintance with the waves
So long as I could see.

Viola. For saying so, there's gold.
Mine own escape unfoldeth to my hope,°
20   Whereto thy speech serves for authority°
The like of him. Know'st thou this country?

Captain. Ay, madam, well, for I was bred and born
Not three hours' travel from this very place.

Viola. Who governs here?

25 *Captain.* A noble duke, in nature as in name.

Viola. What is his name?

Captain. Orsino.

Viola. Orsino! I have heard my father name him.
He was a bachelor then.

30 *Captain.* And so is now, or was so very late;
For but a month ago I went from hence,
And then 'twas fresh in murmur° (as you know
What great ones do, the less will prattle of)
That he did seek the love of fair Olivia.

35 *Viola.* What's she?

Captain. A virtuous maid, the daughter of a count
That died some twelvemonth since, then leaving her
In the protection of his son, her brother,
Who shortly also died; for whose dear love,
40   They say, she hath abjured the sight
And company of men.

Viola.   O that I served that lady,
And might not be delivered° to the world,
Till I had made mine own occasion mellow,
What my estate is.°

Captain.   That were hard to compass,°

19 **unfoldeth to my hope** i.e., reinforces my hope for my brother's safety 20 **serves for authority** i.e., tends to justify 32 **fresh in murmur** i.e., being rumored 42 **delivered** disclosed 43–44 **made mine ... estate is** found an appropriate time to reveal my status 44 **compass** effect

Because she will admit no kind of suit,　　　　　*45*
No, not° the Duke's.
Viola. There is a fair behavior in thee, captain,
And though that° nature with a beauteous wall
Doth oft close in° pollution, yet of thee
I will believe thou hast a mind that suits　　　　*50*
With this thy fair and outward character.°
I prithee (and I'll pay thee bounteously)
Conceal me what I am, and be my aid
For such disguise as haply shall become
The form of my intent.° I'll serve this duke.　　*55*
Thou shalt present me as an eunuch to him;
It may be worth thy pains. For I can sing,
And speak to him in many sorts of music
That will allow° me very worth his service.
What else may hap, to time I will commit;　　　　*60*
Only shape thou thy silence to my wit.°

Captain. Be you his eunuch,° and your mute I'll be;
When my tongue blabs, then let mine eyes not see.

Viola. I thank thee. Lead me on.　　　　　　　　*Exeunt.*

Scene 3. [*Olivia's house.*]

Enter Sir Toby and Maria.

Toby. What a plague means my niece to take the death
of her brother thus? I am sure care's an enemy to
life.

Maria. By my troth, Sir Toby, you must come in

---

46 **not** not even　48 **though that** even though　49 **close in** conceal
51 **character** i.e., appearance and demeanor　54–55 **become/The
form of my intent** i.e., suit my purpose　59 **allow** certify　61 **wit**
i.e., skill in carrying out my plan　62 **Be you his eunuch** (this part of
the plan was not carried out)

5   earlier a' nights. Your cousin,° my lady, takes great
       exceptions to your ill hours.

Toby. Why, let her except before excepted.°

Maria. Ay, but you must confine yourself within the
       modest limits of order.°

10   *Toby.* Confine? I'll confine° myself no finer than I am.
       These clothes are good enough to drink in, and so
       be these boots too. And° they be not, let them hang
       themselves in their own straps.

Maria. That quaffing and drinking will undo you. I
15   heard my lady talk of it yesterday; and of a foolish
       knight that you brought in one night here to be her
       wooer.

Toby. Who? Sir Andrew Aguecheek?

Maria. Ay, he.

20   *Toby.* He's as tall° a man as any's in Illyria.

Maria. What's that to th' purpose?

Toby. Why, he has three thousand ducats a year.

Maria. Ay, but he'll have but a year in all these ducats.
       He's a very fool and a prodigal.

25   *Toby.* Fie that you'll say so! He plays o' th' viol-de-
       gamboys,° and speaks three or four languages word
       for word without book, and hath all the good gifts
       of nature.

Maria. He hath indeed all, most natural;° for, besides
30   that he's a fool, he's a great quarreler; and but that
       he hath the gift of a coward to allay the gust° he
       hath in quarreling, 'tis thought among the prudent
       he would quickly have the gift of a grave.

1.3.5 **cousin** (a term indicating various degrees of kinship; here,
niece)   7 **except before excepted** (Sir Toby parodies the legal jargon
exceptis exceptiendis ["with the exceptions previously noted"] commonly used in leases and contracts)   9 **modest limits of order** reasonable limits of good behavior   10 **confine** i.e., clothe   12 **And** if (a
common Elizabethan usage)   20 **tall** i.e., bold and handsome   25–
26 **viol-de-gamboys** bass viol   29 **natural** i.e., like a natural fool or
idiot   31 **gust** gusto

Toby. By this hand, they are scoundrels and sub-
 stractors° that say so of him. Who are they?   *35*

Maria. They that add, moreover, he's drunk nightly in
 your company.

Toby. With drinking healths to my niece. I'll drink to
 her as long as there is a passage in my throat and
 drink in Illyria. He's a coward and a coistrel° that   *40*
 will not drink to my niece till his brains turn o' th'
 toe like a parish top.° What, wench? *Castiliano
 vulgo;*° for here comes Sir Andrew Agueface.

Enter Sir Andrew.

Andrew. Sir Toby Belch. How now, Sir Toby Belch?

Toby. Sweet Sir Andrew.   *45*

Andrew. Bless you, fair shrew.

Maria. And you too, sir.

Toby. Accost, Sir Andrew, accost.

Andrew. What's that?

Toby. My niece's chambermaid.°   *50*

Andrew. Good Mistress Accost, I desire better acquaintance.

Maria. My name is Mary, sir.

Andrew. Good Mistress Mary Accost.

34–35 **substractors** slanderers 40 **coistrel** knave (literally, a groom
who takes care of a knight's horse) 42 **parish top** (according to
George Steevens, a large top "formerly kept in every village, to be
whipped in frosty weather, that the peasants might be kept warm
by exercise, and out of mischief while they could not work"; however, the allusion may be to the communal top-spinning whose
origins are buried in religious ritual) 42–43 **Castiliano vulgo** (a
phrase of uncertain meaning; perhaps Sir Toby is suggesting that
Maria assume a grave and ceremonial manner—like that of the
notoriously formal Castilians—for Sir Andrew's benefit) 49–50
What's that?/My niece's chambermaid (Sir Andrew asks the meaning of the word "accost," but Sir Toby thinks that he is referring to
Maria. Actually, she was not Olivia's chambermaid, but rather her
companion, or lady in waiting, as is made clear at 1.5.162)

55 *Toby.* You mistake, knight. "Accost" is front her,
    board her, woo her, assail her.

    Andrew. By my troth, I would not undertake her in
    this company. Is that the meaning of "accost"?

    Maria. Fare you well, gentlemen.

60 *Toby.* And thou let part so,° Sir Andrew, would thou
    mightst never draw sword again.

    Andrew. And you part so, mistress, I would I might
    never draw sword again! Fair lady, do you think
    you have fools in hand?°

65 *Maria.* Sir, I have not you by th' hand.

    Andrew. Marry,° but you shall have, and here's my
    hand.

    Maria. Now, sir, thought is free. I pray you, bring
    your hand to th' butt'ry° bar and let it drink.

70 *Andrew.* Wherefore, sweetheart? What's your meta-
    phor?

    Maria. It's dry,° sir.

    Andrew. Why, I think so. I am not such an ass but I
    can keep my hand dry. But what's your jest?

75 *Maria.* A dry jest, sir.

    Andrew. Are you full of them?

    Maria. Ay, sir, I have them at my finger's ends. Marry,
    now I let go your hand, I am barren.°   *Exit Maria.*

    Toby. O knight, thou lack'st a cup of canary!° When
80 did I see thee so put down?

    Andrew. Never in your life, I think, unless you see
    canary put me down. Methinks sometimes I have

60 **so** i.e., without ceremony   64 **have fools in hand** i.e., are dealing
with fools   66 **Marry** indeed (a mild interjection, originally an oath
by the Virgin Mary)   69 **butt'ry** buttery, a storeroom for butts or
casks of liquor   72 **dry** (1) thirsty (2) indicative of impotence
78 **barren** (1) without more jests (2) dull-witted   79 **canary** a sweet
wine from the Canary Islands

no more wit than a Christian or an ordinary man
has. But I am a great eater of beef, and I believe
that does harm to my wit.   *85*

Toby. No question.

Andrew. And I thought that, I'd forswear it. I'll ride
home tomorrow, Sir Toby.

Toby. Pourquoi,° my dear knight?

Andrew. What is *"pourquoi"?* Do, or not do? I would   *90*
I had bestowed that time in the tongues that I have
in fencing, dancing, and bearbaiting, O, had I but
followed the arts!

Toby. Then hadst thou had an excellent head of hair.°

Andrew. Why, would that have mended my hair?   *95*

Toby. Past question, for thou seest it will not curl by
nature.

Andrew. But it becomes me well enough, does't not?

Toby. Excellent. It hangs like flax on a distaff;° and
I hope to see a huswife° take thee between her legs   *100*
and spin it off.

Andrew. Faith, I'll home tomorrow, Sir Toby. Your
niece will not be seen; or if she be, it's four to one
she'll none of me. The Count himself here hard by
woos her.   *105*

Toby. She'll none o' th' Count. She'll not match above
her degree, neither in estate,° years, nor wit; I have
heard her swear't. Tut, there's life in't,° man.

Andrew. I'll stay a month longer. I am a fellow o' th'
strangest mind i' th' world. I delight in masques and   *110*
revels sometimes altogether.

Toby. Art thou good at these kickshawses,° knight?

89 **Pourquoi** why (French). 94 **Then hadst thou had an excellent
head of hair** (perhaps Sir Toby is punning on Sir Andrew's "tongues"
[line 91] as "tongs" or curling irons) 99 **distaff** stick used in spin-
ning 100 **huswife** housewife 107 **estate** fortune 108 **there's life
in't** i.e., there's hope for you yet 112 **kickshawses** trifles (French
quelque chose)

Andrew. As any man in Illyria, whatsoever he be,
under the degree of my betters,° and yet I will not
115 compare with an old° man.

Toby. What is thy excellence in a galliard,° knight?

Andrew. Faith, I can cut a caper.°

Toby. And I can cut the mutton to't.

Andrew. And I think I have the back-trick° simply as
120 strong as any man in Illyria.

Toby. Wherefore are these things hid? Wherefore have
these gifts a curtain before 'em? Are they like to
take° dust, like Mistress Mall's picture? Why dost
thou not go to church in a galliard and come home
125 in a coranto?° My very walk should be a jig. I
would not so much as make water but in a sink-a-
pace.° What dost thou mean? Is it a world to hide
virtues° in? I did think, by the excellent constitution
of thy leg, it was formed under the star of a
130 galliard.°

Andrew. Ay, 'tis strong, and it does indifferent well
in a damned-colored stock.° Shall we set about
some revels?

Toby. What shall we do else? Were we not born under
135 Taurus?°

Andrew. Taurus? That's sides and heart.

114 **under the degree of my betters** i.e., so long as he is not my social
superior 115 **old** i.e., experienced (?) 116 **galliard** lively dance in
triple time 117 **caper** (1) frisky leap (2) spice used to season mutton (hence Sir Toby's remark in the next line) 119 **back-trick** reverse step in dancing 123 **take** gather 125 **coranto** quick running
dance 126–27 **sink-a-pace** cinquepace (French *cinque pas*), a kind
of galliard of five steps (but there is also a scatological pun here)
128 **virtues** talents, accomplishments 129–30 **the star of a galliard**
i.e., a dancing star 132 **damned-colored stock** (of the many emendations proposed for this stocking of uncertain color—"damasked-
colored," "dun-colored," "dove-colored," "damson-colored," and
the like—Rowe's "flame-colored" has been most popular) 135
Taurus the Bull (one of the twelve signs of the zodiac, each of which
was thought to influence a certain part of the human body. Most
authorities assigned Taurus to neither "sides and heart" nor "legs
and thighs," but to neck and throat)

Toby. No, sir; it is legs and thighs. Let me see thee caper. Ha, higher; ha, ha, excellent! *Exeunt.*

Scene 4. [*The Duke's palace.*]

Enter Valentine, and Viola in man's attire.

Valentine. If the Duke continue these favors towards you, Cesario, you are like° to be much advanced. He hath known you but three days and already you are no stranger.

Viola. You either fear his humor° or my negligence, that° you call in question the continuance of his love. Is he inconstant, sir, in his favors? 5

Valentine. No, believe me.

Enter Duke, Curio, and Attendants.

Viola. I thank you. Here comes the Count.

Duke. Who saw Cesario, ho? 10

Viola. On your attendance, my lord, here.

Duke. Stand you awhile aloof. Cesario,
Thou know'st no less but all.° I have unclasped
To thee the book even of my secret soul.
Therefore, good youth, address thy gait° unto her; 15
Be not denied access, stand at her doors,
And tell them there thy fixèd foot shall grow
Till thou have audience.

Viola.   Sure, my noble lord,
If she be so abandoned to her sorrow
As it is spoke, she never will admit me. 20

1.4.5 **humor** changeable disposition   6 **that** in that   13 **no less but all** i.e., everything   15 **address thy gait** direct your steps

Duke. Be clamorous and leap all civil bounds
  Rather than make unprofited° return. ·

Viola. Say I do speak with her, my lord, what then?

Duke. O, then unfold the passion of my love;
25 Surprise her with discourse of my dear° faith;
  It shall become thee well to act my woes.
  She will attend it better in thy youth
  Than in a nuncio's° of more grave aspect.°

Viola. I think not so, my lord.

Duke.   Dear lad, believe it;
30 For they shall yet belie thy happy years
  That say thou art a man. Diana's lip
  Is not more smooth and rubious;° thy small pipe°
  Is as the maiden's organ, shrill and sound,°
  And all is semblative° a woman's part.
35 I know thy constellation° is right apt°
  For this affair. Some four or five attend him,
  All, if you will; for I myself am best
  When least in company. Prosper well in this,
  And thou shalt live as freely as thy lord
  To call his fortunes thine.

40 *Viola.*   I'll do my best
  To woo your lady. [*Aside*] Yet a barful° strife!
  Whoe'er I woo, myself would be his wife.   *Exeunt.*

---

22 **unprofited** unsuccessful 25 **dear** intense 28 **nuncio's** messenger's 28 **aspect** (accent on second syllable) 32 **rubious** ruby-red 32 **pipe** voice 33 **shrill and sound** high and clear 34 **semblative** like 35 **constellation** predetermined qualities 35 **apt** suitable 41 **barful** full of impediments

Scene 5. [*Olivia's house.*]

Enter Maria and Clown.

Maria. Nay, either tell me where thou hast been, or I will not open my lips so wide as a bristle may enter in way of thy excuse. My lady will hang thee for thy absence.

Clown. Let her hang me. He that is well hanged in this world needs to fear no colors.° 5

Maria. Make that good.°

Clown. He shall see none to fear.

Maria. A good lenten° answer. I can tell thee where that saying was born, of "I fear no colors." 10

Clown. Where, good Mistress Mary?

Maria. In the wars; and that may you be bold to say in your foolery.

Clown. Well, God give them wisdom that have it, and those that are fools, let them use their talents.° 15

Maria. Yet you will be hanged for being so long absent, or to be turned away. Is not that as good as a hanging to you?

Clown. Many a good hanging prevents a bad marriage, and for turning away, let summer bear it out.° 20

1.5.6 **fear no colors** i.e., fear nothing (with a pun on "color" meaning "flag" and "collar" meaning "hangman's noose") 7 **Make that good** i.e., explain it 9 **lenten** thin, meager (perhaps an allusion to the colorless, unbleached linen that replaced the customary liturgical purple or violet during Lent) 15 **talents** native intelligence (with perhaps a pun on "talons" meaning "claws") 20 **let summer bear it out** i.e., let the warm weather make it endurable

Maria. You are resolute then?

Clown. Not so, neither; but I am resolved on two
points.°

Maria. That if one break, the other will hold; or if
25   both break, your gaskins° fall.

Clown. Apt, in good faith; very apt. Well, go thy way!
If Sir Toby would leave drinking, thou wert as
witty a piece of Eve's flesh° as any in Illyria.

Maria. Peace, you rogue; no more o' that. Here comes
30   my lady. Make your excuse wisely, you were best.°
                                            [Exit.]

*Enter Lady Olivia with Malvolio
[and other Attendants].*

Clown. Wit, and't° be thy will, put me into good
fooling. Those wits that think they have thee do
very oft prove fools, and I that am sure I lack thee
may pass for a wise man. For what says Quina-
35   palus?° "Better a witty fool than a foolish wit."
God bless thee, lady.

Olivia. Take the fool away.

Clown. Do you not hear, fellows? Take away the lady.

Olivia. Go to,° y' are a dry° fool! I'll no more of you.
40   Besides, you grow dishonest.°

Clown. Two faults, madonna,° that drink and good
counsel will amend. For give the dry° fool drink,
then is the fool not dry. Bid the dishonest man
mend himself: if he mend, he is no longer dishonest;
45   if he cannot, let the botcher° mend him. Anything

23 **points** counts (but Maria takes it in the sense of tagged laces
serving as suspenders) 25 **gaskins** loose breeches 27–28 **thou wert
as witty a piece of Eve's flesh** i.e., you would make as clever a wife
30 **you were best** it would be best for you 31 **and't** if it 34–35 **Quin-
apalus** (a sage of the Clown's invention) 39 **Go to** enough 39 **dry**
stupid 40 **dishonest** unreliable 41 **madonna** my lady 42 **dry**
thirsty 45 **botcher** mender of clothes

that's mended is but patched; virtue that trans-
gresses is but patched with sin, and sin that amends
is but patched with virtue. If that this simple syllo-
gism will serve, so; if it will not, what remedy? As
there is no true cuckold but calamity,° so beauty's   50
a flower. The lady bade take away the fool; therefore, I say again, take her away.

Olivia. Sir, I bade them take away you.

Clown. Misprision in the highest degree.° Lady, *cucullus non facit monachum.*° That's as much to say   55
as, I wear not motley in my brain. Good madonna,
give me leave to prove you a fool.

Olivia. Can you do it?

Clown. Dexteriously,° good madonna.

Olivia. Make your proof.   60

Clown. I must catechize you for it, madonna. Good
my mouse of virtue,° answer me.

Olivia. Well, sir, for want of other idleness,° I'll bide
your proof.

Clown. Good madonna, why mourn'st thou?   65

Olivia. Good fool, for my brother's death.

Clown. I think his soul is in hell, madonna.

Olivia. I know his soul is in heaven, fool.

Clown. The more fool, madonna, to mourn for your
brother's soul, being in heaven. Take away the fool,   70
gentlemen.

50 **there is no true cuckold but calamity** (although the Clown's chat-
ter should not be pressed too hard for significance, Kittredge's para-
phrase of this difficult passage is perhaps the least unsatisfactory:
"Every man is wedded to fortune; hence, when one's fortune is unfaithful, one may in very truth be called a cuckold—the husband of
an unfaithful wife") 54 **Misprision in the highest degree** i.e., an
egregious error in mistaken identity 54–55 **cucullus non facit
monachum** a cowl does not make a monk 59 **Dexteriously** dexterously 61–62 **Good my mouse of virtue** my good virtuous mouse (a
term of playful affection) 63 **idleness** trifling

Olivia. What think you of this fool, Malvolio? Doth he not mend?

Malvolio. Yes, and shall do till the pangs of death
75   shake him. Infirmity, that decays the wise, doth ever make the better fool.

Clown. God send you, sir, a speedy infirmity, for the better increasing your folly. Sir Toby will be sworn that I am no fox,° but he will not pass his word for
80   twopence that you are no fool.

Olivia. How say you to that, Malvolio?

Malvolio. I marvel your ladyship takes delight in such a barren° rascal. I saw him put down the other day with° an ordinary fool that has no more brain than
85   a stone. Look you now, he's out of his guard° already. Unless you laugh and minister occasion° to him, he is gagged. I protest I take these wise men that crow° so at these set° kind of fools no better than the fools' zanies.°

90 *Olivia.* O, you are sick of self-love, Malvolio, and taste with a distempered appetite. To be generous,° guiltless, and of free disposition, is to take those things for birdbolts° that you deem cannon bullets. There is no slander in an allowed° fool, though
95   he do nothing but rail; nor no railing in a known discreet man, though he do nothing but reprove.

Clown. Now Mercury indue thee with leasing,° for thou speak'st well of fools.

Enter Maria.

Maria. Madam, there is at the gate a young gentleman
100   much desires to speak with you.

79 **I am no fox** i.e., sly and dangerous (like you) 83 **barren** stupid
83–84 **put down . . . with** bested . . . by 85 **out of his guard** (defense-
less) 86 **minister occasion** afford opportunity (for his fooling)
88 **crow** i.e., with laughter 88 **set** artificial 89 **zanies** inferior buf-
foons 91 **generous** liberal-minded 93 **birdbolts** blunt arrows 94
allowed licensed, privileged 97 **Mercury indue thee with leasing**
may the god of trickery endow you with the gift of deception.

Olivia. From the Count Orsino, is it?

Maria. I know not, madam. 'Tis a fair young man, and well attended.

Olivia. Who of my people hold him in delay?

Maria. Sir Toby, madam, your kinsman.   *105*

Olivia. Fetch him off, I pray you. He speaks nothing but madman. Fie on him! [*Exit Maria.*] Go you, Malvolio. If it be a suit from the Count, I am sick, or not at home. What you will, to dismiss it. *(Exit Malvolio.)* Now you see, sir, how your fooling *110* grows old,° and people dislike it.

Clown. Thou hast spoke for us, madonna, as if thy eldest son should be a fool; whose skull Jove° cram with brains, for—here he comes—one of thy kin has a most weak pia mater.°   *115*

Enter Sir Toby.

Olivia. By mine honor, half drunk. What is he at the gate, cousin?

Toby. A gentleman.

Olivia. A gentleman? What gentleman?

Toby. 'Tis a gentleman here. A plague o' these pickle- *120* herring!° How now, sot?°

Clown. Good Sir Toby.

Olivia. Cousin,° cousin, how have you come so early by this lethargy?

Toby. Lechery? I defy lechery. There's one at the gate. *125*

Olivia. Ay, marry, what is he?

111 **old** stale, tedious   113 **Jove** (if, as is likely, Shakespeare here and elsewhere wrote "God," the printed text reflects the statute of 1606 that prohibited profane stage allusions to the deity)   115 **pia mater** brain   120–21 **pickle-herring** (to which the drunken Sir Toby attributes his hiccoughing)   121 **sot** fool   123 **Cousin** i.e., uncle (see 1.3.5)

Toby. Let him be the devil and he will, I care not.
Give me faith,° say I. Well, it's all one.   *Exit.*

Olivia. What's a drunken man like, fool?

130 *Clown.* Like a drowned man, a fool, and a madman.
One draught above heat° makes him a fool, the
second mads him, and a third drowns him.

Olivia. Go thou and seek the crowner,° and let him
sit o' my coz;° for he's in the third degree of drink—
135 he's drowned. Go look after him.

Clown. He is but mad yet, madonna, and the fool
shall look to the madman.   [*Exit.*]

Enter Malvolio.

Malvolio. Madam, yond young fellow swears he will
speak with you. I told him you were sick; he takes
140 on him to understand so much, and therefore comes
to speak with you. I told him you were asleep; he
seems to have a foreknowledge of that too, and
therefore comes to speak with you. What is to be
said to him, lady? He's fortified against any denial.

145 *Olivia.* Tell him he shall not speak with me.

Malvolio. H'as° been told so; and he says he'll stand
at your door like a sheriff's post,° and be the supporter to a bench, but° he'll speak with you.

Olivia. What kind o' man is he?

150 *Malvolio.* Why, of mankind.°

Olivia. What manner of man?

Malvolio. Of very ill manner. He'll speak with you,
will you or no.

128 **faith** (in order to resist the devil) 131 **above heat** i.e., above
what is required to make a man normally warm 133 **crowner**
coroner 134 **sit o' my coz** hold an inquest on my kinsman 146 **H'as**
he has 147 **sheriff's post** post set up before a sheriff's door for
placards, notices, and such 148 **but** except 150 **of mankind** i.e.,
like other men

Olivia. Of what personage and years is he?

Malvolio. Not yet old enough for a man nor young   *155*
enough for a boy; as a squash° is before 'tis a
peascod, or a codling° when 'tis almost an apple.
'Tis with him in standing water,° between boy and
man. He is very well-favored and he speaks very
shrewishly.° One would think his mother's milk   *160*
were scarce out of him.

Olivia. Let him approach. Call in my gentlewoman.

Malvolio. Gentlewoman, my lady calls.   *Exit.*

Enter Maria.

Olivia. Give me my veil; come, throw it o'er my face.
We'll once more hear Orsino's embassy.   *165*

Enter Viola.

Viola. The honorable lady of the house, which is she?

Olivia. Speak to me; I shall answer for her. Your will?

Viola. Most radiant, exquisite, and unmatchable beauty
—I pray you tell me if this be the lady of the house,
for I never saw her. I would be loath to cast away   *170*
my speech; for, besides that it is excellently well
penned, I have taken great pains to con° it. Good
beauties, let me sustain no scorn. I am very comptible,° even to the least sinister° usage.

Olivia. Whence came you, sir?   *175*

Viola. I can say little more than I have studied, and
that question's out of my part. Good gentle one,
give me modest° assurance if you be the lady of the
house, that I may proceed in my speech.

156 **squash** unripe peascod (pea pod) 157 **codling** unripe apple
158 **standing water** i.e., at the turning of the tide, between ebb and
flood, when it flows neither way 160 **shrewishly** tartly 172 **con**
learn 173–74 **comptible** sensitive 174 **sinister** discourteous 178
modest reasonable

180 *Olivia.* Are you a comedian?°

Viola. No, my profound heart;° and yet (by the very
fangs of malice I swear) I am not that° I play.
Are you the lady of the house?

Olivia. If I do not usurp° myself, I am.

185 *Viola.* Most certain, if you are she, you do usurp
yourself; for what° is yours to bestow is not yours
to reserve. But this is from my commission.° I will
on with my speech in your praise and then show
you the heart of my message.

190 *Olivia.* Come to what is important in't. I forgive you°
the praise.

Viola. Alas, I took great pains to study it, and 'tis
poetical.

Olivia. It is the more like to be feigned; I pray you
195 keep it in. I heard you were saucy at my gates; and
allowed your approach rather to wonder at you
than to hear you. If you be not mad, be gone; if
you have reason, be brief. 'Tis not that time of
moon with me to make one in so skipping a dia-
200 logue.°

Maria. Will you hoist sail, sir? Here lies your way.

Viola. No, good swabber; I am to hull° here a little
longer. Some mollification for your giant,° sweet
lady. Tell me your mind. I am a messenger.°

205 *Olivia.* Sure you have some hideous matter to deliver,
when the courtesy of it is so fearful.° Speak your
office.°

180 **comedian** actor (because he has had to "con" a "part")   181 **my
profound heart** my sagacious lady (a bantering compliment)
182 **that** that which   184 **usurp** counterfeit (but Viola takes it in the
sense "betray," "wrong")   186 **what** i.e., your hand in marriage
187 **from my commission** beyond my instructions   190 **forgive you**
excuse you from repeating   198–200 **'Tis not ... dialogue** i.e., I am
not in the mood to sustain such aimless banter   202 **hull** lie adrift
203 **giant** (an ironical reference to Maria's small size)   204 **Tell me
your mind. I am a messenger.** (Many editors have divided these
sentences, assigning the first to Olivia and the second to Viola)
206 **when the courtesy of it is so fearful** i.e., since your manner is so
truculent   207 **office** business

Viola. It alone concerns your ear. I bring no overture of war, no taxation of° homage. I hold the olive° in my hand. My words are as full of peace as   *210* matter.°

Olivia. Yet you began rudely. What are you? What would you?

Viola. The rudeness that hath appeared in me have I learned from my entertainment.° What I am, and   *215* what I would, are as secret as maidenhead:° to your ears, divinity;° to any other's, profanation.

Olivia. Give us the place alone; we will hear this divinity. [*Exit Maria and Attendants.*] Now, sir, what is your text?   *220*

Viola. Most sweet lady—

Olivia. A comfortable° doctrine, and much may be said of it. Where lies your text?

Viola. In Orsino's bosom.

Olivia. In his bosom? In what chapter of his bosom?   *225*

Viola. To answer by the method,° in the first of his heart.

Olivia. O, I have read it; it is heresy. Have you no more to say?

Viola. Good madam, let me see your face.   *230*

Olivia. Have you any commission from your lord to negotiate with my face? You are now out of your text.° But we will draw the curtain and show you the picture. [*Unveils.*] Look you, sir, such a one I was this present.° Is't not well done?   *235*

209 **taxation of** demand for   209 **olive** (the symbol of peace)
211 **matter** significant content   215 **entertainment** reception   216
maidenhead maidenhood   217 **divinity** i.e., a sacred message
222 **comfortable** comforting   226 **method** i.e., in the theological
style suggested by "divinity," "profanation," "text," and "doctrine"
232–33 **You are now out of your text** i.e., you have shifted from
talking of your master's heart to asking about my face.   235 **this
present** just now (like portrait painters, Olivia gives the age of the
subject of the "picture" she has just revealed by drawing the "curtain" of a veil from her face)

Viola. Excellently done, if God did all.

Olivia. 'Tis in grain,° sir; 'twill endure wind and weather.

Viola. 'Tis beauty truly blent, whose red and white
240   Nature's own sweet and cunning° hand laid on.
    Lady, you are the cruel'st she alive
    If you will lead these graces to the grave,
    And leave the world no copy.

Olivia. O, sir, I will not be so hard-hearted. I will give
245   out divers schedules° of my beauty. It shall be in-
    ventoried, and every particle and utensil° labeled
    to my will:° as, item,° two lips, indifferent red;
    item, two gray eyes, with lids to them; item,
    one neck, one chin, and so forth. Were you sent hither
250   to praise° me?

Viola. I see you what you are; you are too proud;
    But if° you were the devil, you are fair.
    My lord and master loves you. O, such love
    Could be but recompensed though you were crowned
    The nonpareil of beauty.

255 *Olivia.*   How does he love me?

Viola. With adorations, with fertile° tears,
    With groans that thunder love, with sighs of fire.

Olivia. Your lord does know my mind; I cannot love
    him.
    Yet I suppose him virtuous, know him noble,
260   Of great estate, of fresh and stainless youth;
    In voices well divulged,° free, learned, and valiant,
    And in dimension° and the shape of nature
    A gracious person. But yet I cannot love him.
    He might have took his answer long ago.

265 *Viola.* If I did love you in my master's flame,

237 **in grain** fast-dyed, indelible   240 **cunning** skillful   245 **sched-
ules** statements   246 **utensil** article   246–47 **labeled to my will** i.e.,
added as a codicil   247 **item** also   250 **praise** appraise   252 **if** even
if   256 **fertile** copious   261 **well divulged** i.e., of good repute
262 **dimension** physique

With such a suff'ring, such a deadly° life,
In your denial I would find no sense;
I would not understand it.

Olivia.   Why, what would you?

Viola. Make me a willow° cabin at your gate
And call upon my soul° within the house;   270
Write loyal cantons° of contemnèd° love
And sing them loud even in the dead of night;
Hallo your name to the reverberate° hills
And make the babbling gossip of the air°
Cry out "Olivia!" O, you should not rest   275
Between the elements of air and earth
But° you should pity me.

Olivia. You might do much. What is your parentage?

Viola. Above my fortunes, yet my state° is well.
I am a gentleman.

Olivia.   Get you to your lord.   280
I cannot love him. Let him send no more,
Unless, perchance, you come to me again
To tell me how he takes it. Fare you well.
I thank you for your pains. Spend this for me.

Viola. I am no fee'd post,° lady; keep your purse;   285
My master, not myself, lacks recompense.
Love make his heart of flint that you shall love;°
And let your fervor, like my master's, be
Placed in contempt. Farewell, fair cruelty.   *Exit.*

Olivia. "What is your parentage?"   290
"Above my fortunes, yet my state is well.
I am a gentleman." I'll be sworn thou art.
Thy tongue, thy face, thy limbs, actions, and spirit

266 **deadly** doomed to die   269 **willow** (emblem of a disconsolate
lover)   270 **my soul** i.e., Olivia   271 **cantons** songs   271 **con-
temnèd** rejected   273 **reverberate** reverberating   274 **babbling gossip of the air** i.e., echo   277 **But** but that   279 **state** status   285 **fee'd
post** i.e., lackey to be tipped   287 **Love make ... love** may Love
make the heart of him you love like flint

Do give thee fivefold blazon.° Not too fast; soft,°
    soft,
295   Unless the master were the man. How now?
Even so quickly may one catch the plague?
Methinks I feel this youth's perfections
With an invisible and subtle stealth
To creep in at mine eyes. Well, let it be.
What ho, Malvolio!

Enter Malvolio.

300   *Malvolio.*   Here, madam, at your service.

Olivia. Run after that same peevish° messenger,
    The County's° man. He left this ring behind him,
    Would I or not. Tell him I'll none of it.
    Desire him not to flatter with° his lord
305   Nor hold him up with hopes. I am not for him.
    If that the youth will come this way tomorrow,
    I'll give him reasons for't. Hie thee, Malvolio.

Malvolio. Madam, I will.   *Exit.*

Olivia. I do I know not what, and fear to find
310   Mine eye too great a flatterer for my mind.°
    Fate, show thy force; ourselves we do not owe.°
    What is decreed must be—and be this so!   [*Exit.*]

294 **blazon** heraldic insignia   294 **soft** i.e., take it slowly   301 **peev-ish** truculent impertinent   302 **County's** Count's   304 **flatter with** encourage   310 **Mine eye . . . mind** i.e., my eye, so susceptible to external attractions, will betray my judgment   311 **owe** own

ACT 2

Scene 1. [*The seacoast.*]

Enter Antonio and Sebastian.

Antonio. Will you stay no longer? Nor will you not
that I go with you?

Sebastian. By your patience,° no. My stars shine darkly
over me; the malignancy of my fate might perhaps
distemper° yours. Therefore I shall crave of you   5
your leave, that I may bear my evils alone. It were
a bad recompense for your love to lay any of them
on you.

Antonio. Let me yet know of you whither you are
bound.   10

Sebastian. No, sooth,° sir. My determinate° voyage is
mere extravagancy.° But I perceive in you so excellent a touch of modesty that you will not extort
from me what I am willing to keep in; therefore it
charges me in manners the rather to express myself.°   15
You must know of me then, Antonio, my name is
Sebastian, which I called Roderigo. My father was
that Sebastian of Messaline whom I know you have
heard of. He left behind him myself and a sister,
both born in an hour.° If the heavens had been   20

2.1.3 **patience** permission 5 **distemper** disorder 11 **sooth** truly
11 **determinate** intended 12 **extravagancy** wandering 14–15 **it
charges me ... myself** i.e., civility requires that I give some account
of myself 20 **in an hour** in the same hour

27

pleased, would we had so ended! But you, sir,
altered that, for some hour before you took me
from the breach° of the sea was my sister drowned.

Antonio. Alas the day!

25 *Sebastian.* A lady, sir, though it was said she much
resembled me, was yet of many accounted beautiful.
But though I could not with such estimable wonder°
overfar believe that, yet thus far I will boldly
publish° her: she bore a mind that envy could not
30 but call fair. She is drowned already, sir, with salt
water, though I seem to drown her remembrance
again with more.

Antonio. Pardon me, sir, your bad entertainment.°

Sebastian. O good Antonio, forgive me your trouble.°

35 *Antonio.* If you will not murder me° for my love, let
me be your servant.

Sebastian. If you will not undo what you have done,
that is, kill him whom you have recovered,° desire
it not. Fare ye well at once. My bosom is full of
40 kindness, and I am yet so near the manners of my
mother that, upon the least occasion more, mine
eyes will tell tales of me.° I am bound to the Count
Orsino's court. Farewell. *Exit.*

Antonio. The gentleness of all the gods go with thee.
45 I have many enemies in Orsino's court,
Else would I very shortly see thee there.
But come what may, I do adore thee so
That danger shall seem sport, and I will go. *Exit.*

---

23 **breach** breakers 27 **with such estimable wonder** i.e., with so
much esteem in my appraisal 29 **publish** describe 33 **bad enter-**
tainment i.e., poor reception at my hands 34 **your trouble** the
trouble I have given you 35 **murder me** i.e., by forcing me to part
from you 38 **recovered** saved 40–42 **so near . . . tales of me** i.e.,
so overwrought by my sorrow that, like a woman, I shall weep

Scene 2. [*A street near Olivia's house.*]

Enter Viola and Malvolio at several° doors.

Malvolio. Were not you ev'n now with the Countess
　　Olivia?

Viola. Even now, sir. On a moderate pace I have since
　　arrived but hither.

Malvolio. She returns this ring to you, sir. You might　　5
　　have saved me my pains, to have taken it away
　　yourself. She adds, moreover, that you should put
　　your lord into a desperate assurance° she will none
　　of him. And one thing more, that you be never so
　　hardy to come again in his affairs, unless it be to　　10
　　report your lord's taking of this. Receive it so.

Viola. She took the ring of me.° I'll none of it.

Malvolio. Come, sir, you peevishly threw it to her,
　　and her will is, it should be so returned. If it be
　　worth stooping for, there it lies, in your eye;° if　　15
　　not, be it his that finds it.　　　　　　　　*Exit.*

Viola. I left no ring with her. What means this lady?
　　Fortune forbid my outside have not charmed her.
　　She made good view of me; indeed, so much
　　That sure methought° her eyes had lost her tongue,°　　20
　　For she did speak in starts distractedly.
　　She loves me sure; the cunning° of her passion

2.2.s.d. **several** separate 8 **desperate assurance** hopeless certainty
12 **She took the ring of me** (of the various emendations proposed for
this puzzling line, Malone's "She took no ring of me" is perhaps the
most attractive) 15 **eye** sight 20 **sure methought** ("sure," which
repairs the defective meter of this line, has been adopted from the
Second Folio. Another common emendation is "as methought")
20 **her eyes had lost her tongue** i.e., her fixed gaze made her lose the
power of speech · 22 **cunning** craftiness

Invites me in this churlish messenger.
None of my lord's ring? Why, he sent her none.

25 I am the man.° If it be so, as 'tis,
Poor lady, she were better love a dream.
Disguise, I see thou art a wickedness
Wherein the pregnant enemy° does much.
How easy is it for the proper false°

30 In women's waxen hearts to set their forms!
Alas, our frailty is the cause, not we,
For such as we are made of, such we be.
How will this fadge?° My master loves her dearly;
And I (poor monster)° fond° as much on him;

35 And she (mistaken) seems to dote on me.
What will become of this? As I am man,
My state is desperate° for my master's love.
As I am woman (now alas the day!),
What thriftless° sighs shall poor Olivia breathe?

40 O Time, thou must untangle this, not I;
It is too hard a knot for me t' untie.   [*Exit.*]

Scene 3. [*A room in Olivia's house.*]

Enter Sir Toby and Sir Andrew.

Toby. Approach, Sir Andrew. Not to be abed after
      midnight is to be up betimes; and *"Deliculo sur-*
      gere,"° thou know'st.

Andrew. Nay, by my troth, I know not, but I know
5   to be up late is to be up late.

25 **I am the man** i.e., whom she loves 28 **pregnant enemy** crafty
fiend (i.e., Satan) 29 **proper false** i.e., attractive but deceitful suitors
33 **fadge** turn out 34 **monster** (because of her equivocal position as
both man and woman) 34 **fond** dote 37 **desperate** hopeless 39
thriftless unavailing 2.3.2–3 **Deliculo surgere** i.e., *Diluculo surgere*
saluberrimum est, "it is most healthful to rise early" (a tag from
William Lily's Latin grammar, which was widely used in sixteenth-
century schools)

Toby. A false conclusion; I hate it as an unfilled can.° To be up after midnight, and to go to bed then, is early; so that to go to bed after midnight is to go to bed betimes. Does not our lives consist of the four elements?°

Andrew. Faith, so they say; but I think it rather consists of eating and drinking.

Toby. Th' art a scholar! Let us therefore eat and drink. Marian I say, a stoup° of wine!

Enter Clown.

Andrew. Here comes the fool, i' faith.

Clown. How now, my hearts? Did you never see the picture of We Three?°

Toby. Welcome, ass. Now let's have a catch.°

Andrew. By my troth, the fool has an excellent breast.° I had rather than forty shillings I had such a leg,° and so sweet a breath to sing, as the fool has. In sooth, thou wast in very gracious° fooling last night, when thou spok'st of Pigrogromitus,° of the Vapians° passing the equinoctial of Queubus.° 'Twas very good, i' faith. I sent thee sixpence for thy leman.° Hadst it?

Clown. I did impeticos thy gratillity,° for Malvolio's nose is no whipstock. My lady has a white hand, and the Myrmidons are no bottle-ale houses.°

6 **can** tankard   9–10 **the four elements** i.e., air, fire, earth, and water, which were thought to be the basic ingredients of all things   14 **stoup** cup   16–17 **the picture of We Three** i.e., a picture of two asses, the spectator making the third   18 **catch** round, a simple polyphonic song for several voices   20 **breast** voice   21 **leg** i.e., skill in bowing (?)   22 **gracious** delightful   23–24 **Pigrogromitus, Vapians, Queubus** (presumably words invented by the Clown as specimens of his "gracious fooling" in mock learning)   26 **leman** sweetheart   27 **impeticos thy gratillity** (more of the Clown's fooling, which perhaps means something like "pocket your gratuity")   27–29 **Malvolio's nose ... bottle-ale houses** (probably mere nonsense)

30   *Andrew.* Excellent. Why, this is the best fooling, when
       all is done. Now a song!

     Toby. Come on, there is sixpence for you. Let's have
       a song.

     Andrew. There's a testril° of me too. If one knight
35   give a—°

     Clown. Would you have a love song, or a song of
       good life?°

     Toby. A love song, a love song.

     Andrew. Ay, ay, I care not for good life.

                    Clown sings.

40   O mistress mine, where are you roaming?
            O, stay and hear, your true-love's coming,
                 That can sing both high and low.
            Trip no further, pretty sweeting;
            Journeys end in lovers meeting,
45   Every wise man's son doth know.

     Andrew. Excellent good, i' faith.

     Toby. Good, good.

                    Clown [sings].

            What is love? 'Tis not hereafter;
            Present mirth hath present laughter;
50   What's to come is still° unsure:
            In delay there lies no plenty;
            Then come kiss me, sweet, and twenty,°
                 Youth's a stuff will not endure.

---

34 **testril** tester, sixpence   34–35 **If one knight give a—** (some editors
have tried to supply what seems to be a missing line here, but it is
probable that the Clown breaks in without permitting Sir Andrew
to finish his sentence)   36–37 **of good life** i.e., moral, edifying (?)
50 **still** always   52 **Then come kiss me, sweet, and twenty** i.e., so kiss
me, my sweet, and then kiss me twenty times again (some editors
taking "twenty" as an intensive, read the line as "so kiss me then
my very sweet one")

Andrew. A mellifluous voice, as I am true knight.

Toby. A contagious breath.°   55

Andrew. Very sweet and contagious, i' faith.

Toby. To hear by the nose, it is dulcet in contagion.°
But shall we make the welkin° dance indeed? Shall
we rouse the night owl in a catch that will draw
three souls out of one weaver?° Shall we do that?   60

Andrew. And you love me, let's do't. I am dog° at a
catch.

Clown. By'r Lady, sir, and some dogs will catch well.

Andrew. Most certain. Let our catch be "Thou knave."

Clown. "Hold thy peace, thou knave,"° knight? I   65
shall be constrained in't to call thee knave, knight.

Andrew. 'Tis not the first time I have constrained one
to call me knave. Begin, fool. It begins, "Hold thy
peace."

Clown. I shall never begin if I hold my peace.   70

Andrew. Good, i' faith! Come, begin.

Catch sung. Enter Maria.

Maria. What a caterwauling do you keep here? If my
lady have not called up her steward Malvolio and
bid him turn you out of doors, never trust me.

Toby. My lady's a Cataian, we are politicians,° Mal-   75

55 **contagious breath** catchy song   57 **to hear by the nose, it is dulcet
in contagion** i.e., if we could hear through the nose, the Clown's
"breath" would be sweet and not malodorous, as "contagious"
breaths usually are   58 **welkin** sky   60 **weaver** (weavers were noted
for their singing)   61 **dog** clever (but in the next line the Clown
puns on **dog** i.e., latch, gripping device)   65 **Hold thy peace, thou
knave** (a line from the round proposed by Sir Andrew)   75 **My
lady's a Cataian, we are politicians** (because Sir Toby and his companions are "politicians" [i.e., tricksters, intriguers] they recognize
Maria's warning of Olivia's anger as the ruse of a "Cataian" [i.e.,
native of Cathay, cheater]; hence "Tilly-vally, lady" [line 78], which
means something like "Fiddlesticks, lady")

volio's a Peg-a-Ramsey,° and [*sings*] "Three merry
men be we."° Am not I consanguineous?° Am I
not of her blood? Tilly-vally, lady. [*Sings*] "There
dwelt a man in Babylon, lady, lady."

80 *Clown.* Beshrew° me, the knight's in admirable fooling.

Andrew. Ay, he does well enough if he be disposed,
and so do I too. He does it with a better grace, but
I do it more natural.°

85 *Toby.* [*Sings*] "O the twelfth day of December."

Maria. For the love o' God, peace!

Enter Malvolio.

Malvolio. My masters, are you mad? Or what are you?
Have you no wit,° manners, nor honesty,° but to
gabble like tinkers at this time of night? Do ye
90 make an alehouse of my lady's house, that ye squeak
out your coziers'° catches without any mitigation
or remorse° of voice? Is there no respect of place,
persons, nor time in you?

Toby. We did keep time, sir, in our catches. Sneck up.°

95 *Malvolio.* Sir Toby, I must be round° with you. My
lady bade me tell you that, though she harbors
you as her kinsman, she's nothing allied to your
disorders. If you can separate yourself and your
misdemeanors, you are welcome to the house. If
100 not, and it would please you to take leave of her,
she is very willing to bid you farewell.

76 **Peg-a-Ramsey** (character in an old song whose name Sir Toby
uses apparently as a term of contempt) 76–77 **Three merry men be
we** (like Sir Toby's other snatches, a fragment of an old song)
77 **consanguineous** related, kin (to Olivia) 80 **Beshrew** curse
84 **natural** (with an unintentional pun on "natural" as a term for fool
or idiot; see 1.3.29) 88 **wit** sense 88 **honesty** decency 91 **coziers'**
cobblers' 91–92 **mitigation or remorse** i.e., lowering 94 **Sneck up**
go hang 95 **round** blunt

Toby. [*Sings*] "Farewell, dear heart since I must needs
be gone."°

Maria. Nay, good Sir Toby.

Clown. [*Sings*] "His eyes do show his days are almost
done."

Malvolio. Is't even so?   105

Toby. [*Sings*] "But I will never die."

Clown. [*Sings*] Sir Toby, there you lie.

Malvolio. This is much credit to you.

Toby. [*Sings*] "Shall I bid him go?"

Clown. [*Sings*] "What and if you do?"   110

Toby. [*Sings*] "Shall I bid him go, and spare not?"

Clown. [*Sings*] "O, no, no, no, no, you dare not!"

Toby. Out o' tune, sir? Ye lie.° Art any more than a
steward? Dost thou think, because thou art virtuous,
there shall be no more cakes and ale?   115

Clown. Yes, by Saint Anne, and ginger° shall be hot
i' th' mouth too.

Toby. Th' art i' th' right. —Go, sir, rub your chain
with crumbs.° A stoup of wine, Maria!

Malvolio. Mistress Mary, if you prized my lady's favor   120
at anything more than contempt, you would not
give means for this uncivil rule.° She shall know
of it, by this hand.   *Exit.*

Maria. Go shake your ears.°

---

102 **Farewell ... gone** (what follows, in crude antiphony between
Sir Toby and the Clown, is adapted from a ballad, "Corydon's Farewell to Phyllis")   113 **Out o' tune, sir? Ye lie** (Sir Toby accuses the
Clown of being out of tune, it seems, because he had added an extra
"no" and thus an extra note in line 112, and of lying because he had
questioned his valor in "you dare not." Then he turns to berating
Malvolio)   116 **ginger** (commonly used to spice ale)   118–19 **rub
your chain with crumbs** i.e., polish your steward's chain, your badge
of office   122 **give means for this uncivil rule** i.e., provide liquor for
this brawl   124 **Go shake your ears** i.e., like the ass you are (?)

125 *Andrew.* 'Twere as good a deed as to drink when a
man's ahungry,° to challenge him the field,° and
then to break promise with him and make a fool
of him.

Toby. Do't, knight. I'll write thee a challenge; or I'll
130 deliver thy indignation to him by word of mouth.

Maria. Sweet Sir Toby, be patient for tonight. Since
the youth of the Count's was today with my lady,
she is much out of quiet. For Monsieur Malvolio,
let me alone with him. If I do not gull him into a
135 nayword,° and make him a common recreation, do
not think I have wit enough to lie straight in my
bed. I know I can do it.

Toby. Possess° us, possess us. Tell us something of
him.

140 *Maria.* Marry, sir, sometimes he is a kind of Puritan.°

Andrew. O, if I thought that, I'd beat him like a dog.

Toby. What, for being a Puritan? Thy exquisite
reason, dear knight.

Andrew. I have no exquisite reason for't, but I have
145 reason good enough.

Maria. The devil a Puritan that he is, or anything
constantly° but a time-pleaser;° an affectioned° ass,
that cons state without book° and utters it by great
swarths;° the best persuaded of himself;° so
150 crammed, as he thinks, with excellencies that it is
his grounds of faith that all that look on him love
him; and on that vice in him will my revenge find
notable cause to work.

126 **ahungry** (characteristically, Sir Andrew confuses hunger and
thirst and thus perverts the proverbial expression)   126 **the field** i.e.,
to a duel   135 **nayword** byword   138 **Possess** inform   140 **Puritan**
i.e., a straight-laced, censorious person (in lines 146–47 Maria makes
it clear that she is not using the label in a strict ecclesiastical sense, as
Sir Andrew [line 141] thinks)   147 **constantly** consistently   147
time-pleaser sycophant   147 **affectioned** affected   148 **cons state
without book** i.e., memorizes stately gestures and turns of phrase
149 **swarths** swaths, quantities   149 **the best persuaded of himself**
i.e., who thinks most highly of himself

Toby. What wilt thou do?

Maria. I will drop in his way some obscure epistles of   155
love, wherein by the color of his beard, the shape
of his leg, the manner of his gait, the expressure° of
his eye, forehead, and complexion, he shall find
himself most feelingly personated.° I can write very
like my lady your niece; on a forgotten matter we   160
can hardly make distinction of our hands.

Toby. Excellent. I smell a device.

Andrew. I have 't in my nose too.

Toby. He shall think by the letters that thou wilt drop
that they come from my niece, and that she's in love   165
with him.

Maria. My purpose is indeed a horse of that color.

Andrew. And your horse now would make him an
ass.

Maria. Ass, I doubt not.   170

Andrew. O, 'twill be admirable.

Maria. Sport royal, I warrant you. I know my physic
will work with him. I will plant you two, and let
the fool make a third,° where he shall find the
letter. Observe his construction° of it. For this   175
night, to bed, and dream on the event.° Farewell.

                                              Exit.

Toby. Good night, Penthesilea.°

Andrew. Before me,° she's a good wench.

Toby. She's a beagle° true-bred, and one that adores
me. What o' that?   180

157 **expressure** expression   159 **personated** represented   173–74 **let
the fool make a third** (like the plan to have Viola present herself to
Duke Orsino as a eunuch [1.2.62], this plot device was abandoned; it
is Fabian, not the Clown, who makes the third spectator to Malvolio's exposé)   175 **construction** interpretation   176 **event** outcome
177 **Penthesilea** (in classical mythology, the queen of the Amazons)
178 **Before me** i.e., I swear, with myself as witness   179 **beagle** (one
of several allusions to Maria's small stature)

Andrew. I was adored once too.

Toby. Let's to bed, knight. Thou hadst need send for
more money.

Andrew. If I cannot recover° your niece, I am a foul
185   way out.°

Toby. Send for money, knight. If thou hast her not
i' th' end, call me Cut.°

Andrew. If I do not, never trust me, take it how you
will.

190   *Toby.* Come, come; I'll go burn some sack.° 'Tis too
late to go to bed now. Come, knight; come, knight.
                                                Exeunt.

Scene 4. [*The Duke's palace.*]

Enter Duke, Viola, Curio, and others.

Duke. Give me some music. Now good morrow, friends.
Now, good Cesario, but that piece of song,
That old and antic° song we heard last night.
Methought it did relieve my passion° much,
5   More than light airs and recollected terms°
Of these most brisk and giddy-pacèd times.
Come, but one verse.

Curio. He is not here, so please your lordship, that
should sing it.

10   *Duke.* Who was it?

Curio. Feste the jester, my lord, a fool that the Lady

___

184 **recover** win   184–85 **a foul way out** i.e., badly out of pocket
187 **Cut** i.e., a dock-tailed horse   190 **burn some sack** heat and
spice some Spanish wine   2.4.3 **antic** quaint   4 **passion** suffering
(from unrequited love)   5 **recollected terms** studied phrases

Olivia's father took much delight in. He is about the
house.

Duke. Seek him out, and play the tune the while.
                [*Exit Curio.*] *Music plays.*
Come hither, boy. If ever thou shalt love,   *15*
In the sweet pangs of it remember me;
For such as I am all true lovers are,
Unstaid and skittish in all motions° else
Save in the constant image of the creature
That is beloved. How dost thou like this tune?   *20*

Viola. It gives a very echo to the seat°
Where Love is throned.

Duke.   Thou dost speak masterly.
My life upon't, young though thou art, thine eye
Hath stayed upon some favor° that it loves.
Hath it not, boy?

Viola.   A little, by your favor.   *25*

Duke. What kind of woman is't?

Viola.   Of your complexion.°

Duke. She is not worth thee then. What years, i' faith?

Viola. About your years, my lord.

Duke. Too old, by heaven. Let still° the woman take
An elder than herself: so wears she° to him,   *30*
So sways she level in her husband's heart;°
For, boy, however we do praise ourselves,
Our fancies° are more giddy and unfirm,
More longing, wavering, sooner lost and worn,°
Than women's are.

Viola.   I think it well, my lord.   *35*

Duke. Then let thy love be younger than thyself,

---

18 **motions** emotions   21 **seat** i.e., the heart (see 1.1.38–39)   24 **favor**
face   26 **complexion** temperament   29 **still** always   30 **wears she**
she adapts herself   31 **sways she ... heart** i.e., she keeps steady in
her husband's affections   33 **fancies** loves   34 **worn** (many editors
have adopted the reading "won" from the Second Folio)

Or thy affection cannot hold the bent;°
For women are as roses, whose fair flow'r,
Being once displayed, doth fall that very hour.

40 *Viola.* And so they are; alas, that they are so.
To die, even when they to perfection grow.

Enter Curio and Clown.

Duke. O, fellow, come, the song we had last night.
Mark it, Cesario; it is old and plain.
The spinsters° and the knitters in the sun,
And the free° maids that weave their thread with
45   bones,°
Do use to chant it. It is silly sooth,°
And dallies° with the innocence of love,
Like the old age.°

Clown. Are you ready, sir?

50 *Duke.* I prithee sing.   *Music.*

The Song.

Come away, come away, death,
    And in sad cypress° let me be laid.
Fly away, fly away, breath;
    I am slain by a fair cruel maid.
55 My shroud of white, stuck all with yew,
     O, prepare it.
My part of death, no one so true
     Did share it.

Not a flower, not a flower sweet,
60   On my black coffin let there be strown;
Not a friend, not a friend greet
     My poor corpse, where my bones shall be
       thrown.

37 **hold the bent** i.e., maintain its strength and tension (the image is
that of a bent bow)   44 **spinsters** spinners   45 **free** carefree
45 **bones** i.e., bone bobbins   46 **silly sooth** simple truth   47 **dallies**
deals movingly   48 **the old age** i.e., the good old times   52 **cypress**
a coffin made of cypress wood

A thousand thousand sighs to save,
　　Lay me, O, where
Sad true lover never find my grave,   65
　　To weep there.

Duke. There's for thy pains.

Clown. No pains, sir. I take pleasure in singing, sir.

Duke. I'll pay thy pleasure then.

Clown. Truly, sir, and pleasure will be paid one time   70
or another.

Duke. Give me now leave to leave thee.

Clown. Now the melancholy god protect thee, and the
tailor make thy doublet of changeable° taffeta, for
thy mind is a very opal. I would have men of such   75
constancy put to sea, that their business might be
everything, and their intent everywhere; for that's
it that always makes a good voyage of nothing.
Farewell.   *Exit.*

Duke. Let all the rest give place.°
　　　　　　　[*Exeunt Curio and Attendants.*]
　　　　　　　　　　Once more, Cesario,   80
Get thee to yond same sovereign cruelty.°
Tell her my love, more noble than the world,
Prizes not quantity of dirty lands;
The parts° that fortune hath bestowed upon her
Tell her I hold as giddily° as fortune,   85
But 'tis that miracle and queen of gems°
That nature pranks her in° attracts my soul.

Viola. But if she cannot love you, sir?

Duke. I cannot be so answered.

Viola.   Sooth,° but you must.

---

74 **changeable** i.e., with shifting lights and colors 80 **give place**
withdraw 81 **sovereign cruelty** i.e., peerless and disdainful lady
84 **parts** gifts (of wealth and social status) 85 **giddily** indifferently
86 **queen of gems** i.e., Olivia's beauty 87 **pranks her in** adorns her
with 89 **Sooth** truly

90   Say that some lady, as perhaps there is,
        Hath for your love as great a pang of heart
        As you have for Olivia. You cannot love her.
        You tell her so. Must she not then be answered?

Duke. There is no woman's sides
95   Can bide° the beating of so strong a passion
        As love doth give my heart; no woman's heart
        So big to hold so much; they lack retention.°
        Alas, their love may be called appetite,
        No motion° of the liver° but the palate,
100   That suffer surfeit, cloyment, and revolt;°
        But mine is all as hungry as the sea
        And can digest as much. Make no compare
        Between that love a woman can bear me
        And that I owe Olivia.

Viola.   Ay, but I know—

105 *Duke.* What dost thou know?

Viola. Too well what love women to men may owe.
        In faith, they are as true of heart as we.
        My father had a daughter loved a man
        As it might be perhaps, were I a woman,
        I should your lordship.

110 *Duke.*   And what's her history?

Viola. A blank, my lord. She never told her love,
        But let concealment, like a worm i' th' bud,
        Feed on her damask° cheek. She pined in thought;°
        And, with a green and yellow melancholy,
115   She sat like Patience on a monument,
        Smiling at grief. Was not this love indeed?
        We men may say more, swear more; but indeed
        Our shows are more than will;° for still we prove
        Much in our vows but little in our love.

120 *Duke.* But died thy sister of her love, my boy?

95 **bide** endure 97 **retention** i.e., the ability to retain 99 **motion**
stirring, prompting 99 **liver** (seat of passion) 100 **revolt** revulsion
113 **damask** i.e., like a pink and white damask rose 113 **thought**
brooding 118 **Our shows are more than will** i.e., what we show is
greater than the passion that we feel

Viola. I am all the daughters of my father's house,
  And all the brothers too, and yet I know not.°
  Sir, shall I to this lady?

Duke.   Ay, that's the theme.
  To her in haste. Give her this jewel. Say
  My love can give no place,° bide no denay.°   *125*

                                    Exeunt.

Scene 5. [*Olivia's garden.*]

Enter Sir Toby, Sir Andrew, and Fabian.

Toby. Come thy ways, Signior Fabian.

Fabian. Nay, I'll come. If I lose a scruple° of this
  sport, let me be boiled° to death with melancholy.

Toby. Wouldst thou not be glad to have the niggardly
  rascally sheep-biter° come by some notable shame?   *5*

Fabian. I would exult, man. You know he brought me
  out o' favor with my lady about a bearbaiting here.

Toby. To anger him we'll have the bear again, and we
  will fool him black and blue. Shall we not, Sir
  Andrew?   *10*

Andrew. And we do not, it is pity of our lives.

Enter Maria.

Toby. Here comes the little villain. How now, my
  metal of India?°

122 **I know not** (because she thinks that her brother may be still
alive) 125 **can give no place** cannot yield 125 **denay** denial 2.5.2
scruple smallest part 3 **boiled** (pronounced "biled," quibbling on
"bile," which was thought to be the cause of melancholy) 5 **sheep-
biter** i.e., sneaky dog 13 **metal of India** i.e., golden girl

Maria. Get ye all three into the box tree. Malvolio's
15   coming down this walk. He has been yonder i' the
       sun practicing behavior to his own shadow this half
       hour. Observe him, for the love of mockery; for I
       know this letter will make a contemplative° idiot of
       him. Close,° in the name of jesting. [*The others*
20   *hide.*] Lie thou there [*throws down a letter*]; for
       here comes the trout that must be caught with
       tickling.°   *Exit.*

Enter Malvolio.

Malvolio. 'Tis but fortune; all is fortune. Maria once
       told me she did affect me;° and I have heard herself
25   come thus near, that, should she fancy,° it should
       be one of my complexion. Besides, she uses me with
       a more exalted respect than anyone else that
       follows° her. What should I think on't?

Toby. Here's an overweening rogue.

30 *Fabian.* O, peace! Contemplation makes a rare turkey
       cock of him. How he jets° under his advanced°
       plumes!

Andrew. 'Slight,° I could so beat the rogue.

Toby. Peace, I say.°

35 *Malvolio.* To be Count Malvolio.

Toby. Ah, rogue!

Andrew. Pistol him, pistol him.

Toby. Peace, peace.

Malvolio. There is example for't. The Lady of the
40   Strachy° married the yeoman of the wardrobe.

18 **contemplative** i.e., self-centered   19 **Close** hide   22 **tickling**
stroking, i.e., flattery   24 **she did affect me** i.e., Olivia liked me
25 **fancy** love   28 **follows** serves   31 **jets** struts   31 **advanced** up-
lifted   33 **'Slight** by God's light (a mild oath)   34 **Peace, I say**
(many editors assign this and line 38 to Fabian on the ground that
it is his function throughout the scene to restrain Sir Toby and Sir
Andrew)   39–40 **The Lady of the Strachy** (an unidentified allusion
to a great lady who married beneath her)

Andrew. Fie on him, Jezebel.°

Fabian. O, peace! Now he's deeply in. Look how imagination blows him.°

Malvolio. Having been three months married to her, sitting in my state— 45

Toby. O for a stonebow,° to hit him in the eye!

Malvolio. Calling my officers about me, in my branched° velvet gown; having come from a daybed,° where I have left Olivia sleeping—

Toby. Fire and brimstone! 50

Fabian. O, peace, peace!

Malvolio. And then to have the humor of state;° and after a demure travel of regard,° telling them I know my place, as I would they should do theirs, to ask for my kinsman Toby— 55

Toby. Bolts and shackles!

Fabian. O peace, peace, peace, now, now.

Malvolio. Seven of my people, with an obedient start, make out for° him. I frown the while, and perchance wind up my watch, or play with my—some 60 rich jewel.° Toby approaches; curtsies there to me—

Toby. Shall this fellow live?

Fabian. Though our silence be drawn from us with cars, yet peace.

Malvolio. I extend my hand to him thus, quenching 65 my familiar smile with an austere regard of control°—

41 **Jezebel** (the proud and wicked queen of Ahab, King of Israel, whom Sir Andrew, muddled as usual, regards as Malvolio's prototype in arrogance) 43 **blows him** puffs him up 46 **stonebow** crossbow that shoots stones 48 **branched** embroidered 48–49 **daybed** sofa 52 **to have the humor of state** i.e., to assume an imperious manner 53 **after a demure travel of regard** i.e., having glanced gravely over my retainers 59 **make out for** i.e., go to fetch 60–61 **play with my—some rich jewel** (Malvolio automatically reaches for his steward's chain and then catches himself) 66–67 **an austere regard of control** i.e., a stern look of authority

Toby. And does not Toby take° you a blow o' the lips then?

70 *Malvolio.* Saying, "Cousin Toby, my fortunes having cast me on your niece, give me this prerogative of speech."

Toby. What, what?

Malvolio. "You must amend your drunkenness."

75 *Toby.* Out, scab!

Fabian. Nay, patience, or we break the sinews of our plot.

Malvolio. "Besides, you waste the treasure of your time with a foolish knight"—

80 *Andrew.* That's me, I warrant you.

Malvolio. "One Sir Andrew"—

Andrew. I knew 'twas I, for many do call me fool.

Malvolio. What employment° have we here?
                              [*Takes up the letter.*]

Fabian. Now is the woodcock° near the gin.°

85 *Toby.* O, peace, and the spirit of humors intimate reading aloud to him!

Malvolio. By my life, this is my lady's hand. These be her very C's, her U's, and her T's; and thus makes she her great P's. It is, in contempt of° question,
90 her hand.

Andrew. Her C's, her U's, and her T's? Why that?

Malvolio. [*Reads*] "To the unknown beloved, this, and my good wishes." Her very phrases! By your leave, wax.° Soft,° and the impressure her Lucrece,°

68 **take** give   83 **employment** business   84 **woodcock** (a proverbially stupid bird)   84 **gin** snare   89 **in contempt of** beyond   93–94 **By your leave, wax** i.e., excuse me for breaking the seal   94 **Soft** i.e., take it slowly   94 **the impressure her Lucrece** i.e., the seal depicts Lucrece (noble Roman matron who stabbed herself after she was raped by Tarquin, hence a symbol of chastity)

with which she uses to seal.° 'Tis my lady. To   95
whom should this be?

Fabian. This wins him, liver and all.

Malvolio. [*Reads*]
> "Jove knows I love,
>   But who?
> Lips, do not move;   100
>   No man must know."

"No man must know." What follows? The numbers
altered!° "No man must know." If this should be
thee, Malvolio?

Toby. Marry, hang thee, brock!°   105

Malvolio. [*Reads*]
> "I may command where I adore,
>   But silence, like a Lucrece knife,
> With bloodless stroke my heart doth gore.
>   M. O. A. I. doth sway my life."

Fabian. A fustian° riddle.   110

Toby. Excellent wench,° say I.

Malvolio. "M. O. A. I. doth sway my life." Nay, but
first, let me see, let me see, let me see.

Fabian. What dish o' poison has she dressed° him!

Toby. And with what wing the staniel checks at it!°   115

Malvolio. "I may command where I adore." Why, she
may command me: I serve her; she is my lady.
Why, this is evident to any formal capacity.° There
is no obstruction° in this. And the end; what should
that alphabetical position portend? If I could make   120
that resemble something in me! Softly, "M. O. A. I."

Toby. O, ay, make up that. He is now at a cold scent.

95 **uses to seal** customarily seals   102–103 **The numbers altered** the
meter changed (in the stanza that follows)   105 **brock** badger
110 **fustian** i.e., foolish and pretentious   111 **wench** i.e., Maria
114 **dressed** prepared for   115 **with what wing the staniel checks at
it** i.e., with what speed the kestrel (a kind of hawk) turns to snatch
at the wrong prey   118 **formal capacity** normal intelligence   119
obstruction difficulty

Fabian. Sowter will cry upon't for all this, though it
be as rank as a fox.°

125 *Malvolio.* M.—Malvolio. M.—Why, that begins my
name.

Fabian. Did not I say he would work it out? The cur
is excellent at faults.°

Malvolio. M.—But then there is no consonancy in the
130 sequel.° That suffers under probation.° A should
follow, but O does.

Fabian. And O° shall end, I hope.

Toby. Ay, or I'll cudgel him, and make him cry O.

Malvolio. And then I comes behind.

135 *Fabian.* Ay, and you had any eye behind you, you
might see more detraction at your heels than
fortunes before you.

Malvolio. M, O, A, I. This simulation° is not as the
former; and yet, to crush° this a little, it would bow
140 to me, for every one of these letters are in my name.
Soft, here follows prose.

[*Reads*] "If this falls into thy hand, revolve.° In my
stars° I am above thee, but be not afraid of greatness. Some are born great, some achieve greatness,
145 and some have greatness thrust upon 'em. Thy
Fates open their hands; let thy blood and spirit
embrace them; and to inure° thyself to what thou
art like to be, cast thy humble slough° and appear
fresh. Be opposite with° a kinsman, surly with
150 servants. Let thy tongue tang arguments of state;°
put thyself into the trick of singularity.° She thus

123–24 **Sowter will cry ... as a fox** i.e., the hound will bay after the
false scent even though the deceit is gross and clear   128 **faults**
breaks in the scent   129–30 **consonancy in the sequel** consistency
in what follows   130 **suffers under probation** does not stand up
under scrutiny   132 **O** i.e., sound of lamentation   138 **simulation**
hidden significance   139 **crush** force   142 **revolve** reflect   143 **stars**
fortune   147 **inure** accustom   148 **slough** skin (of a snake)   149
opposite with hostile to   150 **tang arguments of state** i.e., resound
with topics of statecraft   151 **trick of singularity** affectation of
eccentricity

advises thee that sighs for thee. Remember who
commended thy yellow stockings and wished to see
thee ever cross-gartered.° I say, remember. Go to,
thou art made, if thou desir'st to be so. If not, let   155
me see thee a steward still, the fellow of servants,
and not worthy to touch Fortune's fingers. Farewell.
She that would alter services with thee,
                    THE FORTUNATE UNHAPPY."

Daylight and champian° discovers° not more. This   160
is open. I will be proud, I will read politic authors,°
I will baffle° Sir Toby, I will wash off gross° acquaintance, I will be point-devise,° the very man.
I do not now fool myself, to let imagination jade°
me, for every reason excites to this,° that my lady   165
loves me. She did commend my yellow stockings of
late, she did praise my leg being cross-gartered; and
in this she manifests herself to my love, and with
a kind of injunction drives me to these habits of her
liking.° I thank my stars, I am happy. I will be   170
strange,° stout,° in yellow stockings, and cross-
gartered, even with the swiftness of putting on. Jove
and my stars be praised. Here is yet a postscript.
[*Reads*] "Thou canst not choose but know who I
am. If thou entertain'st° my love, let it appear in   175
thy smiling. Thy smiles become thee well. There
fore in my presence still smile, dear my sweet, I
prithee."
Jove, I thank thee. I will smile; I will do everything
that thou wilt have me.   *Exit.*   180

Fabian. I will not give my part of this sport for a
pension of thousands to be paid from the Sophy.°

154 **cross-gartered** i.e., with garters crossed above and below the
knee 160 **champian** champaign, open country 160 **discovers** reveals 161 **politic authors** writers on politics 162 **baffle** publicly
humiliate 162 **gross** low 163 **be point-devise** i.e., follow the advice
in the letter in every detail 164 **jade** trick 165 **excites to this**
i.e., enforces this conclusion 169–170 **these habits of her liking**
this clothing that she likes 171 **strange** haughty 171 **stout** proud
175 **entertain'st** accept 182 **Sophy** Shah of Persia (perhaps with
reference to Sir Anthony Shirley's visit to the Persian court in 1599,
from which he returned laden with gifts and honors)

Toby. I could marry this wench for this device.

Andrew. So could I too.

185 *Toby.* And ask no other dowry with her but such
another jest.

Enter Maria.

Andrew. Nor I neither.

Fabian. Here comes my noble gull-catcher.°

Toby. Wilt thou set thy foot o' my neck?

190 *Andrew.* Or o' mine either?

Toby. Shall I play° my freedom at tray-trip° and
become thy bondslave?

Andrew. I' faith, or I either?

Toby. Why, thou hast put him in such a dream that,
195 when the image of it leaves him, he must run mad.

Maria. Nay, but say true, does it work upon him?

Toby. Like aqua-vitae° with a midwife.

Maria. If you will, then, see the fruits of the sport,
mark his first approach before my lady. He will
200 come to her in yellow stockings, and 'tis a color she
abhors, and cross-gartered, a fashion she detests;
and he will smile upon her which will now be so
unsuitable to her disposition, being addicted to a
melancholy as she is, that it cannot but turn him
205 into a notable contempt. If you will see it, follow
me.

Toby. To the gates of Tartar,° thou most excellent
devil of wit.

Andrew. I'll make one° too.   *Exeunt.*

---

188 **gull-catcher** fool-catcher   191 **play** gamble   191 **tray-trip** (a
dice game)   197 **aqua-vitae** distilled liquors   207 **Tartar** Tartarus
(in classical mythology, the infernal regions)   209 **make one** i.e.,
come

ACT 3

Scene 1. [*Olivia's garden.*]

Enter Viola and Clown [with a tabor].

Viola. Save thee,° friend, and thy music. Dost thou
    live by° thy tabor?°

Clown. No, sir, I live by the church.

Viola. Art thou a churchman?

Clown. No such matter, sir. I do live by the church;   5
    for I do live at my house, and my house doth stand
    by the church.

Viola. So thou mayst say, the king lies° by a beggar,
    if a beggar dwell near him; or, the church stands
    by° thy tabor, if thy tabor stand by the church.   10

Clown. You have said, sir. To see this age! A sen-
    tence is but a chev'ril° glove to a good wit. How
    quickly the wrong side may be turned outward!

Viola. Nay, that's certain. They that dally nicely°
    with words may quickly make them wanton.°   15

Clown. I would therefore my sister had had no name,
    sir.

3.1.1 **Save thee** i.e., God save you   2 **live by** gain a living from (but
the Clown takes it in the sense of "reside near")   2 **tabor** (1) drum
(2) taborn, tavern   8 **lies** sojourns   9–10 **stands by** (1) stands near
(2) upholds   12 **chev'ril** cheveril (i.e., soft kid leather)   14 **dally
nicely** play subtly   15 **wanton** i.e., equivocal in meaning (but the
Clown takes it in the sense of "unchaste")

Viola. Why, man?

Clown. Why, sir, her name's a word, and to dally with
20   that word might make my sister wanton. But indeed
words are very rascals since bonds disgraced them.°

Viola. Thy reason, man?

Clown. Troth,° sir, I can yield you none without
words, and words are grown so false I am loath to
25   prove reason with them.

Viola. I warrant thou art a merry fellow and car'st
for nothing.

Clown. Not so, sir; I do care for something; but in my
conscience, sir, I do not care for you. If that be to
30   care for nothing, sir, I would it would make you
invisible.

Viola. Art not thou the Lady Olivia's fool?

Clown. No, indeed, sir. The Lady Olivia has no folly.
She will keep no fool, sir, till she be married; and
35   fools are as like husbands as pilchers° are to her-
rings—the husband's the bigger. I am indeed not
her fool, but her corrupter of words.

Viola. I saw thee late at the Count Orsino's.

Clown. Foolery, sir, does walk about the orb° like
40   the sun; it shines everywhere. I would be sorry, sir,
but° the fool should be as oft with your master as
with my mistress. I think I saw your wisdom there.

Viola. Nay, and thou pass upon me,° I'll no more
with thee. Hold, there's expenses for thee.

[*Gives a coin.*]

45   *Clown.* Now Jove, in his next commodity° of hair,
send thee a beard.

21 **since bonds disgraced them** i.e., since it was required that a man's
word be guaranteed by a bond (?) 23 **Troth** by my troth
35 **pilchers** pilchards (a kind of small herring) 39 **orb** earth
41 **but** but that 43 **pass upon me** i.e., make me the butt of your
witticisms 45 **commodity** lot, consignment

Viola. By my troth, I'll tell thee, I am almost sick
  for one, though I would not have it grow on my
  chin. Is thy lady within?

Clown. Would not a pair of these° have bred, sir?   50

Viola. Yes, being kept together and put to use.°

Clown. I would play Lord Pandarus of Phrygia, sir,
  to bring a Cressida to this Troilus.°

Viola. I understand you, sir. 'Tis well begged.
                            [*Gives another coin.*]

Clown. The matter, I hope, is not great, sir, begging   55
  but a beggar: Cressida was a beggar.° My lady is
  within, sir. I will conster° to them whence you
  come. Who you are and what you would are out of
  my welkin;° I might say "element," but the word is
  overworn.°   Exit.   60

Viola. This fellow is wise enough to play the fool,
  And to do that well craves° a kind of wit.°
  He must observe their mood on whom he jests,
  The quality of persons, and the time;
  And,° like the haggard,° check at° every feather   65
  That comes before his eye. This is a practice°
  As full of labor as a wise man's art;
  For folly that he wisely shows, is fit;
  But wise men, folly-fall'n,° quite taint their wit.°

---

50 **these** i.e., coins of the sort that Viola had just given him   51 **put
to use** put out at interest   52–53 **I would play ... this Troilus** (in
the story of Troilus and Cressida, which supplied both Chaucer and
Shakespeare the plot for major works, Pandarus was the go-between
in the disastrous love affair)   56 **Cressida was a beggar** (in Robert
Henryson's *Testament of Cressida,* a kind of sequel to Chaucer's
poem, the faithless heroine became a harlot and a beggar)   57 **conster**
explain   59 **welkin** sky   59–60 **I might say ... overworn** (perhaps a
thrust at Ben Jonson, whose fondness for the word "element" had been
ridiculed by other writers)   62 **craves** requires   62 **wit** intelligence
65 **And** (many editors, following Johnson, have emended this to "not")
65 **haggard** untrained hawk   65 **check at** leave the true course and
pursue   66 **practice** skill   69 **folly-fall'n** having fallen into folly   69
taint their wit i.e., betray their common sense

Enter Sir Toby and [Sir] Andrew.

70 *Toby.* Save you, gentleman.

   Viola. And you, sir.

   Andrew. Dieu vous garde, monsieur.

   Viola. Et vous aussi; votre serviteur.°

   Andrew. I hope, sir, you are, and I am yours.

75 *Toby.* Will you encounter° the house? My niece is
   desirous you should enter, if your trade be to° her.

   Viola. I am bound to° your niece, sir; I mean, she is
   the list° of my voyage.

   Toby. Taste° your legs, sir; put them to motion.

80 *Viola.* My legs do better understand° me, sir, than I
   understand what you mean by bidding me taste my
   legs.

   Toby. I mean, to go, sir, to enter.

   Viola. I will answer you with gait and entrance.° But
85 we are prevented.°

Enter Olivia and Gentlewoman [Maria].

   Most excellent accomplished lady, the heavens rain
   odors on you.

   Andrew. That youth's a rare courtier. "Rain odors"—
   well!°

90 *Viola.* My matter hath no voice,° lady, but to your
   own most pregnant and vouchsafed ear.

72–73 **Dieu vous garde . . . votre serviteur** God protect you, sir./And
you also; your servant   75 **encounter** approach   76 **trade be to**
business be with   77 **bound to** bound for (carrying on the metaphor
in "trade")   78 **list** destination   79 **Taste** try   80 **understand** i.e.,
stand under, support   84 **with gait and entrance** by going and enter-
ing (with a pun on "gate")   85 **prevented** anticipated   89 **well**
i.e., well put   90 **matter hath no voice** i.e., business must not be
revealed

Andrew. "Odors," "pregnant," and "vouchsafed"—
I'll get 'em all three all ready.

Olivia. Let the garden door be shut, and leave me to
my hearing. [*Exeunt Sir Toby, Sir Andrew, and*　95
Maria.] Give me your hand, sir.

Viola. My duty, madam, and most humble service.

Olivia. What is your name?

Viola. Cesario is your servant's name, fair princess.

Olivia. My servant, sir? 'Twas never merry world　100
Since lowly feigning° was called compliment.
Y' are servant to the Count Orsino, youth.

Viola. And he is yours, and his must needs be yours.
Your servant's servant is your servant, madam.

Olivia. For° him, I think not on him; for his thoughts　105
Would they were blanks, rather than filled with me.

Viola. Madam, I come to whet your gentle thoughts
On his behalf.

Olivia.　　　　　O, by your leave, I pray you.
I bade you never speak again of him;
But, would you undertake another suit,　110
I had rather hear you to solicit that
Than music from the spheres.°

Viola.　　　　　　　　　　Dear lady—

Olivia. Give me leave,° beseech you. I did send,
After the last enchantment you did here,
A ring in chase of you. So did I abuse°　115
Myself, my servant, and, I fear me, you.
Under your hard construction° must I sit,
To force that on you in a shameful cunning
Which you knew none of yours. What might you
think?

---

101 **lowly feigning** affected humility　105 **For** as for　112 **music
from the spheres** i.e., the alleged celestial harmony of the revolving
stars and planets　113 **Give me leave** i.e., do not interrupt me
115 **abuse** deceive　117 **hard construction** harsh interpretation

120 Have you not set mine honor at the stake
And baited it with all th' unmuzzled thoughts°
That tyrannous heart can think? To one of your
    receiving°
Enough is shown; a cypress,° not a bosom,
Hides my heart. So, let me hear you speak.

Viola. I pity you.

125 *Olivia.*   That's a degree° to love.

Viola. No, not a grize;° for 'tis a vulgar proof°
That very oft we pity enemies.

Olivia. Why then, methinks 'tis time to smile again.
O world, how apt the poor are to be proud.
130 If one should be a prey, how much the better
To fall before the lion than the wolf.   *Clock strikes.*
The clock upbraids me with the waste of time.
Be not afraid, good youth, I will not have you,
And yet, when wit and youth is come to harvest,°
135 Your wife is like to reap a proper° man.
There lies your way, due west.°

Viola.   Then westward ho!°
Grace and good disposition° attend your ladyship.
You'll nothing, madam, to my lord by me?

Olivia. Stay.
140 I prithee tell me what thou think'st of me.

Viola. That you do think you are not what you are.°

Olivia. If I think so, I think the same of you.°

120–121 **set mine honor ... unmuzzled thoughts** (the metaphor is
from the Elizabethan sport of bearbaiting, in which a bear was tied
to a stake and harassed by savage dogs) 122 **receiving** i.e., per-
ception 123 **cypress** gauzelike material 125 **degree** step 126 **grize**
step 126 **vulgar proof** i.e., common knowledge 134 **when wit and
youth is come to harvest** i.e., when you are mature 135 **proper**
handsome 136 **due west** (Olivia is perhaps implying that the sun
of her life—Cesario's love—is about to vanish) 136 **westward ho**
(cry of Thames watermen) 137 **good disposition** i.e., tranquillity
of mind 141 **That you do think you are not what you are** i.e., that
you think you are in love with a man, and are not 142 **If I think
so, I think the same of you** (Olivia misconstrues Viola's remark to
mean that she is out of her mind)

Viola. Then think you right. I am not what I am.

Olivia. I would you were as I would have you be.

Viola. Would it be better, madam, than I am?   *145*
I wish it might, for now I am your fool.°

Olivia. O, what a deal of scorn looks beautiful
In the contempt and anger of his lip.
A murd'rous guilt shows not itself more soon
Than love that would seem hid: love's night is
noon.°   *150*
Cesario, by the roses of the spring,
By maidhood,° honor, truth, and everything,
I love thee so that, maugre° all thy pride,
Nor wit nor reason can my passion hide.
Do not extort thy reasons from this clause,°   *155*
For that° I woo, thou therefore hast no cause;°
But rather reason thus with reason fetter,
Love sought is good, but given unsought is better.

Viola. By innocence I swear, and by my youth,
I have one heart, one bosom, and one truth,   *160*
And that no woman has; nor never none
Shall mistress be of it, save I alone.
And so adieu, good madam. Never more
Will I my master's tears to you deplore.

Olivia. Yet come again; for thou perhaps mayst move   *165*
That heart which now abhors to like his love.

Exeunt.

146 **I am your fool** i.e., you are making a fool of me   150 **love's
night is noon** i.e., love is apparent even when it is hidden   152 **maidhood** maidenhood   153 **maugre** despite   155 **clause** premise   156
For that that because   156 **cause** i.e., to accept my love

Scene 2. [*Olivia's house.*]

Enter Sir Toby, Sir Andrew, and Fabian.

Andrew. No, faith, I'll not stay a jot longer.

Toby. Thy reason, dear venom; give thy reason.

Fabian. You must needs yield° your reason, Sir
Andrew.

5 *Andrew.* Marry, I saw your niece do more favors to
the Count's servingman than ever she bestowed
upon me. I saw't i' th' orchard.

Toby. Did she see thee the while, old boy? Tell me
that.

10 *Andrew.* As plain as I see you now.

Fabian. This was a great argument° of love in her
toward you.

Andrew. 'Slight, will you make an ass o' me?

Fabian. I will prove it legitimate,° sir, upon the oaths
15 of judgment and reason.

Toby. And they have been grand-jurymen since
before Noah was a sailor.

Fabian. She did show favor to the youth in your sight
only to exasperate you, to awake your dormouse°
20 valor, to put fire in your heart and brimstone in
your liver. You should then have accosted her, and
with some excellent jests, fire-new from the mint,
you should have banged the youth into dumbness.
This was looked for at your hand, and this was

3.2.3 **yield** give   11 **great argument** strong evidence   14 **legitimate**
valid   19 **dormouse** i.e., sleepy

balked.° The double gilt° of this opportunity you   25
let time wash off, and you are now sailed into the
North of my lady's opinion,° where you will hang
like an icicle on a Dutchman's beard° unless you do
redeem it by some laudable attempt either of valor
or policy.°   30

Andrew. And't be any way, it must be with valor; for
policy I hate. I had as lief be a Brownist° as a
politician.°

Toby. Why then, build me thy fortunes upon the basis
of valor. Challenge me the Count's youth to fight   35
with him; hurt him in eleven places. My niece shall
take note of it, and assure thyself there is no love-
broker in the world can° more prevail in man's
commendation with woman than report of valor.

Fabian. There is no way but this, Sir Andrew.   40

Andrew. Will either of you bear me a challenge to
him?

Toby. Go, write it in a martial hand. Be curst° and
brief; it is no matter how witty, so it be eloquent
and full of invention. Taunt him with the license of 45
ink.° If thou thou'st° him some thrice, it shall not
be amiss; and as many lies as will lie in thy sheet
of paper, although the sheet were big enough for
the bed of Ware° in England, set 'em down. Go
about it. Let there be gall enough in thy ink, though 50
thou write with a goose-pen, no matter. About it!

Andrew. Where shall I find you?

25 **balked** let slip   25 **gilt** plating   26–27 **the North of my lady's opinion** i.e., her frosty disdain   28 **an icicle on a Dutchman's beard** (perhaps an allusion to the arctic voyage [1596–97] of the Dutchman Willem Barents, an account of which was registered for publication in 1598)   30 **policy** intrigue, trickery   32 **Brownist** follower of William Browne, a reformer who advocated the separation of church and state   33 **politician** schemer   38 **can** i.e., that can   43 **curst** petulant   45–46 **the license of ink** i.e., the freedom that writing permits   46 **thou'st** i.e., use the familiar "thou" instead of the more formal "you"   49 **the bed of Ware** a famous bedstead, almost eleven feet square, formerly in an inn at Ware in Hertfordshire

Toby. We'll call thee at the cubiculo.° Go.
                                              Exit Sir Andrew.

Fabian. This is a dear manikin° to you, Sir Toby.

55 *Toby.* I have been dear to him,° lad, some two thou-
    sand strong or so.

Fabian. We shall have a rare letter from him, but
you'll not deliver't?

Toby. Never trust me then; and by all means stir on
60   the youth to an answer. I think oxen and wain-
    ropes° cannot hale them together. For Andrew,
    if he were opened, and you find so much blood in
    his liver as will clog the foot of a flea, I'll eat the
    rest of th' anatomy.°

65 *Fabian.* And his opposite,° the youth, bears in his
    visage no great presage of cruelty.

                        Enter Maria.

Toby. Look where the youngest wren° of mine° comes.

Maria. If you desire the spleen,° and will laugh your-
    selves into stitches, follow me. Yond gull Malvolio
70   is turned heathen, a very renegado; for there is no
    Christian that means to be saved by believing
    rightly can ever believe such impossible passages
    of grossness.° He's in yellow stockings.

Toby. And cross-gartered?

75 *Maria.* Most villainously; like a pedant that keeps a
    school i' th' church. I have dogged him like his
    murderer. He does obey every point of the letter
    that I dropped to betray him. He does smile his
    face into more lines than is in the new map with

53 **cubiculo** little chamber   54 **manikin** puppet   55 **been dear to him**
i.e., spent his money   60–61 **wainropes** wagon ropes   64 **anatomy**
cadaver   65 **opposite** adversary   67 **youngest wren** i.e., smallest of
small birds   67 **mine** (most editors adopt Theobald's emendation
"nine")   68 **spleen** i.e., a fit of laughter   72–73 **impossible passages
of grossness** i.e., improbabilities

the augmentation of the Indies.° You have not seen   80
such a thing as 'tis. I can hardly forbear hurling
things at him. I know my lady will strike him. If
she do, he'll smile, and take't for a great favor.

Toby. Come bring us, bring us where he is.

                                        Exeunt omnes.

Scene 3. [*A street.*]

Enter Sebastian and Antonio.

Sebastian. I would not by my will have troubled you;
    But since you make your pleasure of your pains,
    I will no further chide you.

Antonio. I could not stay behind you. My desire
    (More sharp than filèd steel) did spur me forth;   5
    And not all love to see you (though so much
    As might have drawn one to a longer voyage)
    But jealousy° what might befall your travel,
    Being skilless in° these parts; which to a stranger,
    Unguided and unfriended, often prove   10
    Rough and unhospitable. My willing love,
    The rather by these arguments of fear,°
    Set forth in your pursuit.

Sebastian.   My kind Antonio,
    I can no longer answer make but thanks,
    And thanks, and ever oft good turns°   15

79–80 **the new map with the augmentation of the Indies** (presumably a map, prepared under the supervision of Richard Hakluyt and others and published about 1600, that employed the principles of projection and showed North America and the East Indies in fuller detail than any earlier map. It was conspicuous for the rhumb lines marking the meridians) 3.3.8 **jealousy** anxiety 9 **skilless in** unacquainted with 12 **The rather by these arguments of fear** i.e., reinforced by my solicitude for your safety 15 **And thanks, and ever oft good turns** (the fact that this line is a foot too short has prompted a wide variety of emendations, the most popular of which has been Theobald's "And thanks, and ever thanks; and oft good turns." Later Folios omit this and the following line altogether)

Are shuffled off with such uncurrent° pay.
But, were my worth° as is my conscience firm,
You should find better dealing. What's to do?
Shall we go see the relics of this town?

20 *Antonio.* Tomorrow, sir; best first go see your lodging.

Sebastian. I am not weary, and 'tis long to night.
I pray you let us satisfy our eyes
With the memorials and the things of fame
That do renown this city.

Antonio.   Would you'ld pardon° me.
25 I do not without danger walk these streets.
Once in a sea-fight 'gainst the Count his galleys°
I did some service; of such note indeed
That, were I ta'en here, it would scarce be answered.°

Sebastian. Belike you slew great number of his people?

30 *Antonio.* Th' offense is not of such a bloody nature,
Albeit the quality° of the time and quarrel
Might well have given us bloody argument.°
It might have since been answered° in repaying
What we took from them, which for traffic's° sake
35 Most of our city did. Only myself stood out;
For which, if I be lapsèd° in this place,
I shall pay dear.

Sebastian.   Do not then walk too open.

Antonio. It doth not fit me. Hold, sir, here's my purse.
In the south suburbs at the Elephant°
40 Is best to lodge. I will bespeak our diet,°
Whiles° you beguile the time and feed your knowledge
With viewing of the town. There shall you have°
me.

16 **uncurrent** worthless 17 **worth** resources 24 **pardon** excuse
26 **the Count his galleys** the Count's warships 28 **answered** defended 31 **quality** circumstances 32 **argument** cause 33 **answered** compensated 34 **traffic's** trade's 36 **lapsèd** surprised and apprehended 39 **Elephant** an inn 40 **bespeak our diet** i.e., arrange for our meals 41 **Whiles** while 42 **have** find

Sebastian. Why I your purse?

Antonio. Haply your eye shall light upon some toy°
     You have desire to purchase, and your store°   *45*
     I think is not for idle markets,° sir.

Sebastian. I'll be your purse-bearer, and leave you for
     An hour.

Antonio.   To th' Elephant.

Sebastian.   I do remember.   *Exeunt.*

Scene 4 [*Olivia's garden.*]

Enter Olivia and Maria.

Olivia. I have sent after him. He says he'll come:°
     How shall I feast him? What bestow of° him?
     For youth is bought more oft than begged or bor-
       rowed.
     I speak too loud. Where's Malvolio? He is sad and
       civil,°
     And suits well for a servant with my fortunes.   *5*
     Where is Malvolio?

Maria. He's coming, madam, but in very strange man-
     ner. He is sure possessed,° madam.

Olivia. Why, what's the matter? Does he rave?

Maria. No, madam, he does nothing but smile. Your   *10*
     ladyship were best to have some guard about you
     if he come, for sure the man is tainted in 's wits.

Olivia. Go call him hither. I am as mad as he,
     If sad and merry madness equal be.

44 **toy** trifle   45 **store** wealth   46 **idle markets** unnecessary pur-
chases   3.4.1 **He says he'll come** suppose he says he'll come   2 **of**
on   4 **sad and civil** grave and formal   8 **possessed** i.e., with a devil,
mad

Enter Malvolio.

15   How now, Malvolio?

Malvolio. Sweet lady, ho, ho!

Olivia. Smil'st thou? I sent for thee upon a sad° occasion.

Malvolio. Sad, lady? I could be sad. This does make
20   some obstruction in the blood, this cross-gartering;
but what of that? If it please the eye of one, it is
with me as the very true sonnet° is, "Please one,
and please all."°

Olivia. Why, how dost thou, man? What is the matter
25   with thee?

Malvolio. Not black in my mind, though yellow in my
legs. It did come to his hands, and commands shall
be executed. I think we do know the sweet Roman
hand.°

30   *Olivia.* Wilt thou go to bed, Malvolio?

Malvolio. To bed? Ay, sweetheart, and I'll come to
thee.

Olivia. God comfort thee. Why dost thou smile so,
and kiss thy hand so oft?

35   *Maria.* How do you, Malvolio?

Malvolio. At your request? Yes, nightingales answer
daws!°

Maria. Why appear you with this ridiculous boldness
before my lady?

40   *Malvolio.* "Be not afraid of greatness." 'Twas well writ.

17 **sad** serious 22 **sonnet** (any short lyric poem) 22–23 **Please
one, and please all** i.e., so long as I please the one I love I do not
care about the rest (from "A prettie newe Ballad, intytuled: The
Crow sits vpon the wall, Please one and please all") 28–29 **the
sweet Roman hand** i.e., italic writing, an elegant cursive script more
fashionable than the crabbed "secretary hand" commonly used in
Shakespeare's time 36–37 **At ... daws** i.e., should I reply to a
mere servant like you? Yes, for sometimes nightingales answer jack-
daws

Olivia. What mean'st thou by that, Malvolio?

Malvolio. "Some are born great."

Olivia. Ha?

Malvolio. "Some achieve greatness."

Olivia. What say'st thou?   45

Malvolio. "And some have greatness thrust upon them."

Olivia. Heaven restore thee!

Malvolio. "Remember who commended thy yellow stockings."   50

Olivia. Thy yellow stockings?

Malvolio. "And wished to see thee cross-gartered."

Olivia. Cross-gartered?

Malvolio. "Go to, thou art made, if thou desir'st to be so."   55

Olivia. Am I made?

Malvolio. "If not, let me see thee a servant still."

Olivia. Why, this is very midsummer madness.°

Enter Servant.

Servant. Madam, the young gentleman of the Count Orsino's is returned. I could hardly entreat him   60 back. He attends your ladyship's pleasure.

Olivia. I'll come to him. [*Exit Servant.*] Good Maria, let this fellow be looked to. Where's my cousin Toby? Let some of my people have a special care of him. I would not have him miscarry° for the   65 half of my dowry.

Exit [Olivia, accompanied by Maria].

58 **midsummer madness** extreme folly, Midsummer Eve (June 23) being traditionally associated with irresponsible and eccentric behavior   65 **miscarry** come to harm

Malvolio. O ho, do you come near me° now? No
worse man than Sir Toby to look to me. This con-
curs directly with the letter. She sends him on pur-
70 pose, that I may appear stubborn° to him; for she
incites me to that in the letter. "Cast thy humble
slough," says she; "be opposite with a kinsman,
surly with servants; let thy tongue tang with arguments of state; put thyself into the trick of singu-
75 larity." And consequently sets down the manner
how: as, a sad face, a reverend carriage, a slow
tongue, in the habit° of some sir° of note, and so
forth. I have limed° her; but it is Jove's doing, and
Jove make me thankful. And when she went away
80 now, "Let this fellow° be looked to." "Fellow."
Not "Malvolio," nor after my degree,° but "fellow." Why, everything adheres together, that no
dram° of a scruple,° no scruple of a scruple, no
obstacle, no incredulous or unsafe° circumstance—
85 what can be said? Nothing that can be can come
between me and the full prospect of my hopes.
Well, Jove, not I, is the doer of this, and he is to
be thanked.

Enter [Sir] Toby, Fabian, and Maria.

Toby. Which way is he, in the name of sanctity? If
90 all the devils of hell be drawn in little,° and
Legion° himself possessed him, yet I'll speak to
him.

Fabian. Here he is, here he is! How is't with you, sir?

---

67 **come near me** i.e., begin to understand my importance   70 **stubborn** hostile   77 **habit** clothing   77 **sir** personage   78 **limed** caught
(as birds are caught with sticky birdlime)   80 **fellow** (1) menial
(2) associate (the sense in which Malvolio takes the word)   81 **after
my degree** according to my status   83 **dram** (1) minute part (2)
apothecary's measure for one-eighth of an ounce   83 **scruple** (1)
doubt (2) apothecary's measure for one-third of a dram   84 **incredulous or unsafe** incredible or doubtful   90 **in little** in small
compass   91 **Legion** a group of devils (see Mark 5:8–9)

Toby. How is't with you, man?°

Malvolio. Go off; I discard you. Let me enjoy my   *95*
private.° Go off.

Maria. Lo, how hollow the fiend speaks within him!
Did not I tell you? Sir Toby, my lady prays you
to have a care of him.

Malvolio. Aha, does she so?   *100*

Toby. Go to, go to; peace, peace; we must deal gently
with him. Let me alone. How do you, Malvolio?
How is't with you? What, man, defy the devil?
Consider, he's an enemy to mankind.

Malvolio. Do you know what you say?   *105*

Maria. La you, and you speak ill of the devil, how he
takes it at heart. Pray God he be not bewitched.

Fabian. Carry his water to th' wise woman.°

Maria. Marry, and it shall be done tomorrow morning if I live. My lady would not lose him for more   *110*
than I'll say.

Malvolio. How now, mistress?

Maria. O Lord.

Toby. Prithee hold thy peace. This is not the way. Do
you not see you move° him? Let me alone with him.   *115*

Fabian. No way but gentleness; gently, gently. The
fiend is rough° and will not be roughly used.

Toby. Why, how now, my bawcock?° How dost thou,
chuck?°

Malvolio. Sir.   *120*

Toby. Ay, biddy, come with me. What, man, 'tis not

94 **How is't with you, man** (the Folio implausibly assigns this speech
to Fabian, but the contemptuous "man" suggests that the speaker
must be Malvolio's social superior)   96 **private** privacy   108 **Carry
his water to th' wise woman** i.e., for analysis   115 **move** agitate
117 **rough** violent   118 **bawcock** fine fellow (French *beau coq*)
119 **chuck** chick

for gravity to play at cherry-pit with Satan.° Hang
him, foul collier!°

Maria. Get him to say his prayers; good Sir Toby, get
125   him to pray.

Malvolio. My prayers, minx?

Maria. No, I warrant you, he will not hear of godli-
ness.

Malvolio. Go hang yourselves all! You are idle° shal-
130   low things; I am not of your element.° You shall
know more hereafter.   *Exit.*

Toby. Is't possible?

Fabian. If this were played upon a stage now, I could
condemn it as an improbable fiction.

135   *Toby.* His very genius° hath taken the infection of the
device, man.

Maria. Nay, pursue him now, lest the device take air
and taint.°

Fabian. Why, we shall make him mad indeed.

140   *Maria.* The house will be the quieter.

Toby. Come, we'll have him in a dark room and
bound. My niece is already in the belief that he's
mad. We may carry it° thus, for our pleasure and
his penance, till our very pastime, tired out of
145   breath, prompt us to have mercy on him; at which
time we will bring the device to the bar and crown
thee for a finder of madmen. But see, but see.

Enter Sir Andrew.

Fabian. More matter for a May morning.°

121-22 **'tis not for gravity . . . Satan** i.e., it is unsuitable for a man of
your dignity to play a children's game with Satan   123 **collier** vendor
of coals   129 **idle** trifling   130 **element** sphere   135 **genius** nature,
personality   137-138 **take air and taint** be exposed and spoiled
143 **carry it** i.e., go on with the joke   148 **More matter for a May
morning** i.e., another subject for a May-Day pageant

Andrew. Here's the challenge; read it. I warrant there's
vinegar and pepper in't.   *150*

Fabian. Is't so saucy?°

Andrew. Ay, is't, I warrant him. Do but read.

Toby. Give me. [*Reads*] "Youth, whatsoever thou art,
thou art but a scurvy fellow."

Fabian. Good, and valiant.   *155*

Toby. [*Reads*] "Wonder not nor admire° not in thy
mind why I do call thee so, for I will show thee no
reason for't."

Fabian. A good note that keeps you from the blow of
the law.   *160*

Toby. [*Reads*] "Thou com'st to the Lady Olivia, and
in my sight she uses thee kindly. But thou liest in
thy throat; that is not the matter I challenge thee
for."

Fabian. Very brief, and to exceeding good sense—   *165*
less.

Toby. [*Reads*] "I will waylay thee going home; where
if it be thy chance to kill me"—

Fabian. Good.

Toby. [*Reads*] "Thou kill'st me like a rogue and a   *170*
villain."

Fabian. Still you keep o' th' windy side of the law.°
Good.

Toby. [*Reads*] "Fare thee well, and God have mercy
upon one of our souls. He may have mercy upon   *175*
mine, but my hope is better, and so look to thyself.
Thy friend, as thou usest him, and thy sworn enemy,
          ANDREW AGUECHEEK."
If this letter move him not, his legs cannot. I'll give't
him.   *180*

151 **saucy** i.e., with "vinegar and pepper"   156 **admire** marvel
172 **o' th' windy side of the law** i.e., safe from prosecution

Maria. You may have very fit occasion for't. He is now in some commerce° with my lady and will by and by depart.

Toby. Go, Sir Andrew. Scout me for him at the corner
185 of the orchard like a bum-baily.° So soon as ever thou seest him, draw; and as thou draw'st, swear horrible; for it comes to pass oft that a terrible oath, with a swaggering accent sharply twanged off, gives manhood more approbation° than ever
190 proof° itself would have earned him. Away!

Andrew. Nay, let me alone for swearing.°   *Exit.*

Toby. Now will not I deliver his letter; for the behavior of the young gentleman gives him out to be of good capacity and breeding; his employment
195 between his lord and my niece confirms no less. Therefore this letter, being so excellently ignorant, will breed no terror in the youth. He will find it comes from a clodpoll.° But, sir, I will deliver his challenge by word of mouth, set upon Aguecheek
200 a notable report of valor, and drive the gentleman (as I know his youth will aptly receive it) into a most hideous opinion of his rage, skill, fury, and impetuosity. This will so fright them both that they will kill one another by the look, like cockatrices.°

Enter Olivia and Viola.

205 *Fabian.* Here he comes with your niece. Give them way till he take leave, and presently after him.°

Toby. I will meditate the while upon some horrid message for a challenge.
          [*Exeunt Sir Toby, Fabian, and Maria.*]

Olivia. I have said too much unto a heart of stone

---

182 **commerce** conversation   185 **bum-baily** bailiff, sheriff's officer
189 **approbation** attestation   190 **proof** actual trial   191 **let me
alone for swearing** i.e., do not worry about my ability at swearing
198 **clodpoll** dunce   204 **cockatrices** fabulous serpents that could
kill with a glance   205–206 **Give them way … after him** i.e., do
not interrupt them until he goes, and then follow him at once

And laid mine honor too unchary° on't.   210
There's something in me that reproves my fault;
But such a headstrong potent fault it is
That it but mocks reproof.

Viola. With the same havior° that your passion bears
Goes on my master's griefs.   215

Olivia. Here, wear this jewel° for me; 'tis my picture.
Refuse it not; it hath no tongue to vex you.
And I beseech you come again tomorrow.
What shall you ask of me that I'll deny,
That honor, saved, may upon asking give?   220

Viola. Nothing but this: your true love for my master.

Olivia. How with mine honor may I give him that
Which I have given to you?

Viola.   I will acquit you.

Olivia. Well, come again tomorrow. Fare thee well.
A fiend like thee° might bear my soul to hell.   225
                         [*Exit.*]

Enter [Sir] Toby and Fabian.

Toby. Gentleman, God save thee.

Viola. And you, sir.

Toby. That defense thou hast, betake thee to't. Of
what nature the wrongs are thou hast done him,
I know not; but thy intercepter, full of despite,°   230
bloody as the hunter,° attends° thee at the orchard
end. Dismount thy tuck,° be yare° in thy prepara-
tion, for thy assailant is quick, skillful, and deadly.

Viola. You mistake, sir. I am sure no man hath any
quarrel to me. My remembrance is very free and   235
clear from any image of offense done to any man.

210 **unchary** carelessly 214 **havior** behavior 216 **jewel** i.e., jeweled
locket (?) 225 **like thee** i.e., with your attractions 230 **despite**
defiance 231 **bloody as the hunter** i.e., bloodthirsty as a hunting
dog 231 **attends** awaits 232 **Dismount thy tuck** unsheathe your
rapier 232 **yare** quick, prompt

Toby. You'll find it otherwise, I assure you. Therefore, if you hold your life at any price, betake you to your guard; for your opposite° hath in him what
240 youth, strength, skill, and wrath can furnish man withal.°

Viola. I pray you, sir, what is he?

Toby. He is knight, dubbed with unhatched° rapier and on carpet consideration,° but he is a devil in
245 private brawl. Souls and bodies hath he divorced three; and his incensement at this moment is so implacable that satisfaction can be none but by pangs of death and sepulcher. "Hob, nob"° is his word; "give't or take't."

250 *Viola.* I will return again into the house and desire some conduct° of the lady. I am no fighter. I have heard of some kind of men that put quarrels purposely on others to taste° their valor. Belike this is a man of that quirk.

255 *Toby.* Sir, no. His indignation derives itself out of a very competent° injury; therefore get you on and give him his desire. Back you shall not to the house, unless you undertake that with me which with as much safety you might answer him. There-
260 fore on, or strip your sword stark naked; for meddle° you must, that's certain, or forswear to wear iron about you.

Viola. This is as uncivil as strange. I beseech you do me this courteous office, as to know of the knight
265 what my offense to him is. It is something of my negligence,° nothing of my purpose.

Toby. I will do so. Signior Fabian, stay you by this gentleman till my return.   *Exit* [*Sir*] *Toby.*

Viola. Pray you, sir, do you know of this matter?

239 **opposite** adversary 241 **withal** with 243 **unhatched** unhacked
244 **on carpet consideration** i.e., not because of his exploits in the
field but through connections at court 248 **Hob, nob** have it, or
have it not 251 **conduct** escort 253 **taste** test 256 **competent**
sufficient 261 **meddle** engage him, fight 265–66 **of my negligence**
unintentional

Fabian. I know the knight is incensed against you, 270
even to a mortal arbitrament;° but nothing of the
circumstance more.

Viola. I beseech you, what manner of man is he?

Fabian. Nothing of that wonderful promise, to read
him by his form, as you are like to find him in the 275
proof of his valor. He is indeed, sir, the most skillful, bloody, and fatal opposite that you could possibly have found in any part of Illyria. Will you
walk towards him? I will make your peace with
him if I can. 280

Viola. I shall be much bound to you for't. I am one
that had rather go with sir priest than sir knight. I
care not who knows so much of my mettle.°

Exeunt.°

Enter [Sir] Toby and [Sir] Andrew.

Toby. Why, man, he's a very devil; I have not seen
such a firago.° I had a pass° with him, rapier, scab- 285
bard, and all, and he gives me the stuck-in° with
such a mortal motion° that it is inevitable; and on
the answer° he pays you as surely as your feet hits
the ground they step on. They say he has been
fencer to the Sophy.° 290

Andrew. Pox on't, I'll not meddle with him.

Toby. Ay, but he will not now be pacified. Fabian
can scarce hold him yonder.

Andrew. Plague on't, and I thought he had been
valiant, and so cunning in fence,° I'd have seen 295

271 **mortal arbitrament** deadly trial 283 **mettle** character, disposition 283 s.d. **Exeunt** (this stage direction, which leaves the stage
empty, properly marks the ending of the scene, but the new scene
that opens with the entrance of Sir Toby and Sir Andrew is not
indicated as such in the Folio) 285 **firago** virago (probably a
phonetic spelling) 285 **pass** bout 286 **stuck-in** stoccado, thrust
287 **mortal motion** deadly pass 288 **answer** return 290 **Sophy**
Shah 295 **in fence** at fencing

him damned ere I'd have challenged him. Let him
let the matter slip, and I'll give him my horse,
gray Capilet.

Toby. I'll make the motion.° Stand here; make a good
300   show on't. This shall end without the perdition of
souls.° [*Aside*] Marry, I'll ride your horse as well
as I ride you.

Enter Fabian and Viola.

I have his horse to take up° the quarrel. I have
persuaded him the youth's a devil.

305 *Fabian.* He is as horribly conceited of him,° and pants
and looks pale, as if a bear were at his heels.

Toby. There's no remedy, sir; he will fight with you
for's oath° sake. Marry, he hath better bethought
him of his quarrel,° and he finds that now scarce
310   to be worth talking of. Therefore draw for the supportance of his vow.° He protests he will not hurt
you.

Viola. [*Aside*] Pray God defend me! A little thing
would make me tell them how much I lack of a
315   man.

Fabian. Give ground if you see him furious.

Toby. Come, Sir Andrew, there's no remedy. The
gentleman will for his honor's sake have one bout
with you; he cannot by the duello° avoid it; but he
320   has promised me, as he is a gentleman and a
soldier, he will not hurt you. Come on, to't.

Andrew. Pray God he keep his oath!   [*Draws.*]

299 **motion** proposal   300–01 **perdition of souls** i.e., loss of life
303 **take up** settle   305 **He is as horribly conceited of him** i.e.,
Cesario has just as terrifying a notion of Sir Andrew   308 **oath**
oath's   309 **his quarrel** the cause of his resentment   310–11 **Therefore draw for the supportance of his vow** i.e., make a show of valor
merely for the satisfaction of his oath   319 **duello** duelling code

Enter Antonio.

Viola. I do assure you 'tis against my will.   [*Draws.*]

Antonio. Put up your sword. If this young gentleman
   Have done offense, I take the fault on me;   325
   If you offend him, I for him defy you.

Toby. You, sir? Why, what are you?

Antonio. [*Draws*] One, sir, that for his love dares yet
   do more
   Than you have heard him brag to you he will.

Toby. Nay, if you be an undertaker,° I am for you.   330
                                [*Draws.*]

Enter Officers.

Fabian. O good Sir Toby, hold. Here come the officers.

Toby. [*To Antonio*] I'll be with you anon.

Viola. [*To Sir Andrew*] Pray, sir, put your sword up,
   if you please.

Andrew. Marry, will I, sir; and for that° I promised   335
   you, I'll be as good as my word. He will bear you
   easily, and reins well.

First Officer. This is the man; do thy office.°

Second Officer. Antonio, I arrest thee at the suit
   Of Count Orsino.

Antonio.   You do mistake me, sir.   340

First Officer. No, sir, no jot. I know your favor°
   well,
   Though now you have no sea-cap on your head.
   Take him away. He knows I know him well.

Antonio. I must obey. [*To Viola*] This comes with
   seeking you.

330 **an undertaker** one who takes up a challenge for another (with
perhaps a pun on "undertaker" as a government agent, i.e., scoun-
drel) 335 **for that** as for what (i.e., his horse, "gray Capilet")
338 **office** duty 341 **favor** face

345   But there's no remedy; I shall answer it.°
        What will you do, now my necessity
        Makes me to ask you for my purse? It grieves me
        Much more for what I cannot do for you
        Than what befalls myself. You stand amazed,
350   But be of comfort.

Second Officer. Come, sir, away.

Antonio. I must entreat of you some of that money.

Viola. What money, sir?
        For the fair kindness you have showed me here,
355   And part° being prompted by your present trouble,
        Out of my lean and low ability
        I'll lend you something. My having is not much.
        I'll make division of my present° with you.
        Hold, there's half my coffer.°

Antonio.   Will you deny me now?
360   Is't possible that my deserts to you
        Can lack persuasion?° Do not tempt my misery,
        Lest that it make me so unsound° a man
        As to upbraid you with those kindnesses
        That I have done for you.

Viola.   I know of none,
365   Nor know I you by voice or any feature.
        I hate ingratitude more in a man
        Than lying, vainness,° babbling, drunkenness,
        Or any taint of vice whose strong corruption
        Inhabits our frail blood.

Antonio.   O heavens themselves!

370 *Second Officer.* Come, sir, I pray you go.

Antonio. Let me speak a little. This youth that you
        see here
        I snatched one half out of the jaws of death;

345 **answer it** i.e., try to defend myself against the accusation
355 **part** partly 358 **present** present resources 359 **coffer** chest,
i.e., money 360–61 **deserts to you/Can lack persuasion** claims on
you can fail to be persuasive 362 **unsound** weak, unmanly
367 **vainness** (1) falseness (2) boasting

Relieved him with such sanctity of love,
And to his image, which methought did promise
Most venerable° worth, did I devotion.   · 375

First Officer. What's that to us? The time goes by.
   Away.

Antonio. But, O, how vild° an idol proves this god!
Thou hast, Sebastian, done good feature° shame.
In nature there's no blemish but the mind;°
None can be called deformed but the unkind.°   380
Virtue is beauty; but the beauteous evil
Are empty trunks,° o'erflourished° by the devil.

First Officer. The man grows mad; away with him!
   Come, come, sir.

Antonio. Lead me on.   *Exit [with Officers].*

Viola. Methinks his words do from such passion fly   385
That he believes himself; so do not I.
Prove true, imagination, O, prove true,
That I, dear brother, be now ta'en for you!

Toby. Come hither, knight; come hither, Fabian. We'll
   whisper o'er a couplet or two of most sage saws.°   390

Viola. He named Sebastian. I my brother know
Yet living in my glass.° Even such and so
In favor was my brother, and he went
Still in this fashion, color, ornament,
For him I imitate. O, if it prove,   395
Tempests are kind, and salt waves fresh in love!
                     [Exit.]

Toby. A very dishonest° paltry boy, and more a
   coward than a hare. His dishonesty appears in
   leaving his friend here in necessity and denying
   him; and for his cowardship, ask Fabian.   400

375 **venerable** worthy of veneration   377 **vild** vile   378 **feature** shape, external appearance   379 **mind** (as distinguished from body or "feature")   380 **unkind** unnatural   382 **trunks** chests   382 **o'er-flourished** decorated with carving and painting   390 **sage saws** wise maxims   392 **living in my glass** i.e., staring at me from my mirror 397 **dishonest** dishonorable

Fabian. A coward, a most devout coward; religious in it.°

Andrew. 'Slid,° I'll after him again and beat him.

Toby. Do; cuff him soundly, but never draw thy
405 sword.

Andrew. And I do not—   [*Exit.*]

Fabian. Come, let's see the event.°

Toby. I dare lay any money 'twill be nothing yet.°
                                        Exit [with Fabian].

401–02 **religious in it** i.e., dedicated to his cowardice (following "devout") 403 **'Slid** by God's eyelid 407 **event** outcome 408 **yet** after all

ACT IV

Scene 1. [*Before Olivia's house.*]

Enter Sebastian and Clown.

Clown. Will you make me believe that I am not sent
for you?

Sebastian. Go to, go to, thou art a foolish fellow. Let
me be clear of thee.

Clown. Well held out,° i' faith! No, I do not know   5
you; nor I am not sent to you by my lady, to bid
you come speak with her; nor your name is not
Master Cesario; nor this is not my nose neither.
Nothing that is so is so.

Sebastian. I prithee vent thy folly somewhere else.   10
Thou know'st not me.

Clown. Vent my folly! He has heard that word of
some great man, and now applies it to a fool. Vent
my folly! I am afraid this great lubber,° the world,
will prove a cockney.° I prithee now, ungird thy   15
strangeness,° and tell me what I shall vent° to my
lady. Shall I vent to her that thou art coming?

Sebastian. I prithee, foolish Greek,° depart from me.

4.1.5 **held out** maintained 14 **lubber** lout 15 **cockney** affected
fop 15–16 **ungird thy strangeness** i.e., abandon your silly pretense
(of not recognizing me) 16 **vent** say 18 **Greek** buffoon

79

There's money for thee. If you tarry longer, I shall
20 give worse payment.

Clown. By my troth, thou hast an open hand. These
wise men that give fools money get themselves a
good report—after fourteen years' purchase.°

Enter [Sir] Andrew, [Sir] Toby, and Fabian.

Andrew. Now, sir, have I met you again? There's for
25 you!   [*Strikes Sebastian.*]

Sebastian. Why, there's for thee, and there, and there!
                                            [*Strikes Sir Andrew.*]
Are all the people mad?

Toby. Hold, sir, or I'll throw your dagger o'er the
house.   [*Seizes Sebastian.*]

30 *Clown.* This will I tell my lady straight.° I would not
be in some of your coats for twopence.   [*Exit.*]

Toby. Come on, sir; hold.

Andrew. Nay, let him alone. I'll go another way to
work with him. I'll have an action of battery against
35 him,° if there be any law in Illyria. Though I
stroke° him first, yet it's no matter for that.

Sebastian. Let go thy hand.

Toby. Come, sir, I will not let you go. Come, my
young soldier, put up your iron. You are well
40 fleshed.° Come on.

Sebastian. I will be free from thee.   [*Frees himself.*]
What wouldst thou now?
If thou dar'st tempt me further, draw thy sword.

Toby. What, what? Nay then, I must have an ounce
or two of this malapert° blood from you. [*Draws.*]

23 **after fourteen years' purchase** i.e., after a long delay, at a high
price   30 **straight** straightaway, at once   34–35 **have an action of
battery against him** charge him with assaulting me   36 **stroke**
struck   39–40 **well fleshed** i.e., made eager for fighting by having
tasted blood   44 **malapert** saucy

Enter Olivia.

Olivia. Hold, Toby! On thy life I charge thee hold!　　　45

Toby. Madam.

Olivia. Will it be ever thus? Ungracious wretch,
　　Fit for the mountains and the barbarous caves,
　　Where manners ne'er were preached! Out of my
　　　sight!
　　Be not offended, dear Cesario.　　　50
　　Rudesby,° begone.
　　　　　　　[*Exeunt Sir Toby, Sir Andrew, and Fabian.*]
　　　　　　　　　　　I prithee gentle friend,
　　Let thy fair wisdom, not thy passion, sway°
　　In this uncivil° and unjust extent°
　　Against thy peace. Go with me to my house,
　　and hear thou there how many fruitless pranks　　　55
　　This ruffian hath botched up,° that thou thereby
　　Mayst smile at this. Thou shalt not choose but go.
　　Do not deny. Beshrew° his soul for me.
　　He started° one poor heart° of mine, in thee.

Sebastian. What relish is in this?° How runs the
　　stream?　　　60
　　Or° I am mad, or else this is a dream.
　　Let fancy still my sense in Lethe° steep;
　　If it be thus to dream, still let me sleep!

Olivia. Nay, come, I prithee. Would thou'dst be ruled
　　by me!

Sebastian. Madam, I will.

Olivia.　　　　　　　O, say so, and so be.　　　65
　　　　　　　　　　　　　　　　　Exeunt.

51 **Rudesby** ruffian　52 **sway** rule　53 **uncivil** barbarous　53 **extent**
display　56 **botched up** clumsily contrived　58 **Beshrew** curse
59 **started** roused　59 **heart** (with a pun on "hart")　60 **What relish
is in this?** i.e., what does this mean?　61 **Or** either　62 **Lethe** in
classical mythology, the river of oblivion in Hades

Scene 2. [*Olivia's house.*]

Enter Maria and Clown.

Maria. Nay, I prithee put on this gown and this beard; make him believe thou art Sir Topas° the curate; do it quickly. I'll call Sir Toby the whilst.°   [*Exit.*]

Clown. Well, I'll put it on, and I will dissemble° my-
5 self in't, and I would I were the first that ever dissembled in such a gown. I am not tall enough to
become the function° well, nor lean enough to be
thought a good student;° but to be said an honest
man and a good housekeeper° goes as fairly as to
10 say a careful° man and a great scholar. The com-
petitors° enter.

Enter [Sir] Toby [and Maria].

Toby. Jove bless thee, Master Parson.

Clown. Bonos dies,° Sir Toby; for, as the old hermit
of Prague,° that never saw pen and ink, very wit-
15 tily said to a niece of King Gorboduc,° "That that
is is"; so, I, being Master Parson, am Master Parson; for what is "that" but that, and "is" but is?

Toby. To him, Sir Topas.

Clown. What ho, I say. Peace in this prison!

20 *Toby.* The knave counterfeits well; a good knave.°

4.2.2 **Sir Topas** (the ridiculous hero of Chaucer's *Rime of Sir Thopas*, a parody of chivalric romances) 3 **the whilst** meanwhile 4 **dissemble** disguise 7 **function** clerical office 8 **student** student 9 **good housekeeper** solid citizen 10 **careful** painstaking 10–11 **competitors** confederates 13 **Bonos dies** good day 13–14 **the old hermit of Prague** (apparently the Clown's nonsensical invention) 15 **King Gorboduc** (a legendary king of Britain) 20 **knave** fellow

Malvolio within.

Malvolio. Who calls there?

Clown. Sir Topas the curate, who comes to visit
Malvolio the lunatic.

Malvolio. Sir Topas, Sir Topas, good Sir Topas, go to
my lady.   25

Clown. Out, hyperbolical° fiend! How vexest thou this
man! Talkest thou nothing but of ladies?

Toby. Well said, Master Parson.

Malvolio. Sir Topas, never was man thus wronged.
Good Sir Topas, do not think I am mad. They have   30
laid me here in hideous darkness.

Clown. Fie, thou dishonest Satan. I call thee by the
most modest° terms, for I am one of those gentle
ones that will use the devil himself with courtesy.
Say'st thou that house° is dark?   35

Malvolio. As hell, Sir Topas.

Clown. Why, it hath bay windows transparent as barricadoes,° and the clerestories° toward the south
north are as lustrous as ebony; and yet complainest
thou of obstruction?   40

Malvolio. I am not mad, Sir Topas. I say to you this
house is dark.

Clown. Madman, thou errest. I say there is no darkness but ignorance, in which thou art more puzzled
than the Egyptians in their fog.°   45

Malvolio. I say this house is as dark as ignorance,
though ignorance were as dark as hell; and I say
there was never man thus abused. I am no more

26 **hyperbolical** boisterous (a term from rhetoric meaning "exag-
gerated in style")   33 **most modest** mildest   35 **house** madman's
cell   37–38 **barricadoes** barricades   38 **clerestories** upper windows
45 **Egyptians in their fog** (to plague the Egyptians Moses brought
a "thick darkness" that lasted three days; see Exodus 10:21–23)

mad than you are. Make the trial of it in any con-
50 stant question.°

Clown. What is the opinion of Pythagoras° concerning
wild fowl?

Malvolio. That the soul of our grandam might hap-
pily° inhabit a bird.

55 *Clown.* What think'st thou of his opinion?

Malvolio. I think nobly of the soul and no way approve
his opinion.

Clown. Fare thee well. Remain thou still in darkness.
Thou shalt hold th' opinion of Pythagoras ere I
60 will allow of thy wits,° and fear to kill a woodcock,° lest thou dispossess the soul of thy grandam.
Fare thee well.

Malvolio. Sir Topas, Sir Topas!

Toby. My most exquisite Sir Topas!

65 *Clown.* Nay, I am for all waters.°

Maria. Thou mightst have done this without thy beard
and gown. He sees thee not.

Toby. To him in thine own voice, and bring me word
how thou find'st him. [*To Maria*] I would we were
70 well rid of this knavery. If he may be conveniently
delivered,° I would he were; for I am now so far
in offense with my niece that I cannot pursue with
any safety this sport to the upshot.° [*To the Clown*]
Come by and by to my chamber.   *Exit* [*with Maria*].

75 *Clown.* [*Sings*] "Hey, Robin, jolly Robin,
                Tell me how thy lady does."°

49–50 **constant question** consistent topic, normal conversation
51 **Pythagoras** (ancient Greek philosopher who expounded the doctrine of the transmigration of souls) 53–54 **happily** haply, perhaps
60 **allow of thy wits** acknowledge your sanity 60–61 **woodcock** (a
proverbially stupid bird) 65 **I am for all waters** i.e., I can turn my
hand to any trade 71 **delivered** released 73 **upshot** conclusion
75–76 **Hey, Robin . . . lady does** (the Clown sings an old ballad)

Malvolio. Fool.

Clown. "My lady is unkind, perdie."°

Malvolio. Fool.

Clown. "Alas, why is she so?"   *80*

Malvolio. Fool, I say.

Clown. "She loves another." Who calls, ha?

Malvolio. Good fool, as ever thou wilt deserve well
at my hand, help me to a candle, and pen, ink, and
paper. As I am a gentleman, I will live to be thank- *85*
ful to thee for't.

Clown. Master Malvolio?

Malvolio. Ay, good fool.

Clown. Alas, sir, how fell you besides your five wits?°

Malvolio. Fool, there was never man so notoriously° *90*
abused. I am as well in my wits, fool, as thou art.

Clown. But as well? Then you are mad indeed, if you
be no better in your wits than a fool.

Malvolio. They have here propertied° me; keep me in
darkness, send ministers to me, asses, and do all *95*
they can to face me out of my wits.°

Clown. Advise you° what you say. The minister is
here.°—Malvolio, Malvolio, thy wits the heavens
restore. Endeavor thyself to sleep and leave thy
vain bibble babble.   *100*

Malvolio. Sir Topas.

Clown. Maintain no words with him, good fellow.

---

78 **perdie** certainly   89 **how fell you besides your five wits?** i.e., how
did you happen to become mad?   90 **notoriously** outrageously
94 **propertied** i.e., used me as a mere object, not a human being
96 **face me out of my wits** i.e., impudently insist that I am mad
97 **Advise you** consider carefully   97–98 **The minister is here** (for
the next few lines the Clown uses two voices, his own and that of Sir
Topas)

—Who, I, sir? Not I, sir. God buy you,° good Sir
Topas.—Marry, amen.—I will, sir, I will.

105 *Malvolio.* Fool, fool, fool, I say!

Clown. Alas, sir, be patient. What say you, sir? I am
shent° for speaking to you.

Malvolio. Good fool, help me to some light and some
paper. I tell thee, I am as well in my wits as any
110 man in Illyria.

Clown. Well-a-day that you were,° sir.

Malvolio. By this hand, I am. Good fool, some ink,
paper, and light; and convey what I will set down
to my lady. It shall advantage thee more than ever
115 the bearing of letter did.

Clown. I will help you to't. But tell me true, are you
not mad indeed, or do you but counterfeit?°

Malvolio. Believe me, I am not. I tell thee true.

Clown. Nay, I'll ne'er believe a madman till I see his
120 brains. I will fetch you light and paper and ink.

Malvolio. Fool, I'll requite it in the highest degree. I
prithee be gone.

Clown. [*Sings*]   I am gone, sir.
                              And anon, sir,
125   I'll be with you again,
                              In a trice,
                              Like to the old Vice,°
                         Your need to sustain.°
                         Who with dagger of lath,
130   In his rage and his wrath,
                              Cries "Ah ha" to the devil.
                         Like a mad lad,

103 **God buy you** God be with you, i.e., good-bye   107 **shent** re-
buked   111 **Well-a-day that you were** alas, if only you were   117
counterfeit pretend   127 **Vice** (in the morality plays, a stock mischievous character who usually carried a wooden dagger)   128 **Your
need to sustain** i.e., in order to help you resist the Devil

                    "Pare thy nails, dad."
                    Adieu, goodman devil.°   *Exit.*

              Scene 3. [*Olivia's garden.*]

                    Enter Sebastian.

Sebastian. This is the air; that is the glorious sun;
    This pearl she gave me, I do feel't and see't;
    And though 'tis wonder that enwraps me thus,
    Yet 'tis not madness. Where's Antonio then?
    I could not find him at the Elephant;   5
    Yet there he was,° and there I found this credit,°
    That he did range the town to seek me out.
    His counsel now might do me golden service;
    For though my soul disputes well with my sense°
    That this may be some error, but no madness,   10
    Yet doth this accident and flood of fortune
    So far exceed all instance,° all discourse,°
    That I am ready to distrust mine eyes
    And wrangle with my reason that persuades me
    To any other trust° but that I am mad,   15
    Or else the lady's mad. Yet, if 'twere so,
    She could not sway° her house, command her
        followers,
    Take and give back affairs and their dispatch°
    With such a smooth, discreet, and stable bearing
    As I perceive she does. There's something in't   20
    That is deceivable.° But here the lady comes.

_____

134 **Adieu, goodman devil** (a much emended line; "goodman" [Folio
"good man"], a title for a yeoman or any man of substance not of
gentle birth, roughly corresponds to our "mister") 4.3.6 **was** had
been 6 **credit** belief 9 **my soul disputes well with my sense** my
reason agrees with the evidence of my senses⁷ 12 **instance** precedent
12 **discourse** reason 15 **trust** belief 17 **sway** rule 18 **Take and
give ... their dispatch** i.e., assume and discharge the management of
affairs 21 **deceivable** deceptive

Enter Olivia and Priest.

Olivia. Blame not this haste of mine. If you mean well,
     Now go with me and with this holy man
     Into the chantry by.° There, before him,
25   And underneath that consecrated roof,
     Plight me the full assurance of your faith,
     That my most jealious° and too doubtful soul
     May live at peace. He shall conceal it
     Whiles° you are willing it shall come to note,°
30   What time we will our celebration keep°
     According to my birth. What do you say?

Sebastian. I'll follow this good man and go with you
     And having sworn truth, ever will be true.

Olivia. Then lead the way, good father, and heavens
          so shine
35   That they may fairly note° this act of mine.

                                              Exeunt.

24 **chantry by** nearby chapel   27 **jealious** jealous, anxious   29 **Whiles**
until   29 **come to note** be made public   30 **our celebration keep**
celebrate our marriage ceremony (as distinguished from the formal
compact of betrothal)   35 **fairly note** look with favor on

ACT V

Scene 1. [*Before Olivia's house.*]

Enter Clown and Fabian.

Fabian. Now as thou lov'st me, let me see his° letter.

Clown. Good Master Fabian, grant me another request.

Fabian. Anything.

Clown. Do not desire to see this letter.   5

Fabian. This is to give a dog, and in recompense desire my dog again.

Enter Duke, Viola, Curio, and Lords.

Duke. Belong you to the Lady Olivia, friends?

Clown. Ay, sir, we are some of her trappings.

Duke. I know thee well. How dost thou, my good   10
fellow?

Clown. Truly, sir, the better for my foes, and the
worse for my friends.

5.1.1 **his** i.e., Malvolio's

Duke. Just the contrary: the better for thy friends.

15 *Clown.* No, sir, the worse.

Duke. How can that be?

Clown. Marry, sir, they praise me and make an ass of
me. Now my foes tell me plainly I am an ass; so
that by my foes, sir, I profit in the knowledge of
20 myself, and by my friends I am abused;° so that,
conclusions to be as kisses,° if your four negatives°
make your two affirmatives,° why then, the worse
for my friends, and the better for my foes.

Duke. Why, this is excellent.

25 *Clown.* By my troth, sir, no, though it please you to
be one of my friends.

Duke. Thou shalt not be the worse for me. There's
gold.

Clown. But that it would be double-dealing,° sir, I
30 would you could make it another.

Duke. O, you give me ill counsel.

Clown. Put your grace° in your pocket, sir, for this
once, and let your flesh and blood obey it.

Duke. Well, I will be so much a sinner to be a double-
35 dealer. There's another.°

Clown. Primo, secundo, tertio° is a good play;° and
the old saying is "The third pays for all." The
triplex,° sir, is a good tripping measure; or the
bells of Saint Bennet,° sir, may put you in mind—
40 one, two, three.

Duke. You can fool no more money out of me at this

20 **abused** deceived   21 **conclusions to be as kisses** i.e., if conclusions
may be compared to kisses (when a coy girl's repeated denials really
mean assent)   21 **negatives** i.e., lips (?)   22 **affirmatives** i.e., mouths
(?)   29 **double-dealing** (1) giving twice (2) duplicity   32 **grace** (1)
title of nobility (2) generosity   35 **another** i.e., coin   36 **Primo,
secundo, tertio** one, two, three   36 **play** child's game (?)   38 **triplex**
triple time in dancing   39 **Saint Bennet** St. Benedict (a church)

throw.° If you will let your lady know I am here
to speak with her, and bring her along with you, it
may awake my bounty further.

Clown. Marry, sir, lullaby to your bounty till I come   *45*
again. I go, sir; but I would not have you to think
that my desire of having is the sin of covetousness.
But, as you say, sir, let your bounty take a nap; I
will awake it anon.   *Exit.*

Enter Antonio and Officers.

Viola. Here comes the man, sir, that did rescue me.   *50*

Duke. That face of his I do remember well;
   Yet when I saw it last, it was besmeared
   As black as Vulcan° in the smoke of war.
   A baubling° vessel was he captain of,
   For shallow draught and bulk unprizable,°   *55*
   With which such scathful° grapple did he make
   With the most noble bottom° of our fleet
   That very envy and the tongue of loss°
   Cried fame and honor on him. What's the matter?

First Officer. Orsino, this is that Antonio   *60*
   That took the *Phoenix* and her fraught° from
     Candy;°
   And this is he that did the *Tiger* board
   When your young nephew Titus lost his leg.
   Here in the streets, desperate of shame and state,°
   In private brabble° did we apprehend him.   *65*

Viola. He did me kindness, sir; drew on my side;°
   But in conclusion put strange speech upon me.°
   I know not what 'twas but distraction.°

42 **throw** throw of the dice   53 **Vulcan** Roman god of fire and
patron of blacksmiths   54 **baubling** insignificant   55 **For shallow
draught and bulk unprizable** i.e., virtually worthless on account of
its small size   56 **scathful** destructive   57 **bottom** ship   58 **very
envy and the tongue of loss** even enmity and the voice of the losers
61 **fraught** freight, cargo   61 **Candy** Candia, Crete   64 **desperate
of shame and state** i.e., recklessly disregarding his shameful past
behavior and the requirements of public order   65 **brabble** brawl
66 **drew on my side** i.e., drew his sword in my defense   67 **put
strange speech upon me** spoke to me so oddly   68 **distraction** madness

Duke. Notable° pirate, thou salt-water thief,
70   What foolish boldness brought thee to their mercies
      Whom thou in terms so bloody and so dear°
      Hast made thine enemies?

Antonio.   Orsino, noble sir,
      Be pleased that I shake off these names you give me.
      Antonio never yet was thief or pirate,
75   Though I confess, on base and ground enough,
      Orsino's enemy. A witchcraft drew me hither.
      That most ingrateful boy there by your side
      From the rude sea's enragèd and foamy mouth
      Did I redeem. A wrack° past hope he was.
80   His life I gave him, and did thereto add
      My love without retention or restraint,
      All his in dedication. For his sake
      Did I expose myself (pure° for his love)
      Into the danger of this adverse° town;
85   Drew to defend him when he was beset;
      Where being apprehended, his false cunning
      (Not meaning to partake with me in danger)
      Taught him to face me out of his acquaintance,°
      And grew a twenty years removèd thing
90   While one would wink; denied me mine own purse,
      Which I had recommended° to his use
      Not half an hour before.

Viola.   How can this be?

Duke. When came he to this town?

Antonio. Today, my lord; and for three months before,
95   No int'rim, not a minute's vacancy,
      Both day and night did we keep company.

                Enter Olivia and Attendants.

Duke. Here comes the Countess; now heaven walks on
      earth.   •

69 **Notable** notorious   71 **dear** grievous   79 **wrack** wreck   83 **pure**
purely   84 **adverse** unfriendly   88 **to face me out of his acquaintance** i.e., brazenly to deny any knowledge of me   91 **recommended**
given

But for° thee, fellow: fellow, thy words are mad-
  ness.
Three months this youth hath tended upon me;
But more of that anon. Take him aside.   *100*

Olivia. What would my lord, but that° he may not
  have,
Wherein Olivia may seem serviceable?
Cesario, you do not keep promise with me.

Viola. Madam?

Duke. Gracious Olivia—   *105*

Olivia. What do you say, Cesario?—Good my lord°—

Viola. My lord would speak; my duty hushes me.

Olivia. If it be aught to the old tune, my lord,
It is as fat and fulsome° to mine ear
As howling after music.

Duke.   Still so cruel?   *110*

Olivia. Still so constant, lord.

Duke. What, to perverseness? You uncivil lady,
To whose ingrate and unauspicious° altars
My soul the faithfull'st off'rings have breathed out
That e'er devotion tendered. What shall I do?   *115*

Olivia. Even what it please my lord, that shall become
  him.

Duke. Why should I not, had I the heart to do it,
Like to th' Egyptian thief° at point of death,
Kill what I love?—a savage jealousy
That sometime savors nobly. But hear me this: *120*
Since you to non-regardance° cast my faith,

98 **But for** as for   101 **but that** except that which (i.e., my love)
106 **Good my lord** i.e., please be silent (so Cesario may speak)
109 **fat and fulsome** gross and repulsive   113 **ingrate and unauspi-
cious** ungrateful and unpropitious   118 **th' Egyptian thief** (in Heli-
odorus' *Ethiopica,* a Greek romance translated by Thomas Under-
down about 1569, the bandit Thyamis, besieged in a cave, plans to
kill the captive princess Clariclea, the object of his hopeless love;
but in the darkness he kills another woman instead)   121 **non-
regardance** neglect

And that° I partly know the instrument
That screws° me from my true place in your favor,
Live you the marble-breasted tyrant still.
125 But this your minion, whom I know you love,
And whom, by heaven I swear, I tender° dearly,
Him will I tear out of that cruel eye
Where he sits crownèd in his master's spite.
Come, boy, with me. My thoughts are ripe in mischief.
130 I'll sacrifice the lamb that I do love.
To spite a raven's heart within a dove.   [*Going.*]

Viola. And I, most jocund, apt,° and willingly,
To do you rest° a thousand deaths would die.
          [*Following.*]

Olivia. Where goes Cesario?

Viola.   After him I love
135 More than I love these eyes, more than my life,
More, by all mores,° than e'er I shall love wife.
If I do feign, you witnesses above
Punish my life for tainting of my love!

Olivia. Ay me detested, how am I beguiled!

Viola. Who does beguile you? Who does do you
140 wrong?

Olivia. Hast thou forgot thyself? Is it so long?
Call forth the holy father.   [*Exit an Attendant.*]

Duke.   [*To Viola*] Come, away!

Olivia. Whither, my lord? Cesario, husband, stay.

Duke. Husband?

Olivia.   Ay, husband. Can he that deny?

Duke. Her husband, sirrah?°

145 *Viola.*   No, my lord, not I.

---

122 **that** since   123 **screws** forces   126 **tender** hold   132 **apt** readily
133 **do you rest** give you peace   136 **mores** i.e., possible comparisons
144 **sirrah** (customary form of address to a menial)

Olivia. Alas, it is the baseness of thy fear
    That makes thee strangle thy propriety.°
    Fear not, Cesario; take thy fortunes up;
    Be that thou know'st thou art, and then thou art
    As great as that° thou fear'st.

Enter Priest.

                  O, welcome, father! *150*
    Father, I charge thee by thy reverence
    Here to unfold—though lately we intended
    To keep in darkness what occasion now
    Reveals before 'tis ripe—what thou dost know
    Hath newly passed between this youth and me.   *155*

Priest. A contract° of eternal bond of love,
    Confirmed by mutual joinder of your hands,
    Attested by the holy close of lips,
    Strength'ned by interchangement of your rings;
    And all the ceremony of this compact°   *160*
    Sealed in my function,° by my testimony;
    Since when, my watch hath told me, toward my
        grave
    I have traveled but two hours.

Duke. O thou dissembling cub, what wilt thou be
    When time hath sowed a grizzle on thy case?°   *165*
    Or will not else thy craft° so quickly grow
    That thine own trip° shall be thine overthrow?
    Farewell, and take her; but direct thy feet
    Where thou and I, henceforth, may never meet.

Viola. My lord, I do protest.

Olivia.   O, do not swear.   *170*
    Hold little° faith, though thou hast too much fear.

Enter Sir Andrew.

147 **strangle thy propriety** deny your identity   150 **that** him who
(i.e., the Duke)   156 **contract** betrothal   160 **compact** (accent on
second syllable)   161 **Sealed in my function** i.e., ratified by me in
my priestly office   165 **a grizzle on thy case** gray hairs on your skin
166 **craft** duplicity   167 **trip** craftiness   171 **little** i.e., at least a little

Andrew. For the love of God, a surgeon! Send one
presently° to Sir Toby.

Olivia. What's the matter?

175 *Andrew.* H'as° broke my head across, and has given
Sir Toby a bloody coxcomb° too. For the love of
God, your help! I had rather than forty pound I
were at home.

Olivia. Who has done this, Sir Andrew?

180 *Andrew.* The Count's gentleman, one Cesario. We
took him for a coward, but he's the very devil
incardinate.°

Duke. My gentleman Cesario?

Andrew. Od's lifelings,° here he is! You broke my
185 head for nothing; and that that I did, I was set on
to do't by Sir Toby.

Viola. Why do you speak to me? I never hurt you.
You drew your sword upon me without cause,
But I bespake you fair° and hurt you not.

Enter [Sir] Toby and Clown.

190 *Andrew.* If a bloody coxcomb be a hurt, you have
hurt me. I think you set nothing by a bloody coxcomb. Here comes Sir Toby halting;° you shall hear
more. But if he had not been in drink, he would
have tickled you othergates° than he did.

195 *Duke.* How now, gentleman? How is't with you?

Toby. That's all one! Has hurt me, and there's th'
end on't. Sot,° didst see Dick Surgeon, sot?

Clown. O, he's drunk, Sir Toby, an hour agone. His
eyes were set° at eight i' th' morning.

173 **presently** immediately   175 **H'as** he has   176 **coxcomb** pate
182 **incardinate** incarnate   184 **Od's lifelings** by God's life   189 **bespake you fair** addressed you courteously   192 **halting** limping
194 **othergates** otherwise   197 **Sot** fool   199 **set** closed

Toby. Then he's a rogue and a passy measures   *200*
pavin.° I hate a drunken rogue.

Olivia. Away with him! Who hath made this havoc
with them?

Andrew. I'll help you, Sir Toby, because we'll be
dressed° together.   *205*

Toby. Will you help—an ass-head and a coxcomb
and a knave, a thin-faced knave, a gull?

Olivia. Get him to bed, and let his hurt be looked to.
[*Exeunt Clown, Fabian, Sir Toby,
and Sir Andrew.*]

Enter Sebastian.

Sebastian. I am sorry, madam, I have hurt your
kinsman;
But had it been the brother of my blood,   *210*
I must have done no less with wit and safety.°
You throw a strange regard° upon me, and by that
I do perceive it hath offended you.
Pardon me, sweet one, even for the vows
We made each other but so late ago.   *215*

Duke. One face, one voice, one habit,° and two
persons—
A natural perspective° that is and is not.

Sebastian. Antonio, O my dear Antonio,
How have the hours racked and tortured me
Since I have lost thee!   *220*

Antonio. Sebastian are you?

Sebastian.   Fear'st thou° that, Antonio?

200–01 **passy measures pavin** i.e., *passamezzo* pavan, a slow and
stately dance of eight bars (hence its relevance to the surgeon whose
eyes had "set at eight") 204–05 **be dressed** have our wounds dressed
211 **with wit and safety** i.e., with a sensible regard for my safety
212 **strange regard** unfriendly look 216 **habit** costume 217 **A
natural perspective** i.e., a natural optical illusion (like that produced
by a stereoscope, which converts two images into one) 221 **Fear'st
thou** do you doubt

Antonio. How have you made division of yourself?
  An apple cleft in two is not more twin
  Than these two creatures. Which is Sebastian?

225 *Olivia.* Most wonderful.

Sebastian. Do I stand there? I never had a brother;
  Nor can there be that deity in my nature
  Of here and everywhere.° I had a sister,
  Whom the blind waves and surges have devoured.
230 Of charity,° what kin are you to me?
  What countryman? What name? What parentage?

Viola. Of Messaline; Sebastian was my father;
  Such a Sebastian was my brother too;
  So went he suited° to his watery tomb.
235 If spirits can assume both form and suit,°
  You come to fright us.

Sebastian.   A spirit I am indeed,
  But am in that dimension grossly clad
  Which from the womb I did participate.°
  Were you a woman, as the rest goes even,°
240 I should my tears let fall upon your cheek
  And say, "Thrice welcome, drownèd Viola!"

Viola. My father had a mole upon his brow.

Sebastian. And so had mine.

Viola. And died that day when Viola from her birth
245 Had numb'red thirteen years.

Sebastian. O, that record° is lively in my soul!
  He finishèd indeed his mortal act
  That day that made my sister thirteen years.

Viola. If nothing lets° to make us happy both
250 But this my masculine usurped attire,

227–28 **Nor can there be ... everywhere** i.e., nor can I, like God, be
everywhere at once   230 **Of charity** out of simple kindness   234
suited clothed   235 **form and suit** body and clothing   237–38 **am in
that dimension ... participate** i.e., clothed in the bodily form that, like
other mortals, I acquired at birth   239 **as the rest goes even** i.e.,
as other circumstances seem to indicate   246 **record** history (accent
on second syllable)   249 **lets** interferes

Do not embrace me till each circumstance
Of place, time, fortune do cohere and jump°
That I am Viola; which to confirm,
I'll bring you to a captain in this town,
Where lie my maiden weeds;° by whose gentle help   255
I was preserved to serve this noble Count.
All the occurrence of my fortune since
Hath been between this lady and this lord.

Sebastian. [*To Olivia*] So comes it, lady, you have
    been mistook.
But nature to her bias drew° in that.   260
You would have been contracted to a maid;
Nor are you therein, by my life, deceived:
You are betrothed both to a maid and man.

Duke. Be not amazed; right noble is his blood.
If this be so, as yet the glass° seems true,   265
I shall have share in this most happy wrack.
[*To Viola*] Boy, thou hast said to me à thousand
    times
Thou never shouldst love woman like to me.

Viola. And all those sayings will I over° swear,
And all those swearings keep as true in soul   270
As doth that orbèd continent° the fire
That severs day from night.

Duke.   Give me thy hand,
And let me see thee in thy woman's weeds.

Viola. The captain that did bring me first on shore
Hath my maid's garments. He upon some action   275
Is now in durance, at Malvolio's suit,°
A gentleman, and follower of my lady's.

Olivia. He shall enlarge° him. Fetch Malvolio hither.

252 **cohere and jump** i.e., fall together and agree   255 **weeds** clothes
260 **nature to her bias drew** i.e., nature followed her normal inclination   265 **glass** i.e., the "natural perspective" of line 217   269 **over**
repeatedly   271 **orbèd continent** in Ptolemaic astronomy, the sphere
of the sun   275–76 **He upon some action ... Malvolio's suit** i.e.,
at Malvolio's instigation he is now imprisoned upon some legal
charge   278 **enlarge** release

And yet alas, now I remember me,
280 They say, poor gentleman, he's much distract.

Enter Clown with a letter, and Fabian.

A most extracting° frenzy of mine own
From my remembrance clearly banished his.
How does he, sirrah?

Clown. Truly, madam, he holds Belzebub at the
285 stave's end° as well as a man in his case° may do.
Has here writ a letter to you; I should have given't
you today morning. But as a madman's epistles are
no gospels, so it skills° not much when they are
delivered.

290 *Olivia.* Open't and read it.

Clown. Look then to be well edified, when the fool
delivers the madman. [*Reads in a loud voice*] "By
the Lord, madam"—

Olivia. How now? Art thou mad?

295 *Clown.* No, madam, I do but read madness. And your
ladyship will have it as it ought to be, you must
allow *vox.*°

Olivia. Prithee read i' thy right wits.

Clown. So I do, madonna; but to read his right wits is
300 to read thus. Therefore perpend,° my princess, and
give ear.

Olivia. [*To Fabian*] Read it you, sirrah.

Fabian. (*Reads*) "By the Lord, madam, you wrong
me, and the world shall know it. Though you have
305 put me into darkness, and given your drunken
cousin rule over me, yet have I the benefit of my
senses as well as your ladyship. I have your own
letter that induced me to the semblance I put on;

281 **extracting** i.e., obliterating (in that it draws me from all thoughts
of Malvolio's "frenzy") 284–85 **he holds Belzebub at the stave's
end** i.e., he keeps the fiend at a distance 285 **case** condition
288 **skills** matters 297 **vox** i.e., an appropriately loud voice 300
perpend pay attention

with the which I doubt not but to do myself much
right, or you much shame. Think of me as you *310*
please. I leave my duty a little unthought of, and
speak out of my injury.
                    THE MADLY USED MALVOLIO."

Olivia. Did he write this?

Clown. Ay, madam.   *315*

Duke. This savors not much of distraction.

Olivia. See him delivered, Fabian; bring him hither.
                              [*Exit Fabian.*]
  My lord, so please you, these things further thought
      on,
  To think me as well a sister as a wife,
  One day shall crown th' alliance on't, so please you, *320*
  Here at my house and at my proper° cost.

Duke. Madam, I am most apt° t' embrace your offer.
  [*To Viola*] Your master quits° you; and for your
      service done him,
  So much against the mettle of your sex,
  So far beneath your soft and tender breeding,   *325*
  And since you called me master for so long,
  Here is my hand; you shall from this time be
  Your master's mistress.

Olivia.   A sister; you are she.

              Enter [Fabian, with] Malvolio.

Duke. Is this the madman?

Olivia.   Ay, my lord, this same.
  How now, Malvolio?

Malvolio.   Madam, you have done me wrong,   *330*
  Notorious° wrong.

Olivia.   Have I, Malvolio? No.

Malvolio. Lady, you have. Pray you peruse that letter.
  You must not now deny it is your hand.

321 **proper** own   322 **apt** ready   323 **quits** releases   331 **Notorious**
notable

Write from it° if you can, in hand or phrase,
335   Or say 'tis not your seal, not your invention.°
You can say none of this. Well, grant it then,
And tell me, in the modesty of honor,°
Why you have given me such clear lights of favor,
Bade me come smiling and cross-gartered to you,
340   To put on yellow stockings, and to frown
Upon Sir Toby and the lighter° people;
And, acting this in an obedient hope,
Why have you suffered me to be imprisoned,
Kept in a dark house, visited by the priest,
345   And made the most notorious geck and gull°
That e'er invention played on? Tell me why.

Olivia. Alas, Malvolio, this is not my writing,
Though I confess much like the character;
But, out of° question, 'tis Maria's hand.
350   And now I do bethink me, it was she
First told me thou wast mad; then cam'st in smiling,
And in such forms which here were presupposed°
Upon thee in the letter. Prithee be content.
This practice hath most shrewdly passed° upon thee;
355   But when we know the grounds and authors of it,
thou shalt be both the plaintiff and the judge
Of thine own cause.

Fabian.   Good madam, hear me speak,
And let no quarrel, nor no brawl to come,
Taint the condition of this present hour,
360   Which I have wond'red at. In hope it shall not,
Most freely I confess myself and Toby
Set this device against Malvolio here,
Upon some stubborn and uncourteous parts°
We had conceived against him. Maria writ
365   The letter, at Sir Toby's great importance,°

---

334 **from it** differently   335 **invention** composition   337 **in the modesty of honor** i.e., with a proper regard to your own honor   341 **lighter** lesser   345 **geck and gull** fool and dupe   349 **out of** beyond   352 **presupposed** imposed   354 **This practice hath most shrewdly passed** i.e., this trick has most mischievously worked   363 **Upon some stubborn and uncourteous parts** i.e., because of some unyielding and discourteous traits of character   365 **importance** importunity

In recompense whereof he hath married her.
How with a sportful malice it was followed
May rather pluck on° laughter than revenge,
If that° the injuries be justly weighed
That have on both sides passed.   370

Olivia. Alas, poor fool,° how have they baffled° thee!

Clown. Why, "some are born great, some achieve
greatness, and some have greatness thrown upon
them." I was one, sir, in this interlude,° one Sir
Topas, sir; but that's all one. "By the Lord, fool, I   375
am not mad!" But do you remember, "Madam, why
laugh you at such a barren rascal? And you smile
not, he's gagged"? And thus the whirligig of time
brings in his revenges.

Malvolio. I'll be revenged on the whole pack of you!   380
                                                    [*Exit.*]

Olivia. He hath been most notoriously abused.

Duke. Pursue him and entreat him to a peace.
He hath not told us of the captain yet.
When that is known, and golden time convents,°
A solemn combination shall be made   385
Of our dear souls. Meantime, sweet sister,
We will not part from hence. Cesario, come—
For so you shall be while you are a man,
But when in other habits you are seen,
Orsino's mistress and his fancy's° queen.   390
                        Exeunt [*all but the Clown*].

Clown sings.°

When that I was and a° little tiny boy,
    With hey, ho, the wind and the rain,
A foolish thing was but a toy,°

368 **pluck on** prompt   369 **If that** if   371 **fool** (here, a term of affection and compassion)   371 **baffled** publicly humiliated   374 **interlude** little play   384 **convents** is suitable (?)   390 **fancy's** love's
s.d. **Clown sings** (since no source has been found for the Clown's
song—which certain editors have inexplicably denounced as dog-
gerel—we may assume that it is Shakespeare's)   391 **and a** a
393 **toy** trifle

For the rain it raineth every day.

395 But when I came to man's estate,
      With hey, ho, the wind and the rain,
    'Gainst knaves and thieves men shut their gate,
      For the rain it raineth every day.

    But when I came, alas, to wive,
400   With hey, ho, the wind and the rain,
    By swaggering could I never thrive,
      For the rain it raineth every day.

    But when I came unto my beds,
      With hey, ho, the wind and the rain,
405 With tosspots° still had drunken heads,
      For the rain it raineth every day.

    A great while ago the world begun,
      Hey, ho, the wind and the rain;
    But that's all one, our play is done,
410   And we'll strive to please you every day.

                                              [*Exit.*]

                      FINIS.

405 tosspots sots

Textual Note

The text of *Twelfth Night*, for which the sole source is the Folio of 1623, is, if not immaculate, so clean and tidy that it presents almost no problems. Apparently set up from the prompt copy or a transcript of it, the Folio of course contains a few misprints (like *incardinate* for *incardinate* at 5.1.182), a few presumed or obvious errors in speech-headings (like those at 2.5.34, 38, where Sir Toby is perhaps confused with Fabian, or at 3.4.24, where Malvolio is assigned a speech that clearly is not his), and a few lines (for example, 2.2.12 and 3.3.15) that seem to need some sort of emendation. Moreover, the fact that the Clown is given all the lovely songs that were perhaps originally Viola's (as suggested at 1.2.57–59 and 2.4.42–43) has been cited as a token of revision. In general, however, the text, as all its editors have gratefully conceded, is one of almost unexampled purity.

In the present edition, therefore, it is followed very closely, even in such forms as *studient, jealious, wrack* (for *wreck*) and *vild,* which preserve, we may suppose, not only Shakespeare's spelling but also his pronunciation. But *prethee, divil, murther, Sathan* (for *Satan*), *Anthonio,* and *berd* (which occurs once for *beard*) are given in modern spelling. A few emendations sanctioned by long and universal approbation—like Pope's *Arion* for *Orion* at 1.2.15, Theobald's inspired *curl by* for *coole my* at 1.3.96, and Hanmer's *staniel* for *stallion* at 2.5.115—have been admitted here, as have one or two superior readings from the later Folios (for example, *tang* for *langer* at 3.4.73). However, such attractive but unnecessary emendations as Pope's *south* for *sound* at 1.1.5 have been rejected, and the few real cruxes have been allowed to stand, so that each reader must struggle all alone with Sir Andrew's *damned colored stock* at 1.3.132, make what he can of the mysterious Lady of the Strachy at 2.5.39–40, and unravel Viola's puzzling pronouncement at 2.2.12 without the aid of emendation.

In this edition the spelling has been modernized (with the exceptions noted above), the Latin act and scene divisions of the Folio translated, the punctuation brought into conformity with modern usage, a few lines that through compositorial error were printed as prose restored to verse (4.2.75–76), and a few stage directions (like the one at 3.4.14) shifted to accommodate the text. At the conclusion of the first, second, and fourth acts, the Folio has *"Finis Actus . . . ,"* here omitted. All editorial interpolations such as the list of characters, indications of place, and stage directions implied by the text but not indicated in the Folio are enclosed in square brackets. Other material departures from the copy text (excluding obvious typographical errors) are listed below in italic type, followed in roman by the Folio reading. It will be apparent that most of them required no agonizing reappraisal.

1.2.15 *Arion* Orion

1.3.29 *all most,* almost   51 *Andrew* Ma.   96 *curl by* coole my   98 *me* we   112 *kickshawses* kicke-chawses   132 *set* sit   136 *That's* That

1.4.28 *nuncio's* Nuntio's

1.5.146 *H'as* Ha's   165 s.d. *Viola* Uiolenta   256 *with fertile tears* fertill teares   302 *County's* Countes

2.2.20 *That sure methought* That me thought   31 *our frailty* O frailtie   32 *of* if

2.3.26 *leman* Lemon   35 *give a*— giue a   134–35 *a nayword* an ayword

2.4.53 *Fly . . . fly* Fye . . . fie   55 *yew* Ew   89 *I* It   104 *know*— know.

2.5.13 *metal* Mettle   115 *staniel* stallion   144 *born* become   144 *achieve* atcheeues   159–60 *thee,* THE FORTUNATE UNHAPPY./*Daylight* thee, tht fortunate vnhappy daylight   177 *dear* deero

3.1.8 *king lies* Kings lyes   69 *wise men* wisemens   84 *gait* gate   93 *all ready* already   114 *here* heare

3.2.8 *see thee the* see the   70 *renegado* Renegatho

3.4.24 *Olivia* Mal.   73 *tang* langer   94 *How is't with you, man* [The Folio

assigns this speech to Fabian]   121 *Ay, biddy* I biddy   152 *Ay, is't,* I, ist?
181 *You . . . for't* Yon . . . fot't   256 *competent* computent

4.2.6 *in* in in   15 *Gorboduc* Gorbodacke   38 *clerestories* cleere stores
73 *sport to the* sport the

5.1.201 *pavin* panyn

The Source of *Twelfth Night*

The plot of *Twelfth Night*—the adventures and misadventures of a pair of identical twins—is so old that its origins are lost in the prehistory of European literature. It had been a commonplace in Greek comedy long before Plautus and Terence imported it to Rome; and when young Shakespeare, at the start of his career, fashionably pillaged Plautus for *The Comedy of Errors,* he was following a distinguished Renaissance tradition of Italian, Spanish, French, and English writers who had worked their artful (and sometimes tedious) changes on the basic situation. One such change was the sexual differentiation of the twins, a refinement affording endless possibilities for intrigue and complication. It may be, as John Manningham suggested in the first known comment on *Twelfth Night* (see p. lxiv n), that for this embellishment he drew on Nicolò Secchi's *Gl'Inganni* (1562), but he could have gone to Secchi's source, which was *Gl'Ingannati* ("The Deceived"), a Plautine comedy, produced at Siena in 1531 and published six years later, that had spawned a dozen translations and adaptations through the later sixteenth century. Despite the formidable scholarship that has been brought to bear upon the question,[1] Shakespeare's knowledge of and obligation to most of this material is still a matter of dispute, but concerning his debt to one late recension of *Gl'Ingannati* there is no dispute whatever. This was Barnabe Rich's "Of Apolonius and Silla," the second of a set of eight prose narratives that was published in 1581 as *Riche his Farewell to Mili-*

---

[1]This scholarship is knowledgeably surveyed by Kenneth Muir, *Shakespeare's Sources*, vol. 1, *Comedies and Tragedies* (1957), pp. 66–77; and Geoffrey Bullough (ed.), *Narrative and Dramatic Sources of Shakespeare*, vol. 2 (1958), pp. 269–285.

*tarie profession: conteinyng verie pleasaunt discourses fit for
a peaceable tyme.*

The genealogy of "Of Apolonius and Silla" is an instructive example of the free and easy ways of sixteenth-century writers: Rich found the tale (which he eked out with incidental and unacknowledged pilferings from William Painter's *Palace of Pleasure*, a big collection of stories first published in 1566) in Pierre de Belleforest's *Histoires Tragiques* (1579), which was translated from Matteo Bandello's *Novelle* (1554), which was based on *Gl'Ingannati*. Although Shakespeare could have read, and perhaps did read, these and other cognate versions of the story, his use of the *Farewell* would seem to be established by the fact that he took from it four words—*coistrel, gaskins, pavin,* and *galliard*—that appear in *Twelfth Night* and not elsewhere in his plays. Moreover, the fifth tale in Rich's collection ("Of Two Brethren and Their Wives") supplies an analogue for the scene (4.2) in which Malvolio is punished, although the subplot of the arrogant steward was apparently Shakespeare's own creation. He may have drawn on other things for this or that detail—for example, on Emanuel Forde's prose romance, *The Famous History of Parismus* (1598), for the shipwreck and for the names of Olivia and Violetta, or on the anonymous play *Sir Clyomon and Clamydes* (1599) for the device (which he himself had used in *The Two Gentlemen of Verona*) of a girl disguised as a man in the service of her lover—but of all the alleged or possible sources, "Of Apolonius and Silla" stands closest to *Twelfth Night*, and therefore it is here reprinted. The text, with modernized spelling and punctuation, is that of the unique copy of the 1581 edition in the Bodleian Library. The bibliographical history of the *Farewell*—a book so popular that it was reprinted in 1583, 1594, and 1606—has been treated by Thomas Mabry Cranfill in his edition of the work (1959), pp. liii–lxxxi.

BARNABE RICH

Of Apolonius and Silla

THE ARGUMENT OF THE SECOND HISTORY

Apolonius Duke, having spent a year's service in the wars against the Turk, returning homeward with his company by sea, was driven by force of weather to the Isle of Cyprus, where he was well received by Pontus, governor of the same Isle; with whom Silla, daughter to Pontus, fell so strangely in love, that after Apolonius was departed to Constantinople, Silla, with one man, followed, and coming to Constantinople, she served Apolonius in the habit of a man, and after many pretty accidents falling out, she was known to Apolonius, who, in requital of her love, married her.

There is no child that is born into this wretched world but before it doth suck the mother's milk it taketh first a sup of the cup of error, which maketh us, when we come to riper years, not only to enter into actions of injury, but many times to stray from that is right and reason; but in all other things, wherein we show ourselves to be most drunken with this poisoned cup, it is in our actions of love; for the lover is so estranged from that is right, and wandereth so wide from the bounds of reason, that he is not able to deem white from black, good from bad, virtue from vice; but only led by the appetite of his own affections, and grounding them on the foolishness of his own fancies, will so settle his liking on such a one as either by desert or unworthiness will merit rather to be loathed than loved.

If a question might be asked, what is the ground indeed of

reasonable love, whereby the knot is knit of true and perfect friendship, I think those that be wise would answer—desert: that is, where the party beloved doth requite us with the like; for otherwise, if the bare show of beauty or the comeliness of personage might be sufficient to confirm us in our love, those that be accustomed to go to fairs and markets might sometimes fall in love with twenty in a day. Desert must then be, of force, the ground of reasonable love; for to love them that hate us, to follow them that fly from us, to fawn on them that frown on us, to curry favor with them that disdain us, to be glad to please them that care not how they offend us, who will not confess this to be an erroneous love, neither grounded upon wit nor reason? Wherefore, right courteous gentlewomen, if it please you with patience to peruse this history following, you shall see Dame Error so play her part with a leash of lovers, a male and two females, as shall work a wonder to your wise judgment, in noting the effect of their amorous devices and conclusions of their actions—the first neglecting the love of a noble dame, young, beautiful, and fair, who only for his goodwill played the part of a serving man, contented to abide any manner of pain only to behold him. He again setting his love of a dame, that despising him (being a noble duke) gave herself to a serving man, as she had thought; but it otherwise fell out, as the substance of this tale shall better describe. And because I have been something tedious in my first discourse [i.e., "Sappho, Duke of Mantona," the first of the eight tales in Rich's *Farewell*], offending your patient ears with the hearing of a circumstance overlong, from henceforth that which I mind to write shall be done with such celerity, as the matter that I pretend to pen may in any wise permit me, and thus followeth the history.

During the time that the famous city of Constantinople remained in the hands of the Christians, amongst many other noblemen that kept their abiding in that flourishing city there was one whose name was Apolonius, a worthy duke, who being but a very young man and even then new come to his possessions, which were very great, levied a mighty band of men at his own proper charges, with whom he served against the Turk during the space of one whole year, in which time, although it were very short, this young duke so behaved himself, as well by prowess and valiance showed with his own hands, as otherwise by his wisdom and liberality used towards his soldiers, that all the world was filled with the fame of this noble duke. When he had thus spent one year's service he caused his trumpet to sound a retreat, and gathering his company together and embarking themselves, he set sail, holding his course towards Constantinople; but, being upon the sea, by the extremity of a tempest which suddenly fell, his fleet was severed, some one way, and some another; but he himself recovered the Isle of Cyprus, where he was worthily received by Pontus, duke and governor of the same isle, with whom he lodged while his ships were new repairing.

This Pontus that was lord and governor of this famous isle was an ancient duke, and had two children, a son and a daughter; his son was named Silvio, of whom hereafter we shall have further occasion to speak, but at this instant he was in the parts of Africa, serving in the wars.

The daughter her name was Silla, whose beauty was so peerless that she had the sovereignty amongst all other dames, as well for her beauty as for the nobleness of her birth. This Silla, having heard of the worthiness of Apolonius, this young duke, who besides his beauty and good graces had a certain natural allurement, that being now in his company in her father's court, she was so strangely attached with the love of Apolonius that there was nothing might content her but his presence and sweet sight; and although she saw no manner of hope to attain to that she most desired, knowing Apolonius to be but a guest, and ready to take the benefit of the next wind and to depart into a strange country, whereby she was bereaved of all possibility ever to see him again, and therefore strived with herself to leave her fondness, but all in vain; it would not be, but, like the fowl which is once limed, the more she striveth, the faster she tieth herself. So Silla was now constrained perforce her will to yield to love, wherefore from time to time she used so great familiarity with him, as her honor might well permit, and fed him with such amorous baits as the modesty of a maid could reasonably afford; which when she perceived did take but small effect, feeling herself outraged with the extremity of her passion, by the only countenance that she bestowed upon

Apolonius, it might have been well perceived that the very eyes pleaded unto him for pity and remorse. But Apolonius, coming but lately from out the field from the chasing of his enemies, and his fury not yet thoroughly dissolved nor purged from his stomach, gave no regard to those amorous enticements, which, by reason of his youth, he had not been acquainted withal. But his mind ran more to hear his pilots bring news of a merry wind, to serve his turn to Constantinople, which in the end came very prosperously; and giving Duke Pontus hearty thanks for his great entertainment, taking his leave of himself and the lady Silla his daughter, departed with his company, and with a happy gale arrived at his desired port. Gentlewomen, according to my promise I will here, for brevity's sake, omit to make repetition of the long and dolorous discourse recorded by Silla for this sudden departure of her Apolonius, knowing you to be as tenderly hearted as Silla herself, whereby you may the better conjecture the fury of her fever.

But Silla, the further that she saw herself bereaved of all hope ever any more to see her beloved Apolonius, so much the more contagious were her passions, and made the greater speed to execute that she had premeditated in her mind, which was this: amongst many servants that did attend upon her, there was one whose name was Pedro, who had a long time waited upon her in her chamber, whereby she was well assured of his fidelity and trust; to that Pedro therefore she bewrayed first the fervency of her love borne to Apolonius, conjuring him in the name of the Goddess of Love herself, and binding him by the duty that a servant ought to have, that tendereth his mistress' safety and good liking, and desiring him with tears trickling down her cheeks that he would give his consent to aid and assist her in that she had determined, which was for that she was fully resolved to go to Constantinople, where she might again take the view of her beloved Apolonius, that he, according to the trust she had reposed in him, would not refuse to give his consent, secretly to convey her from out her father's court according as she would give him direction, and also to make himself partaker of her journey, and to wait upon her, till she had seen the end of her determination.

Pedro, perceiving with what vehemency his lady and mistress had made request unto him, albeit he saw many perils and doubts depending in her pretense, notwithstanding gave his consent to be at her disposition, promising her to further her with his best advice, and to be ready to obey whatsoever she would please to command him. The match being thus agreed upon, and all things prepared in a readiness for their departure, it happened there was a galley of Constantinople ready to depart, which Pedro understanding, came to the captain, desiring him to have passage for himself, and for a poor maid that was his sister, which were bound to Constantinople upon certain urgent affairs; to which request the captain granted, willing him to prepare aboard with all speed, because the wind served him presently to depart.

Pedro now coming to his mistress and telling her how he had handled the matter with the captain, she liking very well of the device, disguising herself into very simple attire, stole away from out her father's court and came with Pedro, whom now she called brother, aboard the galley, where all things being in readiness and the wind serving very well, they launched forth with their oars and set sail. When they were at the sea, the captain of the galley, taking the view of Silla, perceiving her singular beauty he was better pleased in beholding of her face than in taking the height either of the sun or star; and thinking her by the homeliness of her apparel to be but some simple maiden, calling her into his cabin, he began to break with her after the sea fashion, desiring her to use his own cabin for her better ease, and during the time that she remained at the sea she should not want a bed; and then, whispering softly in her ear, he said that for want of a bedfellow he himself would supply that room. Silla, not being acquainted with any such talk, blushed for shame but made him no answer at all. My captain, feeling such bickering within himself, the like whereof he had never endured upon the sea, was like to be taken prisoner aboard his own ship and forced to yield himself captive without any cannon shot; wherefore, to salve all sores, and thinking it the readiest way to speed, he began to break with Silla in the way of marriage, telling her how happy a voyage she had made, to fall into the liking of such a one as himself was, who was able to keep and maintain her like a gentlewoman, and for her sake would likewise take her brother into his fellowship, whom he would by some means prefer in such sort that both of them should have good cause to think themselves thrice happy, she to light of such a husband, and he to light of such a brother. But Silla, nothing pleased with these preferments, desired him to cease his talk, for that she did think herself indeed to be too unworthy such a one as he was, neither was she minded yet to marry, and therefore desired him to fix his fancy upon some that were better worthy than herself was, and that could better like of his courtesy than she could do. The captain, seeing himself thus refused, being in a great chafe, he said as followeth:

"Then, seeing you make so little account of my courtesy proffered to one that is so far unworthy of it, from henceforth I will use the office of my authority; you shall know that I am the captain of this ship and have power to command and dispose of things at my pleasure; and seeing you have so scornfully rejected me to be your loyal husband, I will now take you by force and use you at my will, and so long as it shall please me will keep you for mine own store; there shall be no man able to defend you, nor yet to persuade me from that I have determined." Silla, with these words being stroke into a great fear, did think it now too late to rue her rash attempt, determined rather to die with her own hands than to suffer herself to be abused in such sort; therefore she most humbly desired the captain so much as he could to save her credit, and seeing that she must needs be at his will and disposition, that for that present he would depart and suffer her till night, when in the dark he might take his pleasure without any manner of suspicion to the residue of his company. The captain, thinking now the goal to be more than half won, was contented so far to satisfy her request, and departed out, leaving her alone in his cabin.

Silla, being alone by herself, drew out her knife, ready to strike herself to the heart, and, falling upon her knees, desired God to receive her soul as an acceptable sacrifice for her follies, which she had so willfully committed, craving pardon for her sins; and so forth continuing a long and pitiful reconciliation to God, in the midst whereof there suddenly fell a wonderful storm, the terror whereof was such that there was no man but did think the seas would presently have swallowed them; the billows so suddenly arose with the rage of the wind that they were all glad to fall to heaving out of water, for otherwise their feeble galley had never been able to have brooked the seas. This storm continued all that day and the next night, and they being driven to put romer before the wind [i.e., to let the ship roam where it would] to keep the galley ahead the billow, were driven upon the main shore, where the galley brake all to pieces. There was every man providing to save his own life; some gat upon hatches, boards, and casks, and were driven with the waves to and fro; but the greatest number were drowned, amongst the which Pedro was one; but Silla herself being in the cabin, as you have heard, took hold of a chest that was the captain's, the which by the only providence of God brought her safe to the shore; the which when she had recovered, not knowing what was become of Pedro her man, she deemed that both he and all the rest had been drowned, for that she saw nobody upon the shore but herself; wherefore when she had a while made great lamentations, complaining her mishaps, she began in the end to comfort herself with the hope that she had to see her Apolonius, and found such means that she brake open the chest that brought her to land, wherein she found good store of coin and sundry suits of apparel that were the captain's. And now, to prevent a number of injuries that might be proffered to a woman that was left in her case, she determined to leave her own apparel and to sort herself into some of those suits, that, being taken for a man, she might pass through the country in the better safety; and as she changed her apparel, she thought it likewise convenient to change her name; wherefore, not readily happening of any other, she called herself Silvio, by the name of her own brother, whom you have heard spoken of before.

In this manner she traveled to Constantinople, where she inquired out the palace of the Duke Apolonius; and thinking herself now to be both fit and able to play the serving man, she presented herself to the Duke, craving his service. The Duke, very willing to give succor unto strangers, perceiving him to be a proper smug young man, gave him entertainment. Silla thought herself now more than satisfied for all the casualties that had happened unto her in her journey, that she might at her pleasure take but the view of the Duke

Apolonius, and above the rest of his servants was very diligent and attendant upon him; the which the Duke perceiving, began likewise to grow into good liking with the
diligence of his man, and therefore made him one of his
chamber. Who but Silvio then was most near about him in
helping of him to make him ready in a morning, in the setting of his ruffs, in the keeping of his chamber? Silvio
pleased his master so well that above all the rest of his servants about him he had the greatest credit, and the Duke put
him most in trust.

At this very instant there was remaining in the city a noble
Dame, a widow, whose husband was but lately deceased,
one of the noblest men that were in the parts of Grecia, who
left his lady and wife large possessions and great livings.
This lady's name was called Julina, who besides the abundance of her wealth and the greatness of her revenues had
likewise the sovereignty of all the dames of Constantinople
for her beauty. To this lady Julina, Apolonius became an
earnest suitor; and according to the manner of wooers, besides fair words, sorrowful sighs, and piteous countenances,
there must be sending of loving letters, chains, bracelets,
brooches, rings, tablets, gems, jewels, and presents, I know
not what. So my Duke, who in the time that he remained in
the Isle of Cyprus had no skill at all in the art of love,
although it were more than half proffered unto him, was now
become a scholar in Love's school, and had already learned
his first lesson, that is, to speak pitifully, to look ruthfully, to
promise largely, to serve diligently, and to please carefully;
now he was learning his second lesson, that is, to reward liberally, to give bountifully, to present willingly, and to write
lovingly. Thus Apolonius was so busied in his new study
that I warrant you there was no man that could challenge him
for playing the truant, he followed his profession with so
good a will; and who must be the messenger to carry the
tokens and love letters to the lady Julina but Silvio, his man;
in him the Duke reposed his only confidence, to go between
him and his lady.

Now, gentlewomen, do you think there could have been a
greater torment devised wherewith to afflict the heart of Silla
than herself to be made the instrument to work her own mis-
hap, and to play the attorney in a cause that made so much

against herself? But Silla, altogether desirous to please her master, cared nothing at all to offend herself, followed his business with so good a will as if it had been in her own preferment.

Julina, now having many times taken the gaze of this young youth Silvio, perceiving him to be of such excellent perfect grace, was so entangled with the often sight of this sweet temptation, that she fell into as great a liking with the man as the master was with herself; and on a time, Silvio being sent from his master with a message to the lady Julina, as he began very earnestly to solicit in his master's behalf, Julina, interrupting him in his tale, said: "Silvio, it is enough that you have said for your master; from henceforth either speak for yourself or say nothing at all." Silla, abashed to hear these words, began in her mind to accuse the blindness of love, that Julina, neglecting the good will of so noble a duke, would prefer her love unto such a one as nature itself had denied to recompense her liking.

And now, for a time leaving matters depending as you have heard, it fell out that the right Silvio indeed (whom you have heard spoken of before, the brother of Silla) was come to his father's court into the Isle of Cyprus; where, understanding that his sister was departed in manner as you have heard, conjectured that the very occasion did proceed of some liking had between Pedro her man (that was missing with her) and herself; but Silvio, who loved his sister as dearly as his own life, and the rather for that she was his natural sister, both by father and mother, so the one of them was so like the other in countenance and favor that there was no man able to discern the one from the other by their faces, saving by their apparel, the one being a man, the other a woman.

Silvio therefore vowed to his father not only to seek out his sister Silla but also to revenge the villain which he conceived in Pedro, for the carrying away of his sister; and thus departing, having traveled through many cities and towns without hearing any manner of news of those he went to seek for, at the last he arrived at Constantinople; where, as he was walking in an evening for his own recreation, on a pleasant green yard without the walls of the city, he fortuned to meet with the lady Julina, who likewise had been abroad to take the air; and as she suddenly cast her eyes upon Silvio, thinking him to be her old acquaintance, by reason they were so like one another, as you have heard before, said unto him, "Sir Silvio, if your haste be not the greater, I pray you let me have a little talk with you, seeing I have so luckily met you in this place."

Silvio, wondering to hear himself so rightly named, being but a stranger, not of above two days' continuance in the city, very courteously came towards her, desirous to hear what she would say.

Julina, commanding her train something to stand back, said as followeth: "Seeing my good will and friendly love hath been the only cause to make me so prodigal to offer that I see is so lightly rejected, it maketh me to think that men be of this condition, rather to desire those things which they cannot come by than to esteem or value of that which both largely and liberally is offered unto them; but if the liberality of my proffer hath made to seem less the value of the thing that I meant to present, it is but in your own conceit, considering how many noblemen there hath been here before, and be yet at this present, which hath both served, sued, and most humbly entreated to attain to that which to you of myself I have freely offered, and I perceive is despised, or at the least very lightly regarded."

Silvio, wondering at these words, but more amazed that she could so rightly call him by his name, could not tell what to make of her speeches, assuring himself that she was deceived and did mistake him, did think notwithstanding it had been a point of great simplicity if he should forsake that which fortune had so favorably proffered unto him, perceiving by her train that she was some lady of great honor, and viewing the perfection of her beauty and the excellency of her grace and countenance, did think it unpossible that she should be despised, and therefore answered thus:

"Madam, if before this time I have seemed to forget myself in neglecting your courtesy, which so liberally you have meant unto me, please it you to pardon what is past, and from this day forwards Silvio remaineth ready prest [i.e., eager] to make such reasonable amends as his ability may any ways permit, or as it shall please you to command."

Julina, the gladdest woman that might be to hear this joyful news, said: "Then, my Silvio, see you fail not tomorrow at night to sup with me at my own house, where I will discourse farther with you what amends you shall make me." To which request Silvio gave his glad consent, and thus they departed well pleased. And as Julina did think the time very long till she had reaped the fruit of her desire, so Silvio, he wished for harvest before corn could grow, thinking the time as long till he saw how matters would fall out; but not knowing what lady she might be, he presently (before Julina was out of sight) demanded of one that was walking by what she was and how she was called; who satisfied Silvio in every point, and also in what part of the town her house did stand, whereby he might inquire it out.

Silvio, thus departing to his lodging, passed the night with very unquiet sleeps, and the next morning his mind ran so much of his supper that he never cared, neither for his breakfast nor dinner; and the day to his seeming passed away so slowly that he had thought the stately steeds had been tired that draw the chariot of the sun, or else some other Josua had commanded them again to stand, and wished that Phaeton had been there with a whip.

Julina, on the other side, she had thought the clocksetter had played the knave, the day came no faster forwards; but six o'clock being once stroken, recovered comfort to both parties; and Silvio, hastening himself to the palace of Julina, where by her he was friendly welcomed, and a sumptuous supper being made ready, furnished with sundry sorts of delicate dishes, they sat them down, passing the suppertime with amorous looks, loving countenances, and secret glances conveyed from the one to the other, which did better satisfy them than the feeding of their dainty dishes.

Suppertime being thus spent, Julina did think it very unfitly if she should turn Silvio to go seek his lodging in an evening, desired him therefore that he would take a bed in her house for that night; and, bringing him up into a fair chamber that was very richly furnished, she found such means that when all the rest of her household servants were abed and quiet, she came herself to bear Silvio company, where concluding upon conditions that were in question between them, they passed the night with such joy and contentation as might in that convenient time be wished for; but only that Julina, feeding too much of some one dish above the rest, received a surfeit, whereof she could not be cured in forty weeks after, a natural inclination in all women which are subject to longing and want the reason to use a moderation in their diet. But the morning approaching, Julina took her leave and conveyed herself into her own chamber; and when it was fair daylight, Silvio, making himself ready, departed likewise about his affairs in the town, debating with himself how things had happened, being well assured that Julina had mistaken him; and, therefore, for fear of further evils, determined to come no more there, but took his journey towards other places in the parts of Grecia, to see if he could learn any tidings of his sister Silla.

The Duke Apolonius, having made a long suit and never a whit the nearer of his purpose, came to Julina to crave her direct answer, either to accept of him and of such conditions as he proffered unto her, or else to give him his last farewell.

Julina, as you have heard, had taken an earnest penny of another, whom she had thought had been Silvio, the Duke's man, was at a controversy in herself, what she might do: one while she thought, seeing her occasion served so fit, to crave the Duke's good will for the marrying of his man; then again, she could not tell what displeasure the Duke would conceive, in that she should seem to prefer his man before himself, did think it best therefore to conceal the matter till she might speak with Silvio, to use his opinion how these matters should be handled; and hereupon resolving herself, desiring the Duke to pardon her speeches, said as followeth:

"Sir Duke, for that from this time forwards I am no longer of myself, having given my full power and authority over to another, whose wife I now remain by faithful vow and promise; and albeit I know the world will wonder when they shall understand the fondness of my choice, yet I trust you yourself will nothing dislike with me, sith I have meant no other thing than the satisfying of mine own contentation and liking."

The Duke, hearing these words, answered: "Madam, I must then content myself, although against my will, having the law in your own hands, to like of whom you list and to make choice where it pleaseth you."

Julina, giving the Duke great thanks, that would content himself with such patience, desired him likewise to give his free consent and good will to the party whom she had chosen to be her husband.

"Nay, surely, Madam," quoth the Duke, "I will never give my consent that any other man shall enjoy you than myself; I have made too great account of you than so lightly to pass you away with my good will: but seeing it lieth not in me to let you, having (as you say) made your own choice, so from henceforwards I leave you to your own liking, always willing you well, and thus will take my leave."

The Duke departed towards his own house, very sorrowful that Julina had thus served him; but in the mean space that the Duke had remained in the house of Juliana, some of his servants fell into talk and conference with the servants of Julina; where, debating between them of the likelihood of the marriage between the Duke and the lady, one of the servants of Julina said that he never saw his lady and mistress use so good countenance to the Duke himself as she had done to Silvio, his man, and began to report with what familiarity and courtesy she had received him, feasted him, and lodged him, and that in his opinion, Silvio was like to speed before the Duke or any other that were suitors.

This tale was quickly brought to the Duke himself, who, making better inquiry into the matter, found it to be true that was reported; and better considering of the words which Julina had used towards himself was very well assured that it could be no other than his own man that had thrust his nose so far out of joint; wherefore, without any further respect, caused him to be thrust into a dungeon, where he was kept prisoner, in a very pitiful plight.

Poor Silvio, having got intelligence by some of his fellows what was the cause that the Duke, his master, did bear such displeasure unto him, devised all the means he could, as well by mediation by his fellows, as otherwise by petitions and supplications to the Duke that he would suspend his judgement till perfect proof were had in the matter, and then if any manner of thing did fall out against him, whereby the Duke had cause to take any grief, he would confess himself worthy not only of imprisonment but also of most vile and shameful death. With these petitions he daily plied the

Duke, but all in vain, for the Duke thought he had made so
good proof that he was thoroughly confirmed in his opinion
against his man.

But the lady Julina, wondering what made Silvio that he
was so slack in his visitation, and why he absented himself
so long from her presence, began to think that all was not
well; but in the end, perceiving no decoction of her former
surfeit, received as you have heard, and finding in herself an
unwonted swelling in her belly, assuring herself to be with
child, fearing to become quite bankrout of her honor, did
think it more than time to seek out a father, and made such
secret search and diligent inquiry that she learned the truth
how Silvio was kept in prison by the Duke, his master; and
minding to find a present remedy as well for the love she
bare to Silvio as for the maintenance of her credit and esti-
mation, she speedily hasted to the palace of the Duke, to
whom she said as followeth:

"Sir Duke, it may be that you will think my coming to
your house in this sort doth something pass the limits of
modesty, the which I protest before God, proceedeth of this
desire that the world should know how justly I seek means
to maintain my honor; but to the end I seem not tedious with
prolixity of words, not to use other than direct circumstances, know, sir, that the love I bear to my only beloved
Silvio, whom I do esteem more than all the jewels in the
world, whose personage I regard more than my own life, is
the only cause of my attempted journey, beseeching you that
all the whole displeasure, which I understand you have conceived against him, may be imputed unto my charge, and
that it would please you lovingly to deal with him whom of
myself I have chosen, rather for the satisfaction of mine
honest liking than for the vain preeminences or honorable
dignities looked after by ambitious minds."

The Duke, having heard this discourse, caused Silvio
presently to be sent for and to be brought before him, to
whom he said: "Had it not been sufficient for thee, when I
had reposed myself in thy fidelity and the trustiness of thy
service, that thou shouldst so traitorously deal with me, but
since that time hast not spared still to abuse me with so many
forgeries and perjured protestations, not only hateful unto
me, whose simplicity thou thinkest to be such that by the plot

of thy pleasant tongue thou wouldst make me believe a manifest untruth; but most abominable be thy doings in the presence and sight of God, that hast not spared to blaspheme His holy name, by calling Him to be a witness to maintain thy leasings, and so detestably wouldst thou forswear thyself in a matter that is so openly known."

Poor Silvio, whose innocence was such that he might lawfully swear, seeing Julina to be there in place, answered thus:

"Most noble Duke, well understanding your conceived grief, most humbly I beseech you patiently to hear my excuse, not minding thereby to aggravate or heap up your wrath and displeasure, protesting before God that there is nothing in the world which I regard so much or do esteem so dear as your good grace and favor; but desirous that your Grace should know my innocency, and to clear myself of such impositions wherewith I know I am wrongfully accused, which as I understand should be in the practicing of the lady Julina, who standeth there in place, whose acquittance for my better discharge now I most humbly crave, protesting before the almighty God that neither in thought, word, nor deed I have not otherwise used myself than according to the bond and duty of a servant, that is both willing and desirous to further his master's suits, which I have otherwise said than that is true, you, Madam Julina, who can very well decide the depths of all this doubt, I most humbly beseech you to certify a truth, if I have in anything missaid or have otherwise spoken than is right and just."

Julina, having heard this discourse which Silvio had made, perceiving that he stood in great awe of the Duke's displeasure, answered thus: "Think not, my Silvio, that my coming hither is to accuse you of any misdemeanor towards your master, so I do not deny but in all such embassages wherein towards me you have been employed, you have used the office of a faithful and trusty messenger; neither am I ashamed to confess that the first day that mine eyes did behold the singular behavior, the notable courtesy, and other innumerable gifts wherewith my Silvio is endued; but that beyond all measure my heart was so inflamed, that impossible it was for me to quench the fervent love or extinguish the least part of my conceived torment before I had bewrayed the same unto him, and of my own motion craved his promised faith and loyalty of marriage; and now is the time to manifest the same unto the world, which hath been done before God and between ourselves; knowing that it is not needful to keep secret that which is neither evil done nor hurtful to any person, therefore (as I said before) Silvio is my husband by plighted faith, whom I hope to obtain without offense or displeasure of anyone, trusting that there is no man that will so far forget himself as to restrain that which God hath left at liberty of every wight, or that will seek by cruelty to force ladies to marry otherwise than according to their own liking. Fear not then, my Silvio, to keep your faith and promise which you have made unto me; and as for the rest, I doubt not things will so fall out as you shall have no manner of cause to complain."

Silvio, amazed to hear these words, for that Julina by her speech seemed to confirm that which he most of all desired to be quit of, said: "Who would have thought that a lady of so great honor and reputation would herself be the ambassador of a thing so prejudicial and uncomely for her estate! What plighted promises be these which be spoken of altogether ignorant unto me, which if it be otherwise than I have said, you sacred gods consume me straight with flashing flames of fire. But what words might I use to give credit to the truth and innocency of my cause? Ah, Madam Julina, I desire no other testimony than your own honesty and virtue, thinking that you will not so much blemish the brightness of your honor, knowing that a woman is, or should be, the image of courtesy, continency, and shamefastness, from the which so soon as she stoopeth and leaveth the office of her duty and modesty, besides the degradation of her honor, she thrusteth herself into the pit of perpetual infamy. And as I cannot think you would so far forget yourself, by the refusal of a noble duke, to dim the light of your renown and glory, which hitherto you have maintained amongst the best and noblest ladies, by such a one as I know myself to be, too far unworthy your degree and calling; so most humbly I beseech you to confess a truth, whereto tendeth those vows and promises you speak of, which speeches be so obscure unto me as I know not for my life how I might understand them."

Julina, something nipped with these speeches, said: "And what is the matter that now you make so little account of your Julina, that being my husband indeed, have the face to deny me, to whom thou art contracted by so many solemn oaths? What! Art thou ashamed to have me to thy wife? How much oughtest thou rather to be ashamed to break thy promised faith and to have despised the holy and dreadful name of God, but that time constraineth me to lay open that which shame rather willeth I should dissemble and keep secret. Behold me then here, Silvio, whom thou hast gotten with child; who, if thou be of such honesty, as I trust for all this I shall find, then the thing is done without prejudice or any hurt to my conscience, considering that by the professed faith thou didst account me for thy wife, and I received thee for my spouse and loyal husband, swearing by the almighty God that no other than you have made the conquest and triumph of my chastity, whereof I crave no other witness than yourself and mine own conscience."

I pray you, gentlewomen, was not this a foul oversight of Julina, that would so precisely swear so great an oath, that she was gotten with child by one that was altogether unfurnished with implements for such a turn. For God's love take heed, and let this be an example to you when you be with child, how you swear who is the father before you have had good proof and knowledge of the party; for men be so subtle and full of sleight that God knoweth a woman may quickly be deceived.

But now to return to our Silvio, who, hearing an oath sworn so divinely that he had gotten a woman with child, was like to believe that it had been true in very deed; but remembering his own impediment, thought it impossible that he should commit such an act, and therefore, half in a chafe, he said, "What law is able to restrain the foolish indiscretion of a woman that yieldeth herself to her own desires; what shame is able to bridle or withdraw her from her mind and madness, or with what snaffle is it possible to hold her back from the execution of her filthiness? But what abomination is this, that a lady of such a house should so forget the greatness of her estate, the alliance whereof she is descended, the nobility of her deceased husband, and maketh no conscience to shame and slander herself with such a one as I am, being so far unfit and unseemly for her degree; but how horrible it is to hear the name of God so defaced that we

make no more account, but for the maintenance of our mischiefs we fear no whit at all to forswear His holy name, as
though He were not in all His dealings most righteous, true,
and just and will not only lay open our leasings to the world
but will likewise punish the same with sharp and bitter
scourges."

Julina, not able to endure him to proceed any further in his
sermon, was already surprised with a vehement grief, began
bitterly to cry out, uttering these speeches following:

"Alas, is it possible that the sovereign justice of God can
abide a mischief so great and cursed? Why may I not now
suffer death rather than the infamy which I see to wander
before mine eyes? O happy and more than right happy had I
been if inconstant fortune had not devised this treason
wherein I am surprised and caught! Am I thus become to be
entangled with snares, and in the hands of him, who,
enjoying the spoils of my honor, will openly deprive me of
my fame by making me a common fable to all posterity in
time to come? Ah, traitor and discourteous wretch, is this the
recompense of the honest and firm amity which I have borne
thee? Wherein have I deserved this discourtesy? By loving
thee more than thou art able to deserve? Is it I, arrant thief,
is it I upon whom thou thinkest to work thy mischiefs? Dost
thou think me no better worth, but that thou mayest prodigally waste my honor at thy pleasure? Didst thou dare to
adventure upon me, having thy conscience wounded with so
deadly a treason? Ah, unhappy, and above all other most
unhappy, that have so charely preserved mine honor, and
now am made a prey to satisfy a young man's lust that hath
coveted nothing but the spoil of my chastity and good
name."

Herewithal the tears so gushed down her cheeks that she
was not able to open her mouth to use any further speech.

The Duke, who stood by all this while and heard this
whole discourse, was wonderfully moved with compassion
towards Julina, knowing that from her infancy she had ever
so honorably used herself that there was no man able to
detect her of any misdemeanor otherwise than beseemed a
lady of her estate; wherefore, being fully resolved that
Silvio, his man, had committed this villainy against her, in a
great fury drawing his rapier, he said unto Silvio:

"How canst thou, arrant thief, show thyself so cruel and careless to such as do thee honor? Hast thou so little regard of such a noble lady, as humbleth herself to such a villain as thou art, who, without any respect either of her renown or noble estate, canst be content to seek the wrack and utter ruin of her honor? But frame thyself to make such satisfaction as she requireth, although I know, unworthy wretch, that thou art not able to make her the least part of amends, or I swear by God that thou shalt not escape the death which I will minister to thee with mine own hands, and therefore advise thee well what thou doest."

Silvio, having heard this sharp sentence, fell down on his knees before the Duke, craving for mercy, desiring that he might be suffered to speak with the lady Julina apart, promising to satisfy her according to her own contentation.

"Well," quoth the Duke, "I take thy word; and therewithal I advise thee that thou perform thy promise, or otherwise I protest before God I will make thee such an example to the world that all traitors shall tremble for fear, how they do seek the dishonoring of ladies."

But now Julina had conceived so great grief against Silvio that there was much ado to persuade her to talk with him; but remembering her own case, desirous to hear what excuse he could make, in the end she agreed; and being brought into a place severally by themselves, Silvio began with a piteous voice to say as followeth:

"I know not, madam, of whom I might make complaint, whether of you or of myself, or rather of fortune, which hath conducted and brought us both into so great adversity. I see that you receive great wrong, and I am condemned against all right, you in peril to abide the bruit of spiteful tongues, and I in danger to lose the thing that I most desire; and although I could allege many reasons to prove my sayings true, yet I refer myself to the experience and bounty of your mind." And herewithal loosing his garments down to his stomach, showed Julina his breasts and pretty teats, surmounting far the whiteness of snow itself, saying: "Lo, madam, behold here the party whom you have challenged to be the father of your child; see, I am a woman, the daughter of a noble duke, who only for the love of him, whom you so lightly have shaken off, have forsaken my father, abandoned my country, and, in manner as you see, am become a serving man, satisfying myself but with the only sight of my Apolonius. And now, madam, if my passion were not vehement and my torments without comparison, I would wish that my feigned griefs might be laughed to scorn and my dissembled pains to be rewarded with flouts. But my love being pure, my travail continual, and my griefs endless, I trust, madam, you will not only excuse me of crime, but also pity my distress, the which I protest I would still have kept secret, if my fortune would so have permitted."

Julina did now think herself to be in a worse case than ever she was before, for now she knew not whom to challenge to be the father of her child; wherefore, when she had told the Duke the very certainty of the discourse which Silvio had made unto her, she departed to her own house with such grief and sorrow that she purposed never to come out of her own doors again alive, to be a wonder and mocking stock to the world.

But the Duke, more amazed to hear this strange discourse of Silvio, came unto him; whom when he had viewed with better consideration, perceived indeed that it was Silla, the daughter of Duke Pontus; and embracing her in his arms he said:

"O the branch of all virtue and the flower of courtesy itself, pardon me, I beseech you, of all such discourtesies as I have ignorantly committed towards you: desiring you that without farther memory of ancient griefs, you will accept of me, who is more joyful and better contented with your presence, than if the whole world were at my commandment. Where hath there ever been found such liberality in a lover, which, having been trained up and nourished amongst the delicacies and banquets of the court, accompanied with trains of many fair and noble ladies living in pleasure, and in the midst of delights, would so prodigally adventure yourself, neither fearing mishaps, nor misliking to take such pains, as I know you have not been accustomed unto? O liberality never heard of before! O fact that can never be sufficiently rewarded! O true love most pure and unfeigned!" Herewithal sending for the most artificial workmen, he provided for her sundry suits of sumptuous apparel, and the marriage day appointed, which was celebrated with great triumph through the whole city of Constantinople, everyone praising the nobleness of the Duke, but so many as did behold the excellent beauty of Silla gave her the praise above all the rest of the ladies in the troop.

The matter seemed so wonderful and strange that the bruit was spread throughout all the parts of Grecia, in so much that it came to the hearing of Silvio, who, as you have heard, remained in those parts to inquire of his sister; he being the gladdest man in the world, hasted to Constantinople where, coming to his sister, he was joyfully received, and most lovingly welcomed, and entertained of the Duke, his brother-in-law. After he had remained there two or three days, the Duke revealed unto Silvio the whole discourse how it happened between his sister and the Lady Julina, and how his sister was challenged for getting a woman with child. Silvio, blushing with these words, was stricken with great remorse to make Julina amends; understanding her to be a noble lady, and was left defamed to the world through his default, he therefore bewrayed the whole circumstance to the Duke; whereof the Duke, being very joyful, immediately repaired with Silvio to the house of Julina, whom they found in her chamber, in great lamentation and mourning. To whom the Duke said, "Take courage, madam, for behold here a gentleman that will not stick both to father your child and to take you for his wife; no inferior person, but the son and heir of a noble duke, worthy of your estate and dignity."

Julina, seeing Silvio in place, did know very well that he was the father of her child, and was so ravished with joy that she knew not whether she were awake, or in some dream. Silvio, embracing her in his arms, craving forgiveness of all that was past, concluded with her the marriage day, which was presently accomplished with great joy and contentation to all parties: and thus Silvio, having attained a noble wife, and Silla, his sister, her desired husband, they passed the residue of their days with such delight as those that have accomplished the perfection of their felicities.

Commentaries

SAMUEL JOHNSON

From The Plays of William Shakespeare

"Twelfth Night"

This play is in the graver part elegant and easy, and in some of the lighter scenes exquisitely humorous. Aguecheek is drawn with great propriety, but his character is, in a great measure, that of natural fatuity, and is therefore not the proper prey of a satirist. The soliloquy of Malvolio is truly comic; he is betrayed to ridicule merely by his pride. The marriage of Olivia, and the succeeding perplexity, though well enough contrived to divert on the stage, wants credibility, and fails to produce the proper instruction required in the drama, as it exhibits no just picture of life.

[On Shakespeare's Comedy]

Shakespeare engaged in dramatic poetry with the world open before him; the rules of the ancients were yet known to few; the public judgment was unformed; he had no example of such fame as might force him upon imitation, nor critics of such authority as might restrain his extravagance; he therefore indulged his natural disposition; and his disposition as

From *The Plays of William Shakespeare* (1765). Both selections are from Johnson's edition of Shakespeare's plays, the first from the notes on *Twelfth Night*, the second from the preface to the edition.

Rymer[1] has remarked, led him to comedy. In tragedy he often writes, with great appearance of toil and study, what is written at last with little felicity; but in his comic scenes he seems to produce, without labor, what no labor can improve. In tragedy he is always struggling after some occasion to be comic; but in comedy he seems to repose, or to luxuriate, as in a mode of thinking congenial to his nature. In his tragic scenes there is always something wanting, but his comedy often surpasses expectation or desire. His comedy pleases by the thoughts and the language, and his tragedy for the greater part by incident and action. His tragedy seems to be skill, his comedy to be instinct.

The force of his comic scenes has suffered little diminution from the changes made by a century and a half, in manners or in words. As his personages act upon principles arising from genuine passion, very little modified by particular forms, their pleasures and vexations are communicable to all times and to all places; they are natural, and therefore durable. The adventitious peculiarities of personal habits are only superficial dyes, bright and pleasing for a little while, yet soon fading to a dim tinct, without any remains of former luster; but the discriminations of true passion are the colors of nature; they pervade the whole mass and can only perish with the body that exhibits them. The accidental compositions of heterogeneous modes are dissolved by the chance which combined them; but the uniform simplicity of primitive qualities neither admits increase nor suffers decay. The sand heaped by one flood is scattered by another, but the rock always continues in its place. The stream of time, which is continually washing the dissoluble fabrics of other poets, passes without injury by the adamant of Shakespeare.

---

[1]Thomas Rymer (1641–1713), a critic and scholar of strongly neo-classical bent, whose *Short View of Tragedy* (1692) contains a notorious attack on *Othello*.

WILLIAM HAZLITT

From Characters of Shakespear's Plays

This is justly considered as one of the most delightful of
Shakespear's comedies. It is full of sweetness and pleasantry.
It is perhaps too good-natured for comedy. It has little satire,
and no spleen. It aims at the ludicrous rather than the ridiculous. It makes us laugh at the follies of mankind, not despise
them, and still less bear any ill will towards them. Shakespear's comic genius resembles the bee, rather in its power of
extracting sweets from weeds or poisons than in leaving a
sting behind it. He gives the most amusing exaggeration of
the prevailing foibles of his characters, but in a way that they
themselves, instead of being offended at, would almost join
in to humor; he rather contrives opportunities for them to
show themselves off in the happiest lights than renders them
contemptible in the perverse construction of the wit or malice
of others.—There is a certain stage of society in which people
become conscious of their peculiarities and absurdities, affect
to disguise what they are, and set up pretensions to what they
are not. This gives rise to a corresponding style of comedy,
the object of which is to detect the disguises of self-love, and
to make reprisals on these preposterous assumptions of vanity
by marking the contrast between the real and the affected
character as severely as possible, and denying to those who
would impose on us for what they are not even the merit
which they have. This is the comedy of artificial life, of wit
and satire, such as we see it in Congreve, Wycherley, Van-
brugh, etc. To this succeeds a state of society from which

From William Hazlitt, *Characters of Shakespear's Plays*, 2nd ed.
(London: Taylor & Hessey, 1818.)

the same sort of affectation and pretense are banished by a greater knowledge of the world or by their successful exposure on the stage; and which by neutralizing the materials of comic character, both natural and artificial, leaves no comedy at all—but *the sentimental.* Such is our modern comedy. There is a period in the progress of manners anterior to both these, in which the foibles and follies of individuals are of nature's planting, not the growth of art or study; in which they are therefore unconscious of them themselves, or care not who knows them, if they can but have their whim out; and in which, as there is no attempt at imposition, the spectators rather receive pleasure from humoring the inclinations of the persons they laugh at than wish to give them pain by exposing their absurdity. This may be called the comedy of nature, and it is the comedy which we generally find in Shakespear.— Whether the analysis here given be just or not, the spirit of his comedies is evidently quite distinct from that of the authors above mentioned, as it is in its essence the same with that of Cervantes, and also very frequently of Molière, though he was more systematic in his extravagance than Shakespear. Shakespear's comedy is of a pastoral and poetical cast. Folly is indigenous to the soil, and shoots out with native, happy, unchecked luxuriance. Absurdity has every encouragement afforded it; and nonsense has room to flourish in. Nothing is stunted by the churlish, icy hand of indifference or severity. The poet runs riot in a conceit, and idolizes a quibble. His whole object is to turn the meanest or rudest objects to a pleasurable account. The relish which he has of a pun, or of the quaint humor of a low character, does not interfere with the delight with which he describes a beautiful image, or the most refined love. The clown's forced jests do not spoil the sweetness of the character of Viola; the same house is big enough to hold Malvolio, the Countess, Maria, Sir Toby, and Sir Andrew Aguecheek. For instance, nothing can fall much lower than this last character in intellect or morals: yet how are his weaknesses nursed and dandled by Sir Toby into something "high fantastical" when on Sir Andrew's commendation of himself for dancing and fencing, Sir Toby answers—"Wherefore are these things hid? Wherefore have these gifts a curtain before them? Are they like to take dust like Mistress Moll's picture? Why dost thou not go to church in a galliard, and come home in a coranto? My very walk should be a jig! I would not so much as make water but in a cinque-pace. What dost thou mean? Is this a world to hide virtues in? I did think by the excellent constitution of thy leg, it was framed under the star of a galliard!" How Sir Toby, Sir Andrew, and the Clown afterwards *chirp over their cups,* how they "rouse the night owl in a catch, able to draw three souls out of one weaver!" What can be better than Sir Toby's unanswerable answer to Malvolio, "Dost thou think, because thou art virtuous, there shall be no more cakes and ale?"—In a word, the best turn is given to everything, instead of the worst. There is a constant infusion of the romantic and enthusiastic, in proportion as the characters are natural and sincere: whereas, in the more artificial style of comedy, everything gives way to ridicule and indifference, there being nothing left but affectation on one side, and incredulity on the other.—Much as we like Shakespear's comedies, we cannot agree with Dr. Johnson that they are better than his tragedies; nor do we like them half so well. If his inclination to comedy sometimes led him to trifle with the seriousness of tragedy, the poetical and impassioned passages are the best parts of his comedies. The great and secret charm of *Twelfth Night* is the character of Viola. Much as we like catches and cakes and ale, there is something that we like better. We have a friendship for Sir Toby; we patronize Sir Andrew; we have an understanding with the Clown, a sneaking kindness for Maria and her rogueries; we feel a regard for Malvolio, and sympathize with his gravity, his smiles, his cross garters, his yellow stockings, and imprisonment in the stocks. But there is something that excites in us a stronger feeling than all this—it is Viola's confession of her love.

CHARLES LAMB

[On the Character of Malvolio]

Malvolio is not essentially ludicrous. He becomes comic but by accident. He is cold, austere, repelling; but dignified, consistent, and, for what appears, rather of an overstretched morality. Maria describes him as a sort of Puritan; and he might have worn his gold chain with honor in one of our old Roundhead families, in the service of a Lambert, or a Lady Fairfax. But his morality and his manners are misplaced in Illyria. He is opposed to the proper *levities* of the piece, and falls in the unequal contest. Still his pride, or his gravity, (call it which you will) is inherent, and native to the man, not mock or affected, which latter only are the fit objects to excite laughter. His quality is at the best unlovely, but neither buffoon nor contemptible. His bearing is lofty, a little above his station, but probably not much above his deserts. We see no reason why he should not have been brave, honorable, accomplished. His careless committal of the ring to the ground (which he was commissioned to restore to Cesario) bespeaks a generosity of birth and feeling. His dialect on all occasions is that of a gentleman and a man of education. We must not confound him with the eternal old, low steward of comedy. He is master of the household to a great Princess, a dignity probably conferred upon him for other respects than age or length of service. Olivia, at the first indication of his supposed madness, declares that she "would not have him miscarry for half of her dowry" (3.4.65–6). Does this look as

From "On Some of the Old Actors" in *Elia. Essays which have appeared under the Signature in The London Magazine* by Charles Lamb. (London: Taylor & Hessey, 1823.)

if the character was meant to appear little or insignificant? Once, indeed, she accuses him to his face—of what?—of being "sick of self-love"—but with a gentleness and considerateness which could not have been, if she had not thought that this particular infirmity shaded some virtues. His rebuke to the knight, and his sottish revelers, is sensible and spirited; and when we take into consideration the unprotected condition of his mistress, and the strict regard with which her state of real or dissembled mourning would draw the eyes of the world upon her house affairs, Malvolio might feel the honor of the family in some sort in his keeping; as it appears not that Olivia had any more brothers, or kinsmen, to look to it—for Sir Toby had dropped all such nice respects at the buttery hatch. That Malvolio was meant to be represented as possessing estimable qualities, the expression of the Duke, in his anxiety to have him reconciled, almost infers. "Pursue him, and entreat him to a peace." Even in his abused state of chains and darkness, a sort of greatness seems never to desert him. He argues highly and well with the supposed Sir Topas, and philosophizes gallantly upon his straw. There must have been some shadow of worth about the man; he must have been something more than a mere vapor—a thing of straw, or Jack in office—before Fabian and Maria could have ventured sending him upon a courting errand to Olivia. There was some consonancy (as he would say) in the undertaking, or the jest would have been too bold even for that house of misrule.

Bensley,[1] accordingly, threw over the part an air of Spanish loftiness. He looked, spake, and moved like an old Castilian. He was starch, spruce, opinionated, but his superstructure of pride seemed bottom upon a sense of worth. There was something in it beyond the coxcomb. It was big and swelling, but you could not be sure that it was hollow. You might wish to see it taken down, but you felt that it was upon an elevation. He was magnificent from the outset; but when the decent sobrieties of the character began to give way, and the poison of self-love, in his conceit of the Countess's affection, gradually to work, you would have thought that the hero of La Mancha in person stood before

[1]Robert Bensley (1738?–1817?), a noted actor who retired in 1796.

you. How he went smiling to himself! With what ineffable carelessness would he twirl his gold chain! What a dream it was! You were infected with the illusion and did not wish that it should be removed! You had no room for laughter! If an unseasonable reflection of morality obtruded itself, it was a deep sense of the pitiable infirmity of man's nature, that can lay him open to such frenzies—but in truth you rather admired than pitied the lunacy while it lasted—you felt that an hour of such mistake was worth an age with the eyes open. Who would not wish to live but a day in the conceit of such a lady's love as Olivia? Why, the Duke would have given his principality but for a quarter of a minute, sleeping or waking, to have been so deluded. The man seemed to tread upon air, to taste manna, to walk with his head in the clouds, to mate Hyperion. O! shake not the castles of his pride—endure yet for a season, bright moments of confidence—"stand still ye watches of the element," that Malvolio may be still in fancy fair Olivia's lord—but fate and retribution say no—I hear the mischievous titter of Maria—the witty taunts of Sir Toby—the still more insupportable triumph of the foolish knight—the counterfeit Sir Topas is unmasked—and "thus the whirligig of time," as the true clown hath it, "brings in his revenges." I confess that I never saw the catastrophe of this character, while Bensley played it, without a kind of tragic interest.

HARLEY GRANVILLE-BARKER

[Director's] Preface

This play is classed, as to the period of its writing, with *Much Ado About Nothing, As You Like It*, and *Henry V*. But however close in date, in spirit I am very sure it is far from them. I confess to liking those other three as little as any plays he ever wrote. I find them, so stodgily good, even a little (dare one say it?) vulgar, the work of a successful man who is caring most for success. I can imagine the lovers of his work losing hope in the Shakespeare of that year or two. He was thirty-five and the first impulse of his art had spent itself. He was popular. There was welcome enough, we may be sure, for as many *Much Ado*'s and *As You Like It*'s and jingo history pageants as he'd chose to manufacture. It was a turning point and he might have remained a popular dramatist. But from some rebirth in him that mediocre satisfaction was foregone, and, to our profit at least, came *Hamlet, Macbeth, Lear*, and the rest. *Hamlet*, perhaps, was popular, though Burbage may have claimed a just share in making it so. But I doubt if the great heart of the public would beat any more constantly towards the rarer tragedies in that century and society than it will in this. To the average man or playgoer three hundred or indeed three thousand years are as a day. While we have

From *Twelfth Night. An Acting Edition. With a Producer's Preface by Granville-Barker* (London: William Heinemann, 1912). This preface and two companion pieces written for Heinemann's acting editions of *The Winter's Tale* (1912) and *A Midsummer Night's Dream* were Granville-Barker's first attempts in the form that he later made his own. They were written in conjunction with, and no doubt reflect, his famous Savoy productions of these plays. See C. B. Purdom, *Harley Granville-Barker* (1955), pp. 150–51. Reprinted by permission of the trustees of the Granville-Barker estate.

Shakespeare's own comment even on that "supporter to a state," Polonius (true type of the official mind. And was he not indeed Lord Chamberlain?), that where art is concerned "He's for a jig, or a tale of bawdry, or he sleeps."

Twelfth Night is, to me, the last play of Shakespeare's happy carelessness in the putting together. It is akin to the *Two Gentlemen of Verona* (compare Viola and Julia), it echoes a little to the same tune as the sweeter parts of the *Merchant of Venice*, and its comic spirit is the spirit of the Falstaff scenes of *Henry IV*, that are to my taste the truest comedy he wrote.

There is much to show that the play was designed for performance upon a bare platform stage without traverses or inner rooms or the like. It has the virtues of this method, swiftness and cleanness of writing and simple directness of arrangement even where the plot is least simple. It takes full advantage of the method's convenience. The scene changes constantly from anywhere suitable to anywhere else that is equally so. The time of the play's action is any time that suits the author as he goes along. Scenery is an inconvenience. I am pretty sure that Shakespeare's performance went through without a break. Certainly its conventional arrangement into five acts for the printing of the Folio is neither by Shakespeare's nor any other sensitive hand; it is shockingly bad. If one must have intervals (as the discomforts of most theaters demand), I think the play falls as easily into the three divisions I have marked as any [i.e., intervals after 2.3 and 4.1].

I believe the play was written with a special cast in mind. Who was Shakespeare's clown, a sweet-voiced singer and something much more than a comic actor? He wrote Feste for him, and later the Fool in *Lear*. At least, I can conceive no dramatist risking the writing of such parts unless he knew he had a man to play them. And why a diminutive Maria— Penthesilea, the youngest wren of nine—unless it was only that the actor of the part was to be such a very small boy? I have cudgeled my brains to discover why Maria, as Maria, should be tiny, and finding no reason have ignored the point.

I believe too (this is a commonplace of criticism) that the plan of the play was altered in the writing of it. Shakespeare sets out upon a passionate love romance, perseveres in this until (one detects the moment, it is that jolly midnight revel) Malvolio, Sir Toby and Sir Andrew completely capture him. Even then, perhaps, Maria's notable revenge on the affectioned ass is still to be kept within bounds. But two scenes later he begins to elaborate the new idea. The character of Fabian is added to take Feste's share of the rough practical joke and set him free for subtler wit. Then Shakespeare lets fling and works out the humorous business to his heart's content. That done, little enough space is left him if the play is to be over at the proper hour, and, it may be (if the play was being prepared for an occasion, the famous festivity in the Middle Temple Hall or another), there was little enough time to finish writing it in either. From any cause, we certainly have a scandalously ill-arranged and ill-written last scene, the despair of any stage manager. But one can discover, I believe, amid the chaos scraps of the play he first meant to write. Olivia suffers not so much by the midway change of plan, for it is about her house that the later action of the play proceeds, and she is on her author's hands. It is on Orsino, that interesting romantic, that the blow falls.

> Why should I not, had I the heart to do it,
> Like to the Egyptian thief at point of death,
> Kill what I love?—a savage jealousy
> That sometime savors nobly.

On that fine fury of his—shamefully reduced to those few lines—I believe the last part of the play was to have hung. It is too good a theme to have been meant to be so wasted. And the revelation of Olivia's marriage to his page (as he supposes), his reconciliation with her, and the more vital discovery that his comradely love for Viola is worth more to him after all than any high-sounding passion, is now all muddled up with the final rounding off of the comic relief. The character suffers severely. Orsino remains a finely interesting figure; he might have been a magnificent one. But there, it was Shakespeare's way to come out on the other side of his romance.

The most important aspect of the play must be viewed, to view it rightly, with Elizabethan eyes. Viola was played, and was meant to be played, by a boy. See what this involves. To that original audience the strain of make-believe in the matter ended just where for us it most begins, at Viola's entrance as a page. Shakespeare's audience saw Cesario without effort as Orsino sees him; more importantly they saw him as Olivia sees him; indeed it was over Olivia they had most to make believe. One feels at once how this affects the sympathy and balance of the love scenes of the play. One sees how dramatically right is the delicate still grace of the dialogue between Orsino and Cesario, and how possible it makes the more outspoken passion of the scenes with Olivia. Give to Olivia, as we must do now, all the value of her sex, and to the supposed Cesario none of the value of his, we are naturally quite unmoved by the business. Olivia looks a fool. And it is the common practice for actresses of Viola to seize every chance of reminding the audience that they are girls dressed up, to impress on one moreover, by childish byplay as to legs and petticoats or the absence of them, that this is the play's supreme joke. Now Shakespeare has devised one most carefully placed soliloquy where we are to be forcibly reminded that Cesario is Viola; in it he has as carefully divided the comic from the serious side of the matter. That scene played, the Viola, who does not do her best, as far as the passages with Olivia are concerned, to make us believe, as Olivia believes, that she is a man, shows, to my mind, a lack of imagination and is guilty of dramatic bad manners, knocking, for the sake of a little laughter, the whole of the play's romantic plot on the head.

Let me explain briefly the interpretation I favor of four or five other points.

I do not think that Sir Toby is meant for nothing but a bestial sot. He is a gentleman by birth, or he would not be Olivia's uncle (or cousin, if that is the relationship). He has been, it would seem, a soldier. He is a drinker, and while idleness leads him to excess, the boredom of Olivia's drawing room, where she sits solitary in her mourning, drives him to such jolly companions as he can find: Maria and Fabian and the Fool. He is a poor relation, and has been dear to Sir Andrew some two thousand strong or so (poor Sir Andrew), but as to that he might say he was but anticipating his commission as matrimonial agent. Now, dull though Olivia's house may be, it is free quarters. He is, it seems, in some danger of losing them, but if only by good luck he could see Sir Andrew installed there as master! Not perhaps all one could wish for in an uncle; but to found an interpretation of Sir Toby only upon a study of his unfortunate surname is, I think, for the actor to give us both less and more than Shakespeare meant.

I do not believe that Sir Andrew is meant for a cretinous idiot. His accomplishments may not quite stand to Sir Toby's boast of them; alas! the three or four languages, word for word without book, seem to end at *"Dieu vous garde, Monsieur."* But Sir Andrew, as he would be if he could—the scholar to no purpose, the fine fellow to no end, in short the perfect gentleman—is still the ideal of better men than he who yet can find nothing better to do. One can meet a score of Sir Andrews, in greater or less perfection, any day after a West End London lunch, doing what I believe is called "a slope down Bond."

Fabian, I think, is not a young man, for he hardly treats Sir Toby as his senior; he is the cautious one of the practical jokers, and he has the courage to speak out to Olivia at the end. He treats Sir Andrew with a certain respect. He is a family retainer of some sort; from his talk he has to do with horses and dogs.

Feste, I feel, is not a young man either. There runs through all he says and does that vein of irony by which we may so often mark one of life's self-acknowledged failures. We gather that in those days, for a man of parts without character and with more wit than sense, there was a kindly refuge from the world's struggle as an allowed fool. Nowadays we no longer put them in a livery.

I believe Antonio to be an exact picture of an Elizabethan seaman-adventurer, and Orsino's view of him to be just such as a Spanish grandee would have taken of Drake. "Notable pirate and salt-water thief," he calls him.

> A bawbling vessel was he captain of,
> For shallow draught and bulk unprizable;
> With which such scathful grapple did he make
> With the most noble bottom of the fleet,
> That very envy and the tongue of loss
> Cried fame and honor of him.

And Antonio is a passionate fellow as those West Country-men were. I am always reminded of him by the story of Richard Grenville chewing a wineglass in his rage.

The keynotes of the poetry of the play are that it is passionate and it is exquisite. It is life, I believe, as Shakespeare glimpsed it with the eye of his genius in that half-Italianized court of Elizabeth. Orsino, Olivia, Antonio, Sebastian, Viola are passionate all, and conscious of the worth of their passion in terms of beauty. To have one's full laugh at the play's comedy is no longer possible, even for an audience of Elizabethan experts. Though the humor that is set in character is humor still, so much of the salt of it, its play upon the time and place, can have no savor for us. Instead we have learned editors disputing over the existence and meaning of jokes at which the simplest soul was meant to laugh unthinkingly. I would cut out nothing else, but I think I am justified in cutting those pathetic survivals.

Finally, as to the speaking of the verse and prose. The prose is mostly simple and straightforward. True, he could no more resist a fine-sounding word than, as has been said, he could resist a pun. They abound, but if we have any taste for the flavor of a language he makes us delight in them equally. There is none of that difficult involuted decoration for its own sake in which he reveled in the later plays. The verse is still regular, still lyrical in its inspiration, and it should I think be spoken swiftly. . . .

I think that all Elizabethan dramatic verse must be spoken swiftly, and nothing can make me think otherwise. My fellow workers acting in *The Winter's Tale* were accused by some people (only by some) of gabbling. I readily take that accusation on myself, and I deny it. Gabbling implies hasty speech, but our ideal was speed, nor was the speed universal, nor, but in a dozen well-defined passages, really so great. Unexpected it was, I don't doubt; and once exceed the legal limit, as well accuse you of seventy miles an hour as twenty-one. But I call in question the evidence of mere policemen-critics. I question a little their expertness of hearing, a little too their quickness of understanding Elizabethan English not at its easiest, just a little their lack of delight in anything that is not as they thought it always would be, and I suggest that it is more difficult than they think to look and listen and remember and appraise all in the same flash of time. But be all the shortcomings on one side and that side ours, it is still no proof that the thing come short of is not the right thing. That is the important point to determine, and for much criticism that has been helpful in amending what we did and making clearer what we should strive towards—I tender thanks.

The Winter's Tale, as I see its writing, is complex, vivid, abundant in the variety of its mood and pace and color, now disordered, now at rest, the product of a mind rapid, changing, and overfull. I believe its interpretation should express all that. *Twelfth Night* is quite other. Daily, as we rehearse together, I learn more what it is and should be; the working together of the theater is a fine thing. But, as a man is asked to name his stroke at billiards, I will even now commit myself to this: its serious mood is passionate, its verse is lyrical, the speaking of it needs swiftness and fine tone; not rush, but rhythm, constant and compelling. And now I wait contentedly to be told that less rhythmic speaking of Shakespeare has never been heard.

27 October 1912.

LINDA BAMBER

Comedy, Women, and Development

Many would argue that change, and not the avoidance of
change, is what we value in comedy; but the important
changes in the comedies are collective rather than individual.
Critics who see discovery of identity in the comedies, as even
Northrop Frye claims at times to do,[1] are perhaps displacing
a process that takes place within the social unit onto the individual members of the society. Sherman Hawkins, following
C. L. Barber and Northrop Frye, points out that the action of
Shakespearean comedy opens up a society that was previously closed in on itself;[2] by the end of the story all the characters who matter to us enjoy more freedom than they did to
begin with. But this is not because there have been, as Anne
Barton claims, "self-discoveries, a deepening and development of personality."[3] The discoveries take place at the level
of the plot, not at the level of individual psychology. In
Twelfth Night, for instance, Viola and Sebastian discover
each other's existence, Orsino and Olivia discover that Viola
is a woman and not a man, Malvolio discovers that Olivia is
not, after all, pursuing him. These discoveries and the confu-
sions that precede them realign the whole society for the

From Linda Bamber, *Comic Women, Tragic Men* (Stanford, Cal.: Stanford
University Press, 1982), pp. 129–33.
[1]Northrop Frye, *A Natural Perspective* (New York: Harcourt, Brace and
World, 1965), p. 78.
[2]Sherman Hawkins, "The Two Worlds of Shakespearean Comedy,"
Shakespeare Studies 3 (1967): 69.
[3]Anne Barton, "*As You Like It* and *Twelfth Night*: Shakespeare's Sense of
an Ending," in Malcolm Bradbury and David Palmer, eds., *Stratford-upon-
Avon Studies 14: Shakespearean Comedy* (New York: Crane, Russak & Company, 1972), p. 169.

better; but they do not, as Frye puts it, "lead to a kind of self-knowledge which releases a character from the bondage of his humor."[4] They are of quite a different order from the discoveries of tragedy, which often *do* amount to self-discovery. No recognition in *Twelfth Night* bears comparison to, for instance, Lear's recognition that he is implicated in the suffering of others ("I have ta'en / Too little care of this": 3.4.32–33) or Hamlet's recognition that he cannot create himself through the exercise of will alone ("The readiness is all": 5.2.224).

It is worth examining *Twelfth Night* in some detail because this play is often discussed as a play of self-discovery. No one argues, of course, that Malvolio is "released from the bondage of his humor." Clearly Malvolio is hopeless; at the end of the play he is simply dismissed. Nor is Sir Toby thought to change profoundly, although he is handily brought under control. It is the lovers—Olivia, Orsino, Viola, and even Sebastian—who are seen in terms of self-discovery. Helene Moglen's "Disguise and Development: The Self and Society in *Twelfth Night*" may represent the self-discovery approach to these four characters.[5] For my part, I find nothing that could be called "a deepening and development of personality" in any of them, although I do see some change in one of the four. Not coincidentally, the character who changes is male.

Two kinds of development are discussed in *Twelfth Night* criticism: development of sexuality, and development of a sense of humor as Frey defines the term ("a sense of proportion and a propitiation" related to "the ongoingness of life").[6] In the case of Viola and Sebastian, however, both sexuality and sense of humor seem fully developed from the beginning. Take, for instance, Viola's opening lines:

Viola. My brother he is in Elysium.

Perchance he is not drowned. What think you, sailors?

Captain. It is perchance that you yourself were saved.

[4]Frye, *A Natural Perspective*, p. 79.
[5]Helene Moglen, "Disguise and Development: The Self and Society in *Twelfth Night*," *Literature and Psychology* 13 (1973).
[6]Charles Frey, "The Sweetest Rose: *As You Like It* as Comedy of Reconciliation," *New York Literary Forum* 1 (1978): 167.

Viola. O my poor brother, and so perchance may he be.

(1.2.4–7)

What Viola exhibits here is not what we normally think of as
a sense of humor, but in Frey's terms it is. She has a sense of
proportion about even so painful a fact as the loss of her
brother; she leaves the door open to the comic coincidence
that will resolve the play. "Perchance he is not drowned," of
course, is a nonsequitur; it does not follow from "My brother
he is in Elysium" (4). It is nonsequitur, precisely, that we
depend on in comedy to make things come out right in the
end; Viola speaks in the true illogical spirit of comedy when
she goes straight from her brother's death to the hope for his
life. In her first scene she is firm, forthright, confident, and
even wealthy. She praises the Captain, pays him "bounteously" (52), chooses her disguise, and matter-of-factly
commits herself to time. It is difficult to see her as the uncertain quester that Helene Moglen, for instance, describes.
Moglen says that Viola's disguise is "the adolescent confusion of identity made visible";[7] but in fact it is a consciously
adopted role with which she entertains both herself and the
audience. Neither does Viola's sexuality seem to develop
gradually; she loves her man immediately and constantly
and, given her situation, pursues him as best she can.

Sebastian, similarly, is perfectly sure of his desires from
the beginning. Moglen argues that we see Sebastian turning
gradually from a homosexual attachment to heterosexual
love; but in his very first scene Sebastian decisively turns
away from Antonio, absolutely refusing his service. Sebastian's prose here is almost too virile:

> My stars shine darkly over me; the malignancy of my fate might
> perhaps distemper yours. Therefore I crave of you your leave,
> that I may bear my evils alone. It were a bad recompense for
> your love to lay any of them on you. . . . If you will undo what
> you have done, . . . desire it not. Fare ye well at once . . . I am
> bound to the Count Orsino's court. Farewell.
>
> (2.1.3–8, 37–39, 42–43)

[7]Moglen, "Disguise and Development," p. 15.

Moglen says, "Having endured the loss of his sister, inviting a separation from Antonio, Sebastian seems in growing control of himself";[8] but since the control is there from the start, it is difficult to perceive the growth.

Orsino and Olivia are another story. At the beginning these two characters lack both a sense of proportion and a clarity of desire. Orsino wallows in his own emotions and Olivia has "abjured the sight /And company of men" (1.2.40–41). She is as self-involved in her mourning as Orsino is in his loving. These two characters seem to fit the pattern Sherman Hawkins describes in "The Two Worlds of Shakespearean Comedy": "In the comedies of the alternate pattern [as opposed to those that fit the pattern of New Comedy, where the older generation represses the sexuality of the younger] the heroes and heroines themselves are imprisoned in their inhibitions and aggressions, isolated by fear or repugnance from the general life, cut off not merely from others whom they ought to love but even from themselves."[9] Olivia and Orsino are certainly isolated at the beginning of the play, and by their own actions. But let us look more closely at Olivia in her very first scene. Although she has been three times described as "abandoned to her sorrow" (1.4.19) before we even see her, on her first appearance before us she is no such thing. Her first action is to allow Feste to fool her out of her mourning; her second is to fall madly in love with Cesario. Although Shakespeare may have intended to show development in Olivia, when he gets her onstage he immediately privileges her with perfect comic presence. Olivia explicitly claims both sense of humor and the love-ethic as her own. When Malvolio protests against the liberty of the fool, she says irritably,

> O, you are sick of self-love, Malvolio, and taste with a distempered appetite. To be generous, guiltless, and of free disposition, is to take those things for birdbolts that you deem cannon bullets.   (1.5.90–93)

[8]*Ibid.*, p. 17.
[9]Hawkins, "The Two Worlds," p. 68.

We can find no fault with Olivia's definition of comic freedom: "to take those things for birdbolts that you deem cannon bullets" (92–93). Again, it is a matter of proportion. And when, in the same scene, she finds that she has fallen in love with Cesario, she concludes, "Fate, show thy force: ourselves we do not owe. / What is decreed must be—and be this so!" (308–09). To be of a "free disposition" (92) as a lover is to know, precisely, that "ourselves we do not owe" (311). Before her first appearance Olivia is condemned of a willful attempt to "own" herself, to protect herself from love's uncertainties; but as soon as she appears before us we must withdraw the charges.

Olivia, then, does not seem to change in this play; she is perfectly attuned to comic values right from the start. The change seems to be in the author, not in the character. Shakespeare seems to have meant Olivia as a companion piece to Orsino, a female solipsist. But when he imagines her in action he abandons his plans and showers her with comic privileges. It is perhaps when he imagines her in conversation with Malvolio that he finds himself developing her differently from the way he may have meant to. In Shakespearean comedy the heroine is almost automatically the antithesis of the masculine blocking figure, and perhaps Malvolio's presence in Act 1, scene 5, is responsible for the change of heart about Olivia.

Orsino, however, is truly narcissistic and self-enclosed, truly in need of the challenge of comedy. Orsino does not seduce his author, as Olivia seems to, away from his intentions. And so Orsino does ultimately change. As Hawkins puts it, Orsino learns to allow the intruder into his world: "The force which knocks at the door is love."[10] But although he does answer the knocking, Orsino does not seem to discover himself in the process. He discovers that Viola / Cesario is really a woman and forthwith admits her into his world: "Give me thy hand, /And let me see thee in thy woman's weeds" (5.1.271–72) is all he has to say. Moglen argues that Orsino has developed through a "transitional relationship"[11] with Cesario, but the transition is surely dra-

[10]*Ibid.*, p. 69.
[11]Moglen, "Disguise and Development," p. 16.

matic rather than psychological. It is we who are prepared by their exchanges for Orsino to love Viola, not Orsino himself who is. Orsino's change of allegiance from Olivia to Viola is as daringly conventional, as arbitrary, as unmotivated as anything in the comedies. Since he has known Viola only as his page, the change to loving her as his "mistress" (28) is unrealistically sudden and abrupt.

Orsino, then, changes from a figure of self-enclosure to a prospective bridegroom, and he changes from Olivia's lover to Viola's. Olivia, by contrast, is "of free disposition" (1.5.92) from the first time we see her, and her emotions have a single object. When the Cesario she has married turns out to be Sebastian, there is no need for her to stop loving him on that account. In her case two errors of identity have cancelled each other out. The feminine Other is spared the necessity of change even as she is spared the necessity of choice. She is a constant element in comedy, even when, as in *Twelfth Night*, the scheme of the play suggests that she is there to be redeemed. The feminine is unregenerate in comedy just as she is in tragedy; but in comedy it is unregeneracy we aspire to.

Androgyny in *Twelfth Night*

In *Twelfth Night*, Shakespeare displays much of Viola's person through soliloquies and asides that consider inner as well as surface facts and ironies. Like Rosalind, Viola experiences human freedom and growth in male disguise, but unlike Rosalind, Viola feels self-constricted and self-conscious throughout the play. She is especially conscious of her sexual identity, far more sex-aware, far more troubled by the sex of her sex than is Rosalind. As a result, the girl-as-boy motif is presented as somewhat, though innocently, unnatural, and the effect of Viola's disguise on the play is different from the effect created by Rosalind's. Here Shakespeare openly plays off sexual identity against gender identity in order to suggest with more impact than in *As You Like It* that one must accept one's genetic sex before one can reach toward psychic androgyny. He touches on homosexuality as well as heterosexuality in order to bring home to the audience that androgyny has no necessary connection with any particular kind of sexual orientation. The audience, like Viola, must learn that androgyny is not a physical state, but a state of mind.

Shakespeare summarizes his plot, character, and themes in Viola's soliloquy in the short 2.2: "I left no ring with her. What means this lady? / Fortune forbid my outside have not charmed her" (17–8). When Viola says "Disguise, I see thou art a wickedness" (27), Shakespeare, beyond talking about the rising complication in the play, is mocking the Puri-

Robert Kimbrough, "Androgyny Seen Through Shakespeare's Disguise," *Shakespeare Quarterly* 33 (1982): 17–33; this selection is pages 28–32.

tans whose mounting attack on the impious mummery of satanic players had always been based in part on the abomination of men dressing unnaturally as women—monstrous, indeed. According to Juliet Dusinberre, at the turn of the century some few women were roaming the streets of London dressed as men to taunt protesting Christendom. Surely Shakespeare must have enjoyed for himself the joke of having a girl mockingly apologize for playing a boy. In effect Shakespeare is saying that if that is all small-minded people can think about, so be it. But Viola's self-consciousness about her unnatural transformation leads to a more serious moment as she characterizes herself as a hermaphrodite and a homosexual:

> How will this fadge? My master loves her dearly;
> And I (poor monster) fond as much on him;
> And she (mistaken) seems to dote on me.
> What will become of this? As I am man,
> My state is desperate for my master's love.
> As I am woman (now alas the day!),
> What thriftless sighs shall poor Olivia breathe?
> O Time, thou must untangle this, not I;
> It is too hard a knot for me t' untie.

> (2.2.33–41)

When Viola parenthetically calls herself a "poor monster" (Elizabethan for unnatural) and Olivia "mistaken" (34–35) (both deceived and morally wrong), Shakespeare introduces the concepts of hermaphroditism and homosexuality—to be sure, only fleetingly. A hermaphrodite was unnatural because of the presence of both male and female sex organs, supposedly the result of a kind of monstrous birth like that of Richard, Duke of Gloucester, out of the natural order of things. And, leaving aside any question of actual practice, homosexuality was, of course, automatically stamped unnatural by religious and secular officialdoms.

In spite of her recognition of natural and social aberration, Viola decides to stay in disguise. She could "come out" at this crucial moment, but for the time being what she seeks is freedom within the restrictions of disguise. Liberated from her role as young Lady, she moves into realms of self-discovery.

And having been raised with a twin brother, she knows how to adapt to her adopted sex. The result is Shakespeare's furthest venture into androgyny as seen through disguise.

At the outset, after shipwreck, Viola's normal, sensible course of action upon finding out where she is and whose domain it is would have been to have the captain take her to her father's friend for protection and to arrange her return home as, she thinks, an heiress. But on hearing the name "Orsino," she makes a statement which carries all the weight of a rhetorical question: "He was a bachelor then" (1.2.28–29). Her immediate plan, seen even in the talk about Olivia, is to woo him (or to see if she wishes to), which, paradoxically, she would not be able to do if she presented herself as hapless, for then it would be Orsino's duty to send her right home. So she bribes the captain:

> I prithee (and I'll pay thee bounteously)
> Conceal me what I am, and be my aid
> For such disguise as haply shall become
> The form of my intent. I'll serve this duke.
> Thou shalt present me as an eunuch to him;
> It may be worth thy pains. For I can sing,
> And speak to him in many sorts of music
> That will allow me very worth his service.
> What else may hap, to time I will commit;
> Only shape thou thy silence to my wit.
>
> (522–61)

In disguise, she can exercise that wit which women are not supposed to have, and the role and costume which she chooses are ones for which she is fitted:

> I my brother know
> Yet living in my glass. Even such and so
> In favor was my brother, and he went
> Still in this fashion, color, ornament,
> For him I imitate.   (3.4.391–95)

In acting like her twin brother, she becomes, so to speak, a walking example of Ascham on Imitation: the similar treat-

ment of dissimilar matter. Even though one twin is female and one is male, they share a common humanity. Ex-
tending the rhetorical metaphor, she need not search for the
basis of her *tractatio*; she is herself the basis of her own
invention.

The effect of her disguise on Orsino is like that of Rosalind's on Orlando: men can be relaxedly, if only superfi-
cially, confessional with others of the same sex—the sort of
"just between us" collusion that men easily fall into. Within
Viola's first three days of service, Orsino shows more of his
essential self (though young and in flux) to Cesario than he
has so far been able to show to his neighbor, the distant
Olivia, or would ever reveal to Viola as a stranger of the
opposite sex.

Because he is older than Cesario, Orsino shares his experience in order to teach his young companion (he literally
and figuratively lords it over him). But the lessons learned
are not the ones being taught, as Cesario's responses reveal.
When Orsino, out of the presence of women, confesses that

> boy, however we do praise ourselves,
> our fancies are more giddy and unfirm,
> More longing, wavering, sooner lost and worn,
> Than women's are,   (2.4.32–35)

Viola wisely nods, "I think it well, my lord" (35). And then
not much later in the same scene, Orsino all so humanly and
delightfully contradicts himself:

> There is no woman's sides
> Can bide the beating of so strong a passion
> As love doth give my heart; no woman's heart
> So big to hold so much; they lack retention.
> Alas, their love may be called appetite,
> No motion of the liver but the palate,
> That suffers surfeit, cloyment, and revolt;
> But mine is all as hungry as the sea
> And can digest as much. Make no compare
> Between that love a woman can bear me
> And that I owe Olivia.   (94–104)

To which nonsense Viola can quietly respond, "Ay, but I
know" (104). While indeed she does, she also is coming to
know, as Olivia and Orsino will learn, that many apparent
differences between men and women are dissolvable. When
Orsino asks her what she knows, she answers that women
are as "true of heart as we" (107), where "we" becomes truly
androgynous because it means "we human kinds." And from
her strategic advantage she in her turn can school Orsino
while hiding behind a disguise that cancels out her sexuality,
making her a "blank" (111) (like blank verse, neither feminine nor masculine). from her position and experience, she
knows

> Too well what love women to men may owe.
> In faith, they are as true of heart as we.
> My father had a daughter loved a man
> As it might be perhaps, were I a woman,
> I should your lordship.   (106–09)

In response to Orsino's "And what's her history?" (110)
Viola says:

> A blank, my lord. She never told her love,
> But let concealment, like a worm i' th' bud,
> Feed on her damask cheek. She pined in thought;
> and, with a green and yellow melancholy,
> She sat like Patience on a monument,
> Smiling at grief. Was not this love indeed?
> We men may say more, swear more; but indeed
> Our shows are more than will; for still we prove
> Much in our vows but little in our love.
>   (111–19)

Because she is a man, Viola can turn women's complaints
against masculine infidelity tellingly against that gender.
The lesson she is learning and teaching is one her birth into
life as the twin of a male has already prepared her for: once
sexual differentiation is acknowledged, men and women are
essentially very much alike. She has no trouble playing a
boy, for her childhood has readied her for the role she is now

successful in, even though Orsino remarks that Cesario has all the physical characteristics which would promote the successful portrayal of "a woman's part" (1.4.34).

Thus Shakespeare allows us to see androgyny through disguise. Viola is first of all a woman, but society, being so conscious of sex identity ("what did she have, a boy or a girl?"), assumes she is a man once she puts on male clothing (which is enough to start Sir Andrew quaking). As a result she can be Viola and Sebastian, woman and man, at the same time. Since this is only metaphorically true, she is freed to act out the full range of her human personality. When Shakespeare has Orsino say that Viola could play "a woman's part," he is doing more than calling the audience's attention to her girl-as-boy disguise; he is calling attention to a two-in one nature through the part-acting metaphor.

By giving Viola this metaphor of acting in her dialogue with Olivia—"my speech" (1.5.171), "my part" (177). "I am not that I play"(182)—Shakespeare develops the idea that Viola is Viola at the same time that she is Sebastian. Stated plainly, she does not *become* Sebastian; she *is* Sebastian—but without a penis ("a little thing would make me tell them how much I lack of a man" (3.4.313–15). Such is the nature of successful acting. As an actor, Viola is herself "a natural perspective that is and is not." As Viola-Cesario she can charm Orsino; as Sebastian-Cesario she can charm Olivia. And the audience is just as charmed as are Orsino and Olivia; we are delighted to share with Viola her recognition of her emotional self—"I am almost sick for [a beard]" (3.1.47–48), "I am no fighter" (251), "I am one that had rather go with sir priest than sir knight" (281–82). Because of disguise, the usual social barriers of custom are removed, allowing Orsino and Olivia to get to know the essential Viola-Sebastian. Then, with the arrival of Viola's literal surrogate, her self's other self—"One face, one voice, one habit, and two persons" (5.1.215–16)—the apparent problems afforded by sexual delusion are solved. A happy ending is a natural ending. The marriages are founded on surer ground than if they had been initiated through more artificial means than artifice.

In this sense, Viola's disguise does not turn out to be a total "wickedness." It merely covers those parts of her that too often prevent society from accepting women as human beings. Over the three-month span of the play Orsino develops his instinctive liking of Cesario without having to wrestle with Viola's sex. Meanwhile, Olivia's decision to marry Sebastian is only seemingly sudden. She, too, has had three months to get to know the dominant human aspect of Viola-Sebastian. Not until Sebastian enters does sex—in the form of marriage, of course—enter Olivia's stated plans. Here, as Sebastian says regarding this sexual attraction, "nature to her bias drew in that" (260). But sex is only part of the attraction. Because Viola and Sebastian are twins, Olivia has not really been deceived, a point we should not overlook. Shakespeare has Sebastian say in full:

> So comes it, lady, you have been mistook.
> But nature to her bias drew in that.
> You would have been contracted to a maid;
> Nor are you therein, by my life, deceived:
> You are betrothed both to a maid and man.

> (259–63)

Orsino, too, is betrothed to "a maid and man" (263). Ultimately, there has been no deception. Viola has shown us through her disguise that one can overcome gender differentiation regardless of sex. Olivia and Orsino, who each started the play as the prisoner of gender, are as blessed by disguise as is Viola. They are stimulated by her to draw on their androgynous potential for human growth and to develop toward full, whole, integrated selves.

JEAN E. HOWARD

Cross-dressing in *Twelfth Night*

Undoubtedly, the crossdressed Viola, the woman who can sing both high and low and who is loved by a woman *and* by a man, is a figure who can be read as putting in question the notion of fixed sexual difference. For Catherine Belsey that blurring of sexual difference opens the liberating possibility of undoing all the structures of domination and exploitation premised on binary sexual oppositions.[1] The play therefore seems susceptible to a radical reading. For Stephen Greenblatt, by contrast, Viola's sexual indeterminacy simply signifies the play's projection onto the crossdressed woman of the process of *male* individuation, a stage in "the male trajectory of identity."[2] For Greenblatt the play thus echoes those Renaissance medical discourses of gender that largely erased the question of female subjectivity and rooted masculine privilege in the natural 'fact' "that within differentiated individuals is a single structure, identifiably male" (Greenblatt, p. 93).

I wish to question both readings, first by probing just how thoroughly Viola's gender identity is ever made indeterminate and thereby made threatening *to the theatre audience* (the subjects being addressed by the play's fictions),

From Jean E. Howard, "Crossdressing, the Theatre, and Gender Struggle in Early Modern England," *Shakespeare Quarterly* 39 (1988): 418–40. Used by permission of the author and *Shakespeare Quarterly*.

[1] Catherine Belsey, "Disrupting Sexual Difference: Meaning and Gender in the Comedies," in *Alternative Shakespeares*, ed. John Drakakis (London: Methuen, 1985), pp. 166–90.

[2] Stephen Greenblatt, "Fiction and Friction," in *Shakespearean Negotiations* (Berkeley: University of California Press, 1988), pp. 92–93.

second by calling attention to the degree to which the political threat of female insurgency enters the text not through Viola, the crossdressed woman, but through Olivia, a figure whose sexual and economic independence is ironically reined in *by means of* the crossdressed Viola. The play seems to me to embody a fairly oppressive fable of the containment of gender and class insurgency and the valorization of the "good woman" as the one who has interiorized—whatever her clothing—her essential difference from, and subordinate relations to, the male.[3] Put another way, the play seems to me to applaud a crossdressed woman who does not aspire to the positions of power assigned men, and to discipline a non-crossdressed woman who does.

Discussion of androgyny, or of the erasure of sexual determinacy, always centers with regard to this play on the figure of Viola. Yet the first thing to say about her crossdressing is that it is in no way adopted to protest gender inequities or to prove that "*Custome* is an idiot." Viola adopts male dress as a practical means of survival in an alien environment and, perhaps, as a magical means of keeping alive a brother believed drowned, and of delaying her own entry into the heterosexual arena until that brother returns. In short, for her, crossdressing is not so much a political act as a psychological haven, a holding place. Moreover, and this is a key point, from the time Viola meets Orsino in 1.4 there is no doubt in the audience's mind of her heterosexual sexual orientation or her properly "feminine" subjectivity. As she says when she undertakes to be Orsino's messenger to Olivia, "Whoe'er I woo, myself would be his wife" (42). She never wavers in that resolve even while carrying out the task of wooing Olivia in Orsino's name. The audience always knows that underneath the page's clothes is a "real" woman, one who expresses dislike of her own disguise ("Disguise, I see thou art a wickedness" [2.2.27]), and

[3]For a much less political reading of the play see my own essay, "The Orchestration of *Twelfth Night*" in *Shakespeare's Art of Orchestration* (Urbana: University of Illinois Press, 1984). In that essay, while accurately mapping the actual and metaphorical disguises in the play, I did not explore the political implications of the text's insistence on the return to an "undisguised" state—what that meant for aspiring servants, independent women, etc. In short, I accepted the play's dominant ideologies as a mimesis of the true and natural order of things.

one who freely admits that she has neither the desire nor the aptitude to play the man's part in phallic swordplay. The whole thrust of the dramatic narrative is to release this woman from the prison of her masculine attire and return her to her proper and natural position as wife. Part of the larger ideological consequence of her portrayal, moreover, is to shift the markers of sexual difference inward, from the surface of the body and the apparel which clothes that body, to the interior being of the gendered subject. The play shows that while crossdressing can cause semiotic and sexual confusion, and therefore is to be shunned, it is not truly a problem for the social order if "the heart" is untouched, or, put another way, if not accompanied by the political desire for a redefinition of female rights and powers and a dismantling of a hierarchical gender system. Despite her masculine attire and the confusion it causes in Illyria, Viola's is a properly feminine subjectivity; and this fact countervails the threat posed by her clothes and removes any possibility that she might permanently aspire to masculine privilege and prerogatives. It is fair to say, I think, that Viola's portrayal, along with that of certain other of Shakespeare's crossdressed heroines, marks one of the points of emergence of the feminine subject of the bourgeois era: a woman whose limited freedom is premised on the interiorization of gender difference and the "willing" acceptance of differential access to power and to cultural and economic assets.

Just as clearly, however, the play records the traditional comic disciplining of a woman who lacks such a properly gendered subjectivity. I am referring, of course, to Olivia, whom I regard as the real threat to the hierarchical gender system in this text, Viola being but an *apparent* threat. As Stephen Greenblatt points out, Olivia is a woman of property, headstrong and initially intractable, and she lacks any discernible male relatives, except the disreputable Toby, to control her or her fortune (p. 69). At the beginning of the play she has decided to do without the world of men, and especially to do without Orsino. These are classic marks of unruliness. And in this play she is punished, comically but unmistakably, by being made to fall in love with the cross-dressed Viola. The good woman, Viola, thus becomes the vehicle for humiliating the unruly woman in the eyes of the audience, much as Titania is humiliated in *A Midsummer Night's Dream* by her union with an ass. Not only is the figure of the male-attired woman thus used to enforce a gender system that is challenged in other contexts by that figure, but also, by a bit of theatrical handy-dandy, the oft-repeated fear that boy actors dressed as women leads to sodomy is displaced here upon a woman dressed as a man. It is Viola who provokes the love of Olivia, the same-sex love between women thus functioning as the marker of the "unnatural" in the play and a chief focus of its comedy.

The treatment of Orsino, by contrast, is much less satirical. He, too, initially poses a threat to the Renaissance sex-gender system by languidly abnegating his active role as masculine wooer and drowning in narcissistic self-love. Yet Orsino, while being roundly mocked *within* the play, especially by Feste, is ridiculed only lightly by the play itself, by the punishments meted out to him. His narcissism and potential effeminacy are displaced, respectively, onto Malvolio and Andrew Aguecheek, who suffer fairly severe humiliations for their follies. In contrast, Orsino, the highest-ranking male figure in the play, simply emerges from his claustrophobic house in Act 5 and assumes his "rightful" position as governor of Illyria and future husband of Viola. Moreover, Orsino, in contrast to Olivia, shows no overt sexual interest in the crossdressed Viola until her biological identity is revealed, though his language often betrays an unacknowledged desire for the Diana within the male disguise. The point, however, is that the text makes his attraction to Cesario neither overt nor the object of ridicule.

If, as I have been arguing, this text treats gender relations conservatively, the same is true of its treatment of class. If unruly women and unmanly men are sources of anxiety needing correction, so are upstart crows. The class-jumper Malvolio, who dresses himself up in yellow stockings and cross garters, is savagely punished and humiliated, echoing the more comically managed humiliation of Olivia, the woman who at the beginning of the play jumped gender boundaries to assume control of her house and person and refused her "natural" role in the patriarchal marriage market. The play disciplines independent women like Olivia and upstart crows such as Malvolio and rewards the self-abnegation of a Viola. In the process, female crossdressing is stripped of nearly all of its subversive resonances present in the culture at large. There is no doubt that the play flirts with "dangerous matter": wearing clothes of the opposite sex invites every kind of sexual confusion and "mistaking." But the greatest threat to the sex-gender system is not, I would argue, the potential collapse of biological difference through the figure of Viola but the failure of other characters— namely, Orsino and Olivia—to assume culturally sanctioned positions of dominance and subordination assigned the two genders. As I noted earlier, it is ironic that it is through the crossdressed Viola, with her properly "feminine" subjectivity, that these real threats are removed and both difference and gender hierarchy reinscribed.

SYLVAN BARNET

Twelfth Night on Stage and Screen

Shakespeare wrote at a time when the science of scenic production was in its infancy, and he himself, as he has told us, was
conscious and resentful of its limitations. We have developed
that science, and it is only when Shakespeare's plays are produced with due regard to this development, that they seem to us
works of living art.

—MAX BEERBOHM, reviewing William Poel's production of
Twelfth Night by the Elizabethan Stage Society, 1903

We will talk later about William Poel's attempts to stage
Shakespeare in what he took to be an Elizabethan manner—
that is, to perform the plays without much scenery; here it is
enough to say that Poel was reacting against the tendency
(dominant in the second half of the nineteenth century) to
employ highly illusionistic (and therefore rather bulky)
scenery. Poel's influence was considerable, and healthy, but
directors today almost never are content to use a relatively bare
stage. Instead, in an age that has been characterized as one of
"director's theater," they usually bring a "concept" to the production, and the concept includes an idea for a set. True, the set
today is rarely illusionistic (though every now and then
someone gets the idea of setting *Twelfth Night* in a modern
Adriatic fishing town—the "Illyria" of 1.2.2); most often it is,
in some degree, symbolic, suggestive of some underlying idea.

But what is the underlying idea of this comedy whose title
seems enigmatic, and whose subtitle—"What You Will"—
seems careless? It's easy to say that the play is a "comedy,"
but that word is rather broad. What sort of comedy? A lyrical

164

comedy? Or a satiric comedy? Do we get genial banter or malicious raillery? Among the words one often encounters in reading about *Twelfth Night*, in addition to "lyrical" and "satiric," are "romantic," "wistful" (or "sad"), "romping" (or "boisterous"), and (in an effort to catch both extremes) "bittersweet." Is the heart of the comedy of *Twelfth Night* to be found in the drinking scenes, or in the gulling of Malvolio, or in the unions of lovers at the end of the play, or (now much favored) in Feste's reminders that "youth's a stuff will not endure" (2.3.53) and that "the rain it raineth every day" (5.1.394)? Although Sir Toby's part is the largest, the three dominant roles are those of Viola, Malvolio, and Feste. If one searches Viola's for a statement of the theme, one might come up with "Tempests are kind, and salt waves fresh in love!" (3.4.396), i.e., threatening nature is, finally, benevolent and creative.

In our generation, however, Feste rather than Viola is usually taken to be Shakespeare's spokesperson. Moreover, Feste seems to be getting older, seedier, and grittier (today he usually sings his songs, unaccompanied, in a less than melodious voice), and on occasion his role as a surrogate for the author is indicated by turning him into the stage manager. In 1974 at Ashland, Oregon, for example, he controlled the lighting with magic gestures, and in 1979 at Stratford-upon-Avon he moved scenery and provided cues for actors. This modern emphasis on Feste—and a Feste who is not a youthful joker but an aging ironist—would have surprised nineteenth-century viewers. For them, the key to the play was not a bitter clown but the plucky Viola, a woman whose steadfast devotion to her man was ultimately rewarded.

The stage requirements for *Twelfth Night* are not great—something for Orsino's palace, something for Olivia's garden, and almost nothing for a few less identifiable places. But what shall the set look like? Favorite choices seem to be these: silver or blue (dreamy), gold (autumnal, wistful), brightly varied (carnival), gauzy (Watteauesque). Of all these, golden autumn seems to have been the most popular in the last few decades, with its implication of a world that soon will disappear. And we have even had a winter set: Terry Hands's production for the Royal Shakespeare Company in 1979 showed, at first, bare trees, with a little snow on the ground. Later, some (but by no means many) leaves had sprouted. The rather wintry tone was heightened at the end by a stage picture that did not unite all of the characters; the lovers were grouped in the center, but the rest sat at a distance, facing away from each other. A happier wintry version was given at Yale in December, 1980; it opened with the sound of jingling bells, and with Feste bringing in a Christmas tree, and there was a good deal of Dickensian Christmas jollity.

As with Shakespeare's other plays, we know almost nothing of the earliest productions of *Twelfth Night.* In fact, we have only one record, in 1602 (see above, page lxiv, note 1) of a performance of *Twelfth Night* during Shakespeare's lifetime. In 1618, two years after Shakespeare's death, there is a reference to a performance at court, and in 1623 it was again done at court, under the title *Malvolio.* But despite the paucity of allusions to particular productions, *Twelfth Night* seems to have been popular in the first half of the seventeenth century. A commendatory poem by Leonard Digges, printed in Shakespeare's *Poems* (1640), implies as much:

> The Cockpit galleries, boxes, are all full
> To hear Malvolio, that cross-gartered gull.

In 1642 the theaters in England were closed by act of Parliament, but when Charles II was restored to the throne in 1660, the theaters reopened and *Twelfth Night* was soon staged again. Samuel Pepys recorded in his diary that he saw *Twelfth Night* three times (1661, 1663, and 1669), but he didn't care for it, characterizing it as a "silly play." He probably was speaking of an adaptation, but, equally probably, he would have said the same of the original. In 1703 William Burnaby thoroughly rewrote the play (he kept only about fifty lines of the original), into a work called *Love Betrayed,* intended to be the libretto for an opera, though the venture failed on the stage.

Not until 1741, when David Garrick produced Shakespeare's comedy at Drury Lane, did *Twelfth Night* regain its early popularity. For close to the next eighty years it was given almost annually in London. (The first American production was in Boston, in 1794; the first New York production was in 1804.) During this long run, the chief actor usually played Malvolio; so far as one can tell, in the second decade of the eighteenth century, and in the earliest years of the nineteenth, Malvolio was largely a figure of fun, but a little later in the century he came to assume a semi-tragic status. Charles Lamb's essay on the Malvolio of Robert Bensley (see above, pages 136–38) admirably sets forth this more serious view, but there is some doubt about whether Bensley actually played the role in the way that Lamb attributes to him. According to Lamb, Bensley "threw over the part an air of Spanish loftiness," giving to the overthrow of Malvolio "a kind of tragic interest." Possibly, however, the tragic Malvolio owes more to Lamb than to Bensley. In any case, it did not immediately establish itself as the right way to play the part, for in the middle of the nineteenth century Samuel Phelps, though affecting Spanish gravity, was fatuous and unflappable. (More precisely, Phelps's first Malvolio, in 1848, was comically self-satisfied, neither asking for pity nor evoking it. However, when he played the role again, in 1857, he apparently was less comic and more sympathetic.) Because Phelps's comic Malvolio felt no pain, the audience felt no pain for him. The scene that can be most painful—the one that can most distress a spectator if the actor chooses to convey anguish—is the scene showing Malvolio falsely imprisoned and taunted as a madman (4.2). But Phelps's Malvolio, at least in his first production, did not break when taunted in prison; he retained his (absurd) dignity, did not evoke pity, and remained a comic figure.

Henry Irving, however, in 1884 presented an almost unambiguously tragic Malvolio. Irving, who had never seen the play, seems to have taken his conception of the role chiefly from Lamb's essay. Edward Aveling (amateur actor, theater critic, religious and social reformer, and—for a while—the common-law husband of Karl Marx's daughter, Eleanor) has given us a description of Irving's Malvolio responding to the forged letter, and of Malvolio later in confinement:

> He intended us to pity Malvolio, to weep for if not with him. From the moment when we see how completely he, the sport of others, is self-deceived, a feeling of incipient sympathy takes hold on us. At the end of the scene his exit was not with a pompous swaggering strut; Malvolio passed out with his face

buried in his hands, strangely moved, overwhelmed with his good fortune. Then we began to see what real pain this foolish jest of Maria was . . . about to cause. But how much and how real the pain, was not conceived until Malvolio was seen in prison. The scene is so arranged, with a wall, that of his cell, built down the center line of the stage, that we see both his tor-mentors and the man himself. On the right hand are Maria and the plaguing clown. On the other lies Malvolio. He is in dark-ness. The mental and physical horror of darkness and the longing yearning for deliverance from a prison cell were never so realized, I think, before. And with all this agony (it is liter-ally agony) there is the sense of the grievous wrong done to him, and the utter hopelessness of redress. My readers may be inclined to smile at me, but I declare in all seriousness the effect of this scene from the comedy of *Twelfth Night* on me was that of intense tragedy.

Henry Irving's *Twelfth Night*, even with Ellen Terry as his Viola, was not popular with audiences. Augustin Daly in America, however, in 1869, 1877, and 1893 produced the play successfully—though in an adapted version. Since Daly emphasized the merriment in the play, he deleted Malvolio from the ending, thus avoiding Malvolio's bitter final line: "I'll be revenged on the whole pack of you" (5.1.380), a line that many directors have found hard to fit into a happy ending. Daly also revised the sequence of scenes. Shakespeare's first scene is set in Orsino's palace; the second introduces Viola on the shores of Illyria; the third is in Olivia's house, and the fourth is, again, in Orsino's palace. Daly (like many predecessors, and, for that matter, like many successors) began the play with 1.2 (Viola's ini-tial appearance), and then for his second scene he combined Shakespeare's 1.1 and 1.4 (both in Orsino's palace). Daly's third scene was a combination of Shakespeare's 1.3, 1.5, and 2.2 (all in or near Olivia's house). Such rearrangements, bringing together scenes set in one locale, were necessary because Daly used highly elaborate sets (a magnificent palace for Orsino and a magnificent garden for Olivia), sets that could not easily be erected and struck and erected again without fairly long intervals. To take only the first of these changes: beginning the play not with Orsino's court and talk of music as the food of love but with Viola's entrance from the sea gives added emphasis to the tempest. Doubtless this motif is immensely important, and many directors (for instance John Barton at Stratford in 1969 and Liviu Ciulei at the Guthrie Theater in Minneapolis in 1984) have decided to begin with this scene even when not constrained to do so by their sets. But the rearrangement loses the movement from self-indulgence and sentiment (1.1) to awareness of others and energy (1.2), or, to put it a bit differently, it obscures the sense of a static or somnolent Illyria that suddenly, by an intrusion of tempest-tossed outsiders, gets a shot in the arm.

This essay began with an epigraph drawn from Max Beerbohm's review of William Poel's 1903 production. But that production (given twice, once at the Lecture Hall in Burlington Gardens and once at the Court Theatre in London) was a revival, for Poel and the Elizabethan Stage Society had already done *Twelfth Night* in a more or less Elizabethan style in 1897, in the Hall of the Middle Temple, where the play had been given (see page lxiv, note 1) in Shakespeare's day. Poel erected a raised platform and a proscenium, with two columns on the stage and a raised gallery at the rear, in imitation of the De Witt drawing of the Swan (see page xxviii). A curtain ran from one column to the other, shutting out the rear of the stage when necessary. The raised gallery was not used; it would have been suitable for Malvolio's prison, but in fact Poel cut the scene. Despite this cut (and cuts of some thirty lines on grounds of obscenity), Poel tried to do the play in what he took to be an Elizabethan manner, that is, without cumbersome scenery, and with Elizabethan-style music played on a virginal, a treble and a bass viol, all made in the sixteenth century. For Max Beerbohm, Poel and his associates in the Elizabethan Stage Society were pedants who sacrificed beauty for accuracy. In fact, Poel did not scrupulously try to imitate the Elizabethan theater. For instance, he did not rely on daylight or even on candles (he used electric lights), and he did not use boys to act the female roles. Still, his simple productions—his *Twelfth Night* used only a table and some chairs—and his Elizabethan costumes contrasted sharply with elaborate Victorian and Edwardian productions. Max Beerbohm was not Poel's only severe critic. William

Archer, friend of Shaw and champion of the new drama of Ibsen, saw in Poel's attempts a backward step in the history of drama. In 1895 Archer attacked Poel's Elizabethanism, saying that Shakespeare would not come alive for the modern spectator "by a form of representation which appeals only to the dilettante and the enthusiast." Explaining that he was not defending the excesses of the contemporary theater, Archer went on to say that the excesses scarcely were an argument "forcibly to put back the clock." Scenery and costume, he said, *can* "help and stimulate the imagination of a theatrical audience," whereas "anachronism of costume, and the absence of any sort of pictorial background tend to disconcert and hamper the imagination, and to distract attention from the matter of the play."

Poel's experiment of 1897 did not, of course, immediately put an end to elaborate productions. In 1901 Herbert Beerbohm Tree, Max's half-brother, staged *Twelfth Night* in his usual style, with elaborate sets. (The brothers shared the view that pretty scenery added to the spectator's pleasure.) The sets for *Twelfth Night* included a splendid palace for Orsino and an elaborate garden, with real grass and real fountains, for Olivia's house. But two other points should be mentioned about this production. First, Malvolio was thoroughly comic, even farcical, rather than pathetic or tragic; for instance, making a grand descent down the stairs of Olivia's garden he slipped, landed on his behind, and (as though he had intended to sit in this manner) calmly adjusted his monocle and surveyed the scene. Second, the Feste of this production was not the sweetly lyrical or even the bittersweet minor figure that he usually had been in earlier productions; rather, according to a review by Max Beerbohm, in this production Feste

pervades the whole scheme. It was an excellent idea that he, at the fall of the curtain, should be on the stage, blowing a trill on his secular flute, when the other characters have trooped off to the sound of marriage-bells. "After all," he seems to pipe, "what does it amount to?" just as Shakespeare threw in that *What You Will.* Both as actor and singer, Mr. Courtice Pounds is an admirable Clown, infusing always a touch of sinistry into his mirth.

Here, then, in the reference to the clown's "sinistry," we find a relatively early anticipation of the "dark" *Twelfth Night* that seems in our time nearly to have displaced the "happy" or "comic" *Twelfth Night* of the eighteenth century and probably of the seventeenth. Still, Feste's concluding song was the signal for a dance by the entire company, and so the play ended on an unambiguously harmonious note.

In the nineteenth century, and in the early twentieth, *Twelfth Night* seems to have been moderately popular, but it was not regarded as one of Shakespeare's great plays. A 1912 production by Harley Granville-Barker helped to establish it as a classic. Influenced by Poel, Barker rejected elaborate illusionistic scenery for Shakespeare, partly because such scenery slowed down the play and required shifting of the original order of the scenes, and partly because, in his words, such scenery "swears against everything in the plays." But Granville-Barker did not go as far as Poel in his attempt to revive Elizabethan methods. "It is," he said, too much to ask "an audience to come to the theater so historically sensed as that." Deciding that what was needed for *Twelfth Night* was a set that was "decorative" yet "unencumbrous," he settled on indicating Orsino's palace by some twisted pillars that looked as though they were made out of hard candy, and indicating Olivia's garden by some topiary trees that looked as though they had been assembled out of construction paper or came from a child's box of Noah's ark toys. In effect Granville-Barker established the modern practice of using a decorative setting with some suggestions of locale, a practice somewhere between the utterly unlocalized neutral setting of Poel and the realistic settings of most Victorian and Edwardian productions. Physical action—especially in the clowning of Sir Andrew and Sir Toby—was relatively restrained. The play ended with Feste singing while Olivia's garden gates closed; according to reviewers, the gist of the idea was that for a while we had wandered in a delightful fairyland but now the time had come to leave it. Ever since Granville-Barker's production, which was enthusiastically received, the play has been constantly in the repertory.

We have already glanced at productions in Minneapolis, New Haven, and Stratford. Of the innumerable modern productions, there is space now to look at only three more, all by the Royal Shakespeare Company: Peter Hall's at Stratford-upon-Avon in 1958; John Barton's, also at Stratford, in 1969, revived in Australia and London in 1970, and again at Stratford in 1971 and 1972; and John Caird's, also at Stratford, in 1983.

Hall's production, with Dorothy Tutin as Viola and Mark Dignam as Malvolio, was notably autumnal: Illyria was represented by a golden setting—for the viewer, a now-lost golden age—with white trees and autumn flowers; Cesario wore amber, Olivia (after putting aside her mourning garb) wore light brown and red, and the men, costumed as cavaliers, wore purple, mauve, silver, and brown velvet or satin. (The cavalier costumes, i.e. the Royalist costumes of the middle of the seventeenth century, had autumnal implications, since the king was soon to be executed and the cavaliers defeated by the Puritans.) Reviewers and spectators found Hall's production "Chekhovian."

Barton's production of 1969, with a barer setting (it thus seemed more Elizabethan) was even more melancholy, though Donald Sinden's Malvolio was said to be comic as well as heroic. In one especially delightful comic bit Malvolio noticed the sundial in Olivia's garden and rotated the dial to make it conform to his watch. (For Sinden's interpretation of his role, see his essay in *Players of Shakespeare,* ed. Philip Brockbank.) During the 202 performances, over four years, it is said that the comedy in the production increased somewhat, but the chief idea seems consistently to have been taken from Feste's song asserting that "Youth's a stuff will not endure" (2.3.53). At the end the melancholy was emphasized by separating Antonio—the lonely outsider—from the happy couples. (Barton's *Twelfth Night,* widely regarded as one of the great productions of the century, is discussed in some detail in Stanley Wells, *Royal Shakespeare* and in Lois Potter, *Twelfth Night: Text and Performance.*)

The sadness characteristic of these productions was even more marked in Caird's production of 1983. The program quoted Sonnet 12 ("Nothing 'gainst Time's scythe can make defense"); the set showed a ruined garden, part graveyard, with rusting gates; and the play diminished all of the characters—even Viola (Zoë Wanamaker), whose grief for her brother almost overwhelmed her. (Most readers of the play will notice that the melancholy she shows in 1.2.3–7 soon yields to a delightful energy, in lines 19–64.) Something of the production's dark side can be seen in the fact that Olivia actually struck Malvolio in the cross-garter scene. True, Maria in 3.2.83 says, "I know my lady will strike him," but perhaps not until 1983 did Olivia actually do so. The dueling was similarly unusual in its violence, and Toby kicked Sebastian, provoking Olivia to strike Toby. None of this was quite redeemed by the broad comedy of Malvolio or, at the end, by the passionate kiss of Viola and Orsino, which was followed by a clap of thunder and a flash of lightning—the rain of which Feste sings.

Although Chekhovian or "dark" versions seem dominant, with an emphasis on the isolation of the individual, symbolized especially in Feste but also (as has just been mentioned) by separating Antonio from the others, sunny versions are still occasionally found. For instance, in Marcia Taylor's production at Santa Cruz in 1986, when Feste sings his final song he was alone for only the first two stanzas. When Feste sang of coming "to wive" (5.1.399), Viola (restored to her "woman's weeds," as Orsino requests in 273) entered with Orsino; when Feste sang of "swaggering" (401), Toby and Maria entered; at "a great while ago the world begun" (407), the rest of the cast—with Malvolio at the very end—entered, so that the final impression (at "But that's all one, our play is done" [409]) was of a festive reunion.

Before glancing briefly at a television version and a movie, we should mention an engaging 1996 musical adaptation, *Play On!*, by Sheldon Epps and Cheryl L. West, with songs by Duke Ellington. (Many of Ellington's songs deal with the paradox of love, for instance "I Aint Got Nothin' but the Blues" and "I Got It Bad and that Aint Good.") Epps, an artist-in-residence at the Old Globe Theater in San Diego, originally intended to stage *Twelfth Night* with an incidental score of Ellington's songs, but ultimately he decided to thoroughly adapt the play, setting it in Harlem in the 1940s: Vy, a young black woman from the South, travels to Harlem, where she hopes to become a songwriter. To succeed in a business where a female songwriter is not taken seriously, she adopts a disguise. She falls in love with Duke, a composer and bandleader, who is in love with Lady Liv, a singer at the Cotton Club (a famous black night club, which in fact closed in 1936). Liv's manager—the equivalent of Malvolio—is an arrogant fellow called Rev, who is tricked into wearing a yellow zoot suit (the equivalent of Malvolio's yellow garters). The success of the production in San Diego inspired a move to New York in 1997, where it received mixed reviews.

The 1980 BBC television version of *Twelfth Night*, by contrast, of course stays close to the text. Like all of the other BBC productions, it uses Renaissance costume (the BBC was committed to this approach, except for the plays set in ancient Rome or Greece, and for the English history plays); if it offers a surprise, the surprise is that it is basically a happy, festive version, where, for instance, the gender confusion causes amusement rather than apprehension. A 1996 film version, set in the nineteenth century, directed by Trevor Nunn, is very different, decidedly melancholy. An introductory voice-over tells us that Messaline and Illyria are at war, and throughout the film we see men in uniform on patrol. The early scenes are dark—the shipwreck takes place at night, the households of Orsino and Olivia seem gloomy, and the season seems to be late autumn. When we first see Feste (Ben Kingsley), who probably owes much to Samuel Beckett's tramps, he is in an austere landscape setting and he seems menacing, almost a Grim Reaper. A lonely, aging figure, not at all the singer with the "mellifluous voice" of the text (2.3.54), he is the outsider, a bitter (rather than a funny) commentator on the action.

Samuel Pepys, we recall, in the 1660s characterized *Twelfth Night* as a "silly play." Our own century seems so intent on regarding it as a dark and profound play about alienation that there is some danger the comedy will be lost. Perhaps Barton's production was the one that best combined comedy and profundity, or, rather, that did not lose the comedy while treating the play as more than a silly trifle.

Bibliographic Note: For material on *Twelfth Night* on the stage, in addition to the references cited in this discussion, see especially the works by Ralph Berry, Michael Billington, and Laurie E. Osborne, listed in the Suggested References on pages 179 and 187–88.

Suggested References

The number of possible references is vast and grows alarmingly. (The *Shakespeare Quarterly* devotes one issue each year to a list of the previous year's work, and *Shakespeare Survey*—an annual publication—includes a substantial review of biographical, critical, and textual studies, as well as a survey of performances.) The vast bibliography is best approached through James Harner, *The World Shakespeare Bibliography on CD-Rom: 1900–Present*. The first release, in 1996, included more than 12,000 annotated items from 1990–93, plus references to several thousand book reviews, productions, films, and audio recordings. The plan is to update the publication annually, moving forward one year and backward three years. Thus, the second issue (1997), with 24,700 entries, and another 35,000 or so references to reviews, newspaper pieces, and so on, covered 1987–94.

Though no works are indispensable, those listed below have been found especially helpful. The arrangement is as follows:

1. Shakespeare's Times
2. Shakespeare's Life
3. Shakespeare's Theater
4. Shakespeare on Stage and Screen
5. Miscellaneous Reference Works
6. Shakespeare's Plays: General Studies
7. The Comedies
8. The Romances
9. The Tragedies
10. The Histories
11. *Twelfth Night*

The titles in the first five sections are accompanied by brief explanatory annotations.

1. Shakespeare's Times

Andrews, John F., ed. *William Shakespeare: His World, His Work, His Influence,* 3 vols. (1985). Sixty articles, dealing not only with such subjects as "The State," "The Church," "Law," "Science, Magic, and Folklore," but also with the plays and poems themselves and Shakespeare's influence (e.g., translations, films, reputation)

Byrne, Muriel St. Clare. *Elizabethan Life in Town and Country* (8th ed., 1970). Chapters on manners, beliefs, education, etc., with illustrations.

Dollimore, John, and Alan Sinfield, eds. *Political Shakespeare: New Essays in Cultural Materialism* (1985). Essays on such topics as the subordination of women and colonialism, presented in connection with some of Shakespeare's plays.

Greenblatt, Stephen. *Representing the English Renaissance* (1988). New Historicist essays, especially on connections between political and aesthetic matters, statecraft and stagecraft.

Joseph, B. L. *Shakespeare's Eden: the Commonwealth of England 1558–1629* (1971). An account of the social, political, economic, and cultural life of England.

Kernan, Alvin. *Shakespeare, the King's Playwright: Theater in the Stuart Court 1603–1613* (1995). The social setting and the politics of the court of James I, in relation to *Hamlet, Measure for Measure, Macbeth, King Lear, Antony and Cleopatra, Coriolanus,* and *The Tempest.*

Montrose, Louis. *The Purpose of Playing: Shakespeare and the Cultural Politics of the Elizabethan Theatre* (1996). A poststructuralist view, discussing the professional theater "within the ideological and material frameworks of Elizabethan culture and society," with an extended analysis of *A Midsummer Night's Dream.*

Mullaney, Steven. *The Place of the Stage: License, Play, and Power in Renaissance England* (1988). New Historicist analysis, arguing that popular drama became a cultural institution "only by . . . taking up a place on the margins of society."

Schoenbaum, S. *Shakespeare: The Globe and the World*

(1979). A readable, abundantly illustrated introductory book on the world of the Elizabethans.

Shakespeare's England, 2 vols. (1916). A large collection of scholarly essays on a wide variety of topics, e.g., astrology, costume, gardening, horsemanship, with special attention to Shakespeare's references to these topics.

2. Shakespeare's Life

Andrews, John F., ed. *William Shakespeare: His World, His Work, His Influence,* 3 vols. (1985). See the description above.

Bentley, Gerald E. *Shakespeare: A Biographical Handbook* (1961). The facts about Shakespeare, with virtually no conjecture intermingled.

Chambers, E. K. *William Shakespeare: A Study of Facts and Problems,* 2 vols. (1930). The fullest collection of data.

Fraser, Russell. *Young Shakespeare* (1988). A highly readable account that simultaneously considers Shakespeare's life and Shakespeare's art.

————. *Shakespeare: The Later Years* (1992).

Schoenbaum, S. *Shakespeare's Lives* (1970). A review of the evidence and an examination of many biographies, including those of Baconians and other heretics.

————. *William Shakespeare: A Compact Documentary Life* (1977). An abbreviated version, in a smaller format, of the next title. The compact version reproduces some fifty documents in reduced form. A readable presentation of all that the documents tell us about Shakespeare.

————. *William Shakespeare: A Documentary Life* (1975). A large-format book setting forth the biography with facsimiles of more than two hundred documents, and with transcriptions and commentaries.

3. Shakespeare's Theater

Astington, John H., ed. *The Development of Shakespeare's Theater* (1992). Eight specialized essays on theatrical companies, playing spaces, and performance.

Beckerman, Bernard. *Shakespeare at the Globe, 1599–1609* (1962). On the playhouse and on Elizabethan dramaturgy, acting, and staging.

Bentley, Gerald E. *The Profession of Dramatist in Shakespeare's Time* (1971). An account of the dramatist's status in the Elizabethan period.

———. *The Profession of Player in Shakespeare's Time, 1590–1642* (1984). An account of the status of members of London companies (sharers, hired men, apprentices, managers) and a discussion of conditions when they toured.

Berry, Herbert. *Shakespeare's Playhouses* (1987). Usefully emphasizes how little we know about the construction of Elizabethan theaters.

Brown, John Russell. *Shakespeare's Plays in Performance* (1966). A speculative and practical analysis relevant to all of the plays, but with emphasis on *The Merchant of Venice, Richard II, Hamlet, Romeo and Juliet,* and *Twelfth Night.*

———. *William Shakespeare: Writing for Performance* (1996). A discussion aimed at helping readers to develop theatrically conscious habits of reading.

Chambers, E. K. *The Elizabethan Stage*, 4 vols. (1945). A major reference work on theaters, theatrical companies, and staging at court.

Cook, Ann Jennalie. *The Privileged Playgoers of Shakespeare's London, 1576–1642* (1981). Sees Shakespeare's audience as wealthier, more middle-class, and more intellectual than Harbage (below) does.

Dessen, Alan C. *Elizabethan Drama and the Viewer's Eye* (1977). On how certain scenes may have looked to spectators in an Elizabethan theater.

Gurr, Andrew. *Playgoing in Shakespeare's London* (1987). Something of a middle ground between Cook (above) and Harbage (below).

———. *The Shakespearean Stage, 1579–1642* (2nd ed., 1980). On the acting companies, the actors, the playhouses, the stages, and the audiences.

Harbage, Alfred. *Shakespeare's Audience* (1941). A study of the size and nature of the theatrical public, emphasizing the representativeness of its working class and middle-class audience.

Hodges, C. Walter. *The Globe Restored* (1968). A conjectural restoration, with lucid drawings.

Hosley, Richard. "The Playhouses," in *The Revels History of Drama in English*, vol. 3, general editors Clifford Leech and T. W. Craik (1975). An essay of a hundred pages on the physical aspects of the playhouses.

Howard, Jane E. "Crossdressing, the Theatre, and Gender Struggle in Early Modern England," *Shakespeare Quarterly* 39 (1988): 418–40. Judicious comments on the effects of boys playing female roles.

Orrell, John. *The Human Stage: English Theatre Design, 1567–1640* (1988). Argues that the public, private, and court playhouses are less indebted to popular structures (e.g., innyards and bear-baiting pits) than to banqueting halls and to Renaissance conceptions of Roman amphitheaters.

Slater, Ann Pasternak. *Shakespeare the Director* (1982). An analysis of theatrical effects (e.g., kissing, kneeling) in stage directions and dialogue.

Styan, J. L. *Shakespeare's Stagecraft* (1967). An introduction to Shakespeare's visual and aural stagecraft, with chapters on such topics as acting conventions, stage groupings, and speech.

Thompson, Peter. *Shakespeare's Professional Career* (1992). An examination of patronage and related theatrical conditions.

———. *Shakespeare's Theatre* (1983). A discussion of how plays were staged in Shakespeare's time.

4. Shakespeare on Stage and Screen

Bate, Jonathan, and Russell Jackson, eds. *Shakespeare: An Illustrated Stage History* (1996). Highly readable essays on stage productions from the Renaissance to the present.

Berry, Ralph. *Changing Styles in Shakespeare* (1981). Discusses productions of six plays (*Coriolanus, Hamlet, Henry V, Measure for Measure, The Tempest*, and *Twelfth Night*) on the English stage, chiefly 1950–1980.

————. *On Directing Shakespeare: Interviews with Contemporary Directors* (1989). An enlarged edition of a book first published in 1977, this version includes the seven interviews from the early 1970s and adds five interviews conducted in 1988.

Brockbank, Philip, ed. *Players of Shakespeare: Essays in Shakespearean Performance* (1985). Comments by twelve actors, reporting their experiences with roles. See also the entry for Russell Jackson (below).

Bulman, J. C., and H. R. Coursen, eds. *Shakespeare on Television* (1988). An anthology of general and theoretical essays, essays on individual productions, and shorter reviews, with a bibliography and a videography listing cassettes that may be rented.

Coursen, H. P. *Watching Shakespeare on Television* (1993). Analyses not only of TV versions but also of films and videotapes of stage presentations that are shown on television.

Davies, Anthony, and Stanley Wells, eds. *Shakespeare and the Moving Image: The Plays on Film and Television* (1994). General essays (e.g., on the comedies) as well as essays devoted entirely to *Hamlet, King Lear,* and *Macbeth.*

Dawson, Anthony B. *Watching Shakespeare: A Playgoer's Guide* (1988). About half of the plays are discussed, chiefly in terms of decisions that actors and directors make in putting the works onto the stage.

Dessen, Alan. *Elizabethan Stage Conventions and Modern Interpretations* (1984). On interpreting conventions such as the representation of light and darkness and stage violence (duels, battles).

Donaldson, Peter. *Shakespearean Films/Shakespearean Directors* (1990). Postmodernist analyses, drawing on Freudianism, Feminism, Deconstruction, and Queer Theory.

Jackson, Russell, and Robert Smallwood, eds. *Players of Shakespeare 2: Further Essays in Shakespearean Performance by Players with the Royal Shakespeare Company* (1988). Fourteen actors discuss their roles in productions between 1982 and 1987.

————. *Players of Shakespeare 3: Further Essays in Shakespearean *Performance by Players with the Royal Shakespeare Company* (1993). Comments by thirteen performers.

Jorgens, Jack. *Shakespeare on Film* (1977). Fairly detailed studies of eighteen films, preceded by an introductory chapter addressing such issues as music, and whether to "open" the play by including scenes of landscape.

Kennedy, Dennis. *Looking at Shakespeare: A Visual History of Twentieth-Century Performance* (1993). Lucid descriptions (with 170 photographs) of European, British, and American performances.

Leiter, Samuel L. *Shakespeare Around the Globe: A Guide to Notable Postwar Revivals* (1986). For each play there are about two pages of introductory comments, then discussions (about five hundred words per production) of ten or so productions, and finally bibliographic references.

McMurty, Jo. *Shakespeare Films in the Classroom* (1994). Useful evaluations of the chief films most likely to be shown in undergraduate courses.

Rothwell, Kenneth, and Annabelle Henkin Melzer. *Shakespeare on Screen: An International Filmography and Videography* (1990). A reference guide to several hundred films and videos produced between 1899 and 1989, including spinoffs such as musicals and dance versions.

Sprague, Arthur Colby. *Shakespeare and the Actors* (1944). Detailed discussions of stage business (gestures, etc.) over the years.

Willis, Susan. *The BBC Shakespeare Plays: Making the Televised Canon* (1991). A history of the series, with interviews and production diaries for some plays.

5. Miscellaneous Reference Works

Abbott, E. A. *A Shakespearean Grammar* (new edition, 1877). An examination of differences between Elizabethan and modern grammar.

Allen, Michael J. B., and Kenneth Muir, eds. *Shakespeare's Plays in Quarto* (1981). One volume containing facsimiles of the plays issued in small format before they were collected in the First Folio of 1623.

Bevington, David. *Shakespeare* (1978). A short guide to hundreds of important writings on the subject.

Blake, Norman. *Shakespeare's Language: An Introduction* (1983). On vocabulary, parts of speech, and word order.

Bullough, Geoffrey. *Narrative and Dramatic Sources of Shakespeare*, 8 vols. (1957–75). A collection of many of the books Shakespeare drew on, with judicious comments.

Campbell, Oscar James, and Edward G. Quinn, eds. *The Reader's Encyclopedia of Shakespeare* (1966). Old, but still the most useful single reference work on Shakespeare.

Cercignani, Fausto. *Shakespeare's Works and Elizabethan Pronunciation* (1981). Considered the best work on the topic, but remains controversial.

Dent, R. W. *Shakespeare's Proverbial Language: An Index* (1981). An index of proverbs, with an introduction concerning a form Shakespeare frequently drew on.

Greg, W. W. *The Shakespeare First Folio* (1955). A detailed yet readable history of the first collection (1623) of Shakespeare's plays.

Harner, James. *The World Shakespeare Bibliography*. See headnote to Suggested References.

Hosley, Richard. *Shakespeare's Holinshed* (1968). Valuable presentation of one of Shakespeare's major sources.

Kökeritz, Helge. *Shakespeare's Names* (1959). A guide to pronouncing some 1,800 names appearing in Shakespeare.

———. *Shakespeare's Pronunciation* (1953). Contains much information about puns and rhymes, but see Cercignani (above).

Muir, Kenneth. *The Sources of Shakespeare's Plays* (1978). An account of Shakespeare's use of his reading. It covers all the plays, in chronological order.

Miriam Joseph, Sister. *Shakespeare's Use of the Arts of Language* (1947). A study of Shakespeare's use of rhetorical devices, reprinted in part as *Rhetoric in Shakespeare's Time* (1962).

The Norton Facsimile: The First Folio of Shakespeare's Plays (1968). A handsome and accurate facsimile of the first collection (1623) of Shakespeare's plays, with a valuable introduction by Charlton Hinman.

Onions, C. T. *A Shakespeare Glossary*, rev. and enlarged by

R. D. Eagleson (1986). Definitions of words (or senses of words) now obsolete.

Partridge, Eric. *Shakespeare's Bawdy*, rev. ed. (1955). Relatively brief dictionary of bawdy words; useful, but see Williams, below.

Shakespeare Quarterly. See headnote to Suggested References.

Shakespeare Survey. See headnote to Suggested References.

Spevack, Marvin. *The Harvard Concordance to Shakespeare* (1973). An index to Shakespeare's words.

Vickers, Brian. *Appropriating Shakespeare: Contemporary Critical Quarrels* (1993). A survey—chiefly hostile—of recent schools of criticism.

Wells, Stanley, ed. *Shakespeare: A Bibliographical Guide* (new edition, 1990). Nineteen chapters (some devoted to single plays, others devoted to groups of related plays) on recent scholarship on the life and all of the works.

Williams, Gordon. *A Dictionary of Sexual Language and Imagery in Shakespearean and Stuart Literature*, 3 vols. (1994). Extended discussions of words and passages; much fuller than Partridge, cited above.

6. Shakespeare's Plays: General Studies

Bamber, Linda. *Comic Women, Tragic Men: A Study of Gender and Genre in Shakespeare* (1982).

Barnet, Sylvan. *A Short Guide to Shakespeare* (1974).

Callaghan, Dympna, Lorraine Helms, and Jyotsna Singh. *The Weyward Sisters: Shakespeare and Feminist Politics* (1994).

Clemen, Wolfgang H. *The Development of Shakespeare's Imagery* (1951).

Cook, Ann Jennalie. *Making a Match: Courtship in Shakespeare and His Society* (1991).

Dollimore, Jonathan, and Alan Sinfield. *Political Shakespeare: New Essays in Cultural Materialism* (1985).

Dusinberre, Juliet. *Shakespeare and the Nature of Women* (1975).

Granville-Barker, Harley. *Prefaces to Shakespeare*, 2 vols. (1946–47; volume 1 contains essays on *Hamlet, King*

Lear, Merchant of Venice, Antony and Cleopatra, and *Cymbeline*; volume 2 contains essays on *Othello, Coriolanus, Julius Caesar, Romeo and Juliet, Love's Labor's Lost*).

————. *More Prefaces to Shakespeare* (1974; essays on *Twelfth Night, A Midsummer Night's Dream, The Winter's Tale, Macbeth*).

Harbage, Alfred. *William Shakespeare: A Reader's Guide* (1963).

Howard, Jean E. *Shakespeare's Art of Orchestration: Stage Technique and Audience Response* (1984).

Jones, Emrys. *Scenic Form in Shakespeare* (1971).

Lenz, Carolyn Ruth Swift, Gayle Greene, and Carol Thomas Neely, eds. *The Woman's Part: Feminist Criticism of Shakespeare* (1980).

Novy, Marianne. *Love's Argument: Gender Relations in Shakespeare* (1984).

Rose, Mark. *Shakespearean Design* (1972).

Scragg, Leah. *Discovering Shakespeare's Meaning* (1994).

————. *Shakespeare's "Mouldy Tales": Recurrent Plot Motifs in Shakespearean Drama* (1992).

Traub, Valerie. *Desire and Anxiety: Circulations of Sexuality in Shakespearean Drama* (1992).

Traversi, D. A. *An Approach to Shakespeare*, 2 vols. (3rd rev. ed, 1968–69)..

Vickers, Brian. *The Artistry of Shakespeare's Prose* (1968).

Wells, Stanley. *Shakespeare: A Dramatic Life* (1994).

Wright, George T. *Shakespeare's Metrical Art* (1988).

7. The Comedies

Barber, C. L. *Shakespeare's Festive Comedy* (1959; discusses *Love's Labor's Lost, A Midsummer Night's Dream, The Merchant of Venice, As You Like It, Twelfth Night*).

Barton, Anne. *The Names of Comedy* (1990).

Berry, Ralph. *Shakespeare's Comedy: Explorations in Form* (1972).

Bradbury, Malcolm, and David Palmer, eds. *Shakespearean Comedy* (1972).

Bryant, J. A., Jr. *Shakespeare and the Uses of Comedy* (1986).

Carroll, William. *The Metamorphoses of Shakespearean Comedy* (1985).

Champion, Larry S. *The Evolution of Shakespeare's Comedy* (1970).

Evans, Bertrand. *Shakespeare's Comedies* (1960).

Frye, Northrop. *Shakespearean Comedy and Romance* (1965).

Leggatt, Alexander. *Shakespeare's Comedy of Love* (1974).

Miola, Robert S. *Shakespeare and Classical Comedy: The Influence of Plautus and Terence* (1994).

Nevo, Ruth. *Comic Transformations in Shakespeare* (1980).

Ornstein, Robert. *Shakespeare's Comedies: From Roman Farce to Romantic Mystery* (1986).

Richman, David. *Laughter, Pain, and Wonder: Shakespeare's Comedies and the Audience in the Theater* (1990).

Salingar, Leo. *Shakespeare and the Traditions of Comedy* (1974).

Slights, Camille Wells. *Shakespeare's Comic Commonwealths* (1993).

Waller, Gary, ed. *Shakespeare's Comedies* (1991).

Westlund, Joseph. *Shakespeare's Reparative Comedies: A Psychoanalytic View of the Middle Plays* (1984).

Williamson, Marilyn. *The Patriarchy of Shakespeare's Comedies* (1986).

8. The Romances (*Pericles, Cymbeline, The Winter's Tale, The Tempest, The Two Noble Kinsmen*)

Adams, Robert M. *Shakespeare: The Four Romances* (1989).

Felperin, Howard. *Shakespearean Romance* (1972).

Frye, Northrop. *A Natural Perspective: The Development of Shakespearean Comedy and Romance* (1965).

Mowat, Barbara. *The Dramaturgy of Shakespeare's Romances* (1976).

Warren, Roger. *Staging Shakespeare's Late Plays* (1990).

Young, David. *The Heart's Forest: A Study of Shakespeare's Pastoral Plays* (1972).

9. The Tragedies

Bradley, A. C. *Shakespearean Tragedy* (1904).

Brooke, Nicholas. *Shakespeare's Early Tragedies* (1968).

Champion, Larry. *Shakespeare's Tragic Perspective* (1976).

Drakakis, John, ed. *Shakespearean Tragedy* (1992).

Evans, Bertrand. *Shakespeare's Tragic Practice* (1979).

Everett, Barbara. *Young Hamlet: Essays on Shakespeare's Tragedies* (1989).

Foakes, R. A. *Hamlet versus Lear: Cultural Politics and Shakespeare's Art* (1993).

Frye, Northrop. *Fools of Time: Studies in Shakespearean Tragedy* (1967).

Harbage, Alfred, ed. *Shakespeare: The Tragedies* (1964).

Mack, Maynard. *Everybody's Shakespeare: Reflections Chiefly on the Tragedies* (1993).

McAlindon, T. *Shakespeare's Tragic Cosmos* (1991).

Miola, Robert S. *Shakespeare and Classical Tragedy: The Influence of Seneca* (1992).

————. *Shakespeare's Rome* (1983).

Nevo, Ruth. *Tragic Form in Shakespeare* (1972).

Rackin, Phyllis. *Shakespeare's Tragedies* (1978).

Rose, Mark, ed. *Shakespeare's Early Tragedies: A Collection of Critical Essays* (1995).

Rosen, William. *Shakespeare and the Craft of Tragedy* (1960).

Snyder, Susan. *The Comic Matrix of Shakespeare's Tragedies* (1979).

Wofford, Susanne. *Shakespeare's Late Tragedies: A Collection of Critical Essays* (1996).

Young, David. *The Action to the Word: Structure and Style in Shakespearean Tragedy* (1990).

————. *Shakespeare's Middle Tragedies: A Collection of Critical Essays* (1993).

10. The Histories

Blanpied, John W. *Time and the Artist in Shakespeare's English Histories* (1983).

Campbell, Lily B. *Shakespeare's "Histories": Mirrors of Elizabethan Policy* (1947).

Champion, Larry S. *Perspective in Shakespeare's English Histories* (1980).

Hodgdon, Barbara. *The End Crowns All: Closure and Contradiction in Shakespeare's History* (1991).

Holderness, Graham. *Shakespeare Recycled: The Making of Historical Drama* (1992).

—————, ed. *Shakespeare's History Plays: "Richard II" to "Henry V"* (1992).

Leggatt, Alexander. *Shakespeare's Political Drama: The History Plays and the Roman Plays* (1988).

Ornstein, Robert. *A Kingdom for a Stage: The Achievement of Shakespeare's History Plays* (1972).

Rackin, Phyllis. *Stages of History: Shakespeare's English Chronicles* (1990).

Saccio, Peter. *Shakespeare's English Kings: History, Chronicle, and Drama* (1977).

Tillyard, E. M. W. *Shakespeare's History Plays* (1944).

Velz, John W., ed. *Shakespeare's English Histories: A Quest for Form and Genre* (1996).

11. *Twelfth Night*

In addition to the titles listed above in Section 7, The Comedies, see the following:

Barnet, Sylvan. "Charles Lamb and the Tragic Malvolio." *Philological Quarterly* 33 (1954): 177–88.

Belsey, Catherine. "Disrupting Sexual Difference: Meaning and Gender in the Comedies." In *Alternative Shakespeares,* ed. John Drakakis (1985), pp. 166–90.

Billington, Michael. *RSC Directors' Shakespeare: Approaches to "Twelfth Night."* (1990).

Greenblatt, Stephen. *Shakespearean Negotiations: The Circulation of Social Energy in Renaissance England.* (1988).

Greif, Karen. "A Star Is Born: Feste on the Modern Stage," *Shakespeare Quarterly* 39 (1988): 56–78.

Hayles, Nancy K. "Sexual Disguise in *As You Like It* and *Twelfth Night*," *Shakespeare Survey* 32 (1979): 63–72.

Hollander, John. "*Twelfth Night* and the Morality of Indulgence," *Sewanee Review* 67 (1959): 220–38.

Jardine, Lisa. "Twins and Travesties: *Twelfth Night*." In *Erotic Politics*, ed. Susan Zimmerman (1993), pp. 27–38.

Jenkins, Harold. "Shakespeare's *Twelfth Night*," *Rice Institute Pamphlet* 45 (1959): 19–42.

Kermode, Frank. "The Mature Comedies." In *Stratford-upon-Avon Studies 3: The Early Shakespeare*, eds. John Russell Brown and Bernard Harris (1961), pp. 211–27.

Lewalski, Barbara. "Thematic Patterns in *Twelfth Night*," *Shakespeare Studies* 1 (1965): 168–81.

Malcolmson, Christina. " 'What You Will': Social Mobility and Gender in *Twelfth Night*." In *The Matter of Difference: Materialist Feminist Criticism of Shakespeare*, ed. Valerie Wayne (1991), pp. 29–57.

Mallin, Eric S. *Inscribing the Time: Shakespeare and the End of Elizabethan England* (1995).

Osborne, Laurie E. *The Trick of Singularity: "Twelfth Night" and the Performance Editions* (1996).

Potter, Lois. *Twelfth Night* (1985).

Traub, Valerie. *Desire and Anxiety: Circulations of Sexuality in Shakespearean Drama* (1992).

Yearling, Elizabeth M. "Language, Theme, and Character in *Twelfth Night*," *Shakespeare Survey* 35 (1982): 79–86.

SIGNET CLASSICS

The Signet Classics Shakespeare Series:

The Histories

*extensively revised and updated expert commentary
provides more enjoyment through a greater
understanding of the texts*

HENRY IV: PART I, Maynard Mack, ed.

HENRY IV: PART II, Norman Holland, ed.

HENRY V, John Russell Brown, ed.

*HENRY VI: PARTS I, II, & III, Lawrence V. Ryan,
Arthur Freeman, & Milton Crane, ed.*

RICHARD II, Kenneth Muir, ed.

RICHARD III, Mark Eccles, ed.

**Available wherever books are sold or at
signetclassics.com**